SOUNDBITE CULTURE

SOUNDBITE CULTURE

THE
DEATH
OF
DISCOURSE

IN A

WIRED
WORLD

DAVID SLAYDEN
RITA KIRK WHILLOCK
EDITORS

SAGE Publications
International Educational and Professional Publisher
Thousand Oaks   London   New Delhi

For information:

SAGE Publications, Inc.
2455 Teller Road
Thousand Oaks, California 91320
E-mail: order@sagepub.com

SAGE Publications Ltd.
m6 Bonhill Street
London EC2A 4PU
United Kingdom

SAGE Publications India Pvt. Ltd.
M-32 Market
Greater Kailash I
New Delhi 110 048 India

Printed in the United States of America

Library of Congress Cataloging-in-Publication Data

Main entry under title:

Soundbite culture: The death of discourse in a wired world/
edited by David Slayden and Rita Kirk Whillock.
  p.   cm.
  ISBN 0-7619-0871-4 (cloth: alk. paper)
  ISBN 0-7619-0872-2 (pbk.: alk. paper)
  1. Communication—Social aspects. 2. Mass media—
Social aspects. 3. Language and culture. 4. Language and
education. 5. Civilization, Modern—20th century. 6. Postmodernism. I. Slayden, David. II. Whillock, Rita Kirk.
  HM258.S648 1999
  302.2—dc21   98-40180

99 00 01 02 03 04 10 9 8 7 6 5 4 3 2 1

Acquiring Editor:	Margaret H. Seawell
Editorial Assistant:	Reneé Piernot
Production Editor:	Denise Santoyo
Typesetter/Designer:	Marion Warren
Indexer:	Jeanne Casalegano
Cover Designer:	Candice Harman

Contents

Acknowledgments   vii

Introduction   ix
    David Slayden and Rita Kirk Whillock

PART I: SMOKE AND MIRRORS: MARKETS, PUBLICS,
AND CITIZEN-CONSUMERS   1

  1 **Giant Sucking Sounds: Politics as Illusion**   5
    Rita Kirk Whillock

  2 **Call and Response: Sports, Talk Radio, and the
    Death of Democracy**   29
    David Theo Goldberg

  3 **Democratic Delusions: The Town Meeting in an
    Electronic Age**   43
    Dale Herbeck

PART II: CENSORED AND SILENCED:
ACTS OF RESISTANCE AND POPULISM   65

  4 **Reading the Writing on the Wall: Graffiti in the
    Racialized City**   69
    Les Back, Michael Keith, and John Solomos

  5 **The Art of Subversive Image Making**   103
    Carol Becker

6 Resisting Whiteness: Revolutionary
   Multiculturalism as Counterhegemonic Praxis   113
   Peter L. McLaren

PART III: BORDERS AND BOUNDARIES: THE
ACADEMY AT THE EDGE OF DISCOURSE   151

7 The Death of Discourse in Our Own (Chat)
   Room: "Sextext," Skillful Discussion, and
   Virtual Communities   155
   Peter M. Kellett and H. L. Goodall, Jr.

8 Performing Cultural Studies
   as a Pedagogical Practice   191
   Henry A. Giroux

9 Rethinking Harmful Words: The Demise
   of the Critical Education Model and
   Discourse in the Schoolhouse   203
   Charles N. Davis

PART IV: MASTER AND SLAVE: POPULAR MEDIA
AND THE SHAPING OF BEHAVIOR   225

10 Negotiable Realities: Chaotic Attractors
    of Our Understanding   229
    David Everett Whillock

11 Worlds at GWAR: Celebrations of Juvenile
    Resistance in Post-Punk Pop   247
    Glenn C. Geiser-Getz

12 Vicarious Realities: Internet Discourses and
    Narratives of the Future   267
    David Slayden

Index   289

Acknowledgments

In these few words, we hope to give public honor to the private communication that has sustained us through the publishing process. Denise Hulce and David Whillock are truly communication enablers. They question, critique, laugh, pause, and sit quietly with us. For their companionship and intellectual compassion, we thank them.

Two others willingly assisted us in the sometimes tedious communication that accompanies this kind of collaborative effort: Crissy Cohen and Tiffany Hartgraves, our student assistants for this project. Their attention to detail in the early stages of reviewing the manuscripts, editing, and checking citations cannot be praised more highly. They are rare gems who are sure to make a lasting impression on those they meet.

Margaret Seawell, our Southern gem of an editor, is quite special to us. From the time we first pitched the idea through the completion of the manuscript, she has found ways to make this a better book. Her humor and high standards are equaled only by her charm.

Finally, we wish to thank the entire support crew at Sage. They have been dedicated to a quality execution of this project, and we are thankful for their input and encouragement.

Introduction

This book emerged from the recognition of an enigma: At a time when there are more means of facilitating discourse than ever before, less real communication is taking place, particularly if one assumes communication to be a reasoned exchange of views (reached through a process of thought and reflection) with a spirit of give-and-take, of point and counterpoint, characterized by a verbalized expression and representation of the self. Indeed, we would argue that discourse, as such, has been subsumed by ritualistic and stylistic performances, frequently dictated by the channels of discourse themselves, and that the conception and presentation of the self have become both increasingly fluid and imagistic, shaped by the demands of the mediated environments in which such performances take place. Discourse has become so transformed and marginalized by the exigencies of facilitation (media technologies and their markets) that it has effectively disappeared; dialogue has evaporated into narcissistic images. To an environment of postmodern premillennial angst characterized by forecasting, dreading, and celebrating ends, this book—*Soundbite Culture*—suggests that the rise of the image and the decline of the word have been accompanied by a reconstitution of actuated selves and communities into image-oriented performances, products, and presentations. Where exchange once existed—as an actuality or an ideal—there is now the illusion of discourse.

Soundbite Culture combines theory with case analysis to describe and account for the environment within which discourse may become extinct. Beyond merely decrying an end, once we admit that discourse as a "reasoned exchange" rarely exists in our mediated culture, we can examine what has replaced it and why. We can, for example, see that cultural conventions have been replaced by production codes wherein points of cultural reference emanate from the produced realm of film and television, rather than from a shared experience of the everyday physical world. We can explore how acts of resistance and populism—graffiti provides one example—are routinely censored and silenced through commercial assimilation. We become aware of the role played by opinion polls, consumer surveys, and ratings in transforming publics into markets and citizens into consumers. Because we live in a period when cognitive habits are encouraged and dominated more by photography, television, computers, and film than by language, we can focus on the impact of these practices and the issues raised by them. Readers will come to understand that, in the age of information, we are witnessing the end of personal, communicative exchange: possibly the death of discourse.

Any number of recent examples would lend support to such a conclusion, but two critiques from vastly different perspectives support the argument not only that discourse is dying or seriously ill but that recognition of this condition extends beyond the realm of academic writing, which in recent years has itself been criticized for lack of exchange, a postmodern loop of talking about talking.

The first comes from a cartoonist, Tom Tomorrow, whose four-frame strip "This Modern World" is syndicated mostly in alternative papers—a term that can itself be misleading because these papers include weeklies with large urban audiences, such as *The Observer* in Dallas. The first frame of the cartoon shows a reporter interviewing two "youths" with boxer shorts on their heads. His questions are framed to give social and political significance to the youths' apparently nonsensical act. To these questions, the youths respond with meaninglessly appropriate "whatevers." In the next two frames, we witness the rise and fall of a movement, "The Boxer Rebellion," with cover stories by *Newsweek* and *Time*. By the end of the series of cartoon frames, the same two youths have removed the boxer shorts from their heads and are now wearing socks on their ears. The same reporter is interviewing them. We can expect the phenomenon to recycle itself, with the news media eschewing fact and exploiting demographics to identify and offer interpretations of the latest trend. This moment of humor is, of course, a serious criticism of the media's noncoverage of real events and the hyping of non-events for commercial gain. Readers become markets, and what is reported is determined primarily by what has the highest entertainment value to a demographic with desirable spending habits.

The second example comes from Thich Nhat Hanh's *Living Buddha, Living Christ* (1995). Thich Nhat Hanh is a Vietnamese monk who was chairman of the Vietnamese Buddhist Peace Delegation during the Vietnam War, and for this work he was nominated by Dr. Martin Luther King, Jr. for the Nobel Peace Price. Thich Nhat Hahn has been described as "a rare combination of mystic, scholar, and activist," and his works have been translated and read internationally. Explaining the importance of exchange to the process of understanding and peace, he writes:

> In a true dialogue, both sides are willing to change. We have to appreciate that truth can be received outside of—not only within—our own group. If we do not believe that, entering into dialogue would be a waste of time. If we think we monopolize the truth and we still organize a dialogue, it is not authentic. We have to believe that by engaging in dialogue with the other person, we have the possibility of making a change within ourselves, that we can become deeper. Dialogue is not a means for assimilation in the sense that one side expands and incorporates the other into its "self." Dialogue must be practiced on the basis of "non-self." We have to allow what is good, beautiful, and meaningful in the other's tradition to transform us. (p. 9)

Thich Nhat Hanh's words reveal to ourselves how and why *Soundbite Culture* has grown out of our previous book *Hate Speech* (Whillock & Slayden, 1995), in which we wrote about how hate functions as an essential tool for the construction of identity and the acquisition of power. The various chapters of *Hate Speech*

> recognize and discuss hate as a tool used to assert—either actively or symboli-cally—one identity and annihilate another. . . . An underlying question about this operation—hate as a symbolic expression of identity—is the acceptance of an aggressive confrontational imperative: Why must one identity be achieved at the expense of another? And if expressions of hate are in fact destructive, annihilistic in their very shape and intent, why do we argue that they must be admitted as part of public discourse? (pp. xiii-xiv)

In *Hate Speech,* we argued that only through the airing of opposing views—however repugnant they might be—could conflict be resolved because a necessary step to resolution of a conflict is its identification. And discourse not allowed will find other means of expression and engagement: the bombing of abortion clinics, the bombing of the Murrah Federal Building in Oklahoma City, and so on. So *Soundbite Culture* follows and extends from *Hate Speech* in its concern over the breakdown of exchange and the very real consequence that can result from such breakdowns.

But *Soundbite Culture* also recognizes the benefits that are possible from a reemergence of engaged discourse in public life, from personal to organizational, social, and political transformation. The various subjects and sites in this book are contiguously related, with the range and context showing just how widespread is the absence of genuine dialogue. If it critiques the negative possibilities of where we are now—a dystopic view of a technological future comparable to Terry Gilliam's film *Brazil*—it also offers hope for a positive vision of an enlivened public dialogue.

For years, pessimists have decried changes that revolutionize their lifestyles, fearing that such changes were somehow inherently evil and stand the potential to rip civilized society apart. We do not subscribe to that view. But we do find that how people adapt to those changes can have either positive or negative consequences.

One consequence of the social science revolution early in the 20th century was a rush to embrace new media technologies without much thought given to the implications of media use on the part of the consumer. Sellers were much more focused and directed in their efforts to adapt media usage to specific ends.

The advent of mass media was accompanied by the introduction of a new communication model. Lasswell's model (who says what to whom with what effect) became the basis for measurement schemes that could isolate communication variables, thereby permitting businesses ways of targeting communication more effectively. The result of those efforts was the creation of a consumer society. Such consumer societies, according to Simpson (1994), establish and maintain themselves because they "have the capacity to sell the attention of mass audiences to advertisers, who use that attention to promote their goods and services" (p. 19).

To push products or services, the media were used to promote lifestyles and worldviews. Indeed, much current research indicates that consumers view product purchases as social markers, as indicators of persona. "Thus," as Simpson (1994) says,

> the (professed) ability to measure mass media messages and the responses they trigger became one necessary prerequisite to a much broader social shift, a shift in which modern consumer culture displaced existing [traditional] social forms. That process, moreover, consistently has been marked by great violence, frequently including genocide, as the "modern" world overwhelms indigenous cultures and peoples. (p. 20)

At one and the same time, two worlds exist: the world we live in and "plastique," the world we pretend to possess—the world often existing only as a promise or a projection through the narratives, parables, and representations of the culture industry and its domain—the media.

The organization of this book, divided into four parts, can be said to echo the dichotomous arrangement of these two worlds: the real, lived world and "plastique," with its contrasting titles that suggest some fundamental oppositions in current society; these oppositions suggest courses of experience and presentation that are often parallel but occasionally intersect willy-nilly, with both confusing and illuminating instances. Part I, "Smoke and Mirrors: Markets, Publics, and Citizen-Consumers," examines the varieties of reified experience in the public realm made possible by media coverage of politics and sports, along with the accompanying, deceptive, and often absurd or inapplicable appeals to community and democracy. In these arenas—both of sports and of politics—meaningful experience resulting from tangible actions and personal exchange has been replaced by stylized and hollow ritual. The authors here examine how their own experience of politics and sports—whose origins are tangible, local, and democratic but now come to us from a mediated distance—has been packaged and marketed to communities that also, like the planned communities or gated communities of recent years, seem equally apart from the authentic lived experience of a neighborhood. Both message and receivers of the message seem oddly unreal.

Part II, "Censored and Silenced: Acts of Resistance and Populism," offers examples of practices of resistance to the commodifying of expression in matters racial, artistic, and social and suggests that the seamless web of postindustrial capitalism may indeed be not so seamless after all. The different yet converging realms of art, personal politics, and graffiti offer compelling evidence and practices for surmounting the numbing effects of current mainstream hegemony.

Part III, "Borders and Boundaries: The Academy at the Edge of Discourse," focuses on our own backyard, so to speak, by scrutinizing various current discursive practices and attitudes within the academy. Three chapters offer commentary that suggests the marginal position now occupied by academic discourse may be the result of academic discourse. Following the overquoted and paraphrased insight of Pogo that we are ourselves the enemy, academe's current discursive atrophy stems, in many cases, from an unwillingness even to get so far as meeting the enemy. Certainly, each chapter in this part suggests a compelling lack of, and respect for, exchange within a modern academy characterized by careerism and intolerance.

Part IV, "Master and Slave: Popular Media and the Shaping of Behavior," revisits an old theme in regard to machines and culture, looking at the ambiguous power relationships between humans and the machines designed and built to serve them. It is a theme often explored in popular culture from 19th-century fictional explorations of technological utopias and dystopias to *fin de siecle* cinematic treatments. In this regard, the final part reiterates the fundamental question asked throughout the book from a variety of perspectives about the nature of our current relation with the mediated environment.

The structure of this book, then, is dialogic, calling for and situating or allowing one voice to be heard next to another—divergent, possibly disagreeable, yet a necessity if we as a society are to go beyond the noise and entertainment that characterize the current communications environment and participate in genuine discourse.

DAVID SLAYDEN
RITA KIRK WHILLOCK

REFERENCES

Hanh, T-N. (1995). *Living Buddha, living Christ*. New York: Riverhead.
Simpson, C. (1994). *Science of coercion: Communication research and psychological warfare 1945-1960*. Oxford, UK: Oxford University Press.
Whillock, R. K., & Slayden, D. (Eds.). (1995). *Hate speech*. Thousand Oaks, CA: Sage.

PART I

SMOKE AND MIRRORS: MARKETS, PUBLICS, AND CITIZEN-CONSUMERS

And talking to themselves, they muttered,

> "No one cares!" "I am not a crook."
> "No one thinks." "They are all crooks."
> "No one has it." "Money talks, so if you have it, flaunt it. If you don't, then fake it."
> "No one believes it." "Be all that you can [pretend to] be."
> "No one wants it." "He's not my [president, senator, governor, mayor, boss]. I didn't vote for him."
> "Everyone fears it." "Only [Rush, Jenny, Geraldo . . .] really cares about what people say."

Underneath the public musings of discouragement, people need to hope. Perhaps it is because we find ourselves fatally flawed. Pointing to others who are more "perfect" or clearly worse somehow makes us feel less conspicuous.

The conspicuous are in the public fray by choice, and they dominate much of what passes for public talk. They are not like "us," so we can discuss "them" around the watercooler with impunity. Our lives, our choices, our behavior is vastly different, we often say as we climb into our

$30,000 cars, meet the family for dinner at a local restaurant, and compare the day's sound bites.

The authors in this section analyze two areas of public talk in which the stories of heroes and gods, power and religion, fame and fortune weave themselves into everyday discourse: politics and sports. These two realms of public talk dominate much of the public airwaves. So how do we talk? What do we talk about? Whom do we talk to? Most important, how do we connect with people with whom we share little common experience or background?

In both politics and sports, the mythos says that our heroes are locals with special talents. We root for their success because, in a sense, it is rooting for us, for our communities. It is intensely American. We put the winners on billboards welcoming visitors to town and plaster their insignias on our water towers as monuments of achievement. Just as quickly, we forget their names by the time the paint fades and replace them with new icons for today's dreams.

In Chapter 1, Rita Whillock's title ("Giant Sucking Sounds") parodies an argument used by Ross Perot in the 1996 presidential campaign. Perot argued that if Congress passed NAFTA legislation, then American jobs would flow south of the border. The argument was not as compelling as the language: "All we will hear is giant sucking sounds." Few people will remember the Perot platform. The more memorable aspect of the campaign was his colorful use of language. In her chapter, Whillock argues that colorful language and images have replaced substantive public dialogue— hence, the subtitle "Politics as Illusion." Whillock argues that political correctness has paralyzed public judgment. People no longer know how to engage in public criticism. Second, she contends that mass media marketing has developed a standard whereby public language appeals to everyone and offends no one. In this way, everyone is the same and no one is different; no *one* person matters anymore. Finally, Whillock suggests that although people are using more channels of expression, political dialogue is decidedly lacking. Lacking is an exchange of ideas, an appreciation for compromise, and an ability to articulate difference.

David Goldberg takes a different approach in Chapter 2. He suggests that sports radio has become the common ground for a white male community of like-minded virtual friends. Because this previously dominant culture has diminished influence in the political sphere, the friends have moved into a realm of sports talk. Against this field of battle, sports becomes a surrogate topic for almost anything elsewhere. The listener-participants rant and rave about sometimes only tangentially related sports themes. But, in the end, it isn't really about talk at all. As Goldberg contends, it "adds up now to little more than the commitment to purchase marketed merchandise, to root for the same team no matter how exploitative of fan sentimentality." This reflective critique forces the reader to consider the masked purposes driving sports talk and asks us to consider this an aneurysm in the body politic.

In Chapter 3, Dale Herbeck advances the argument a step further. He argues that our leaders (and their spinmeisters) recognize the breakdown of public competence in political argument. In an attempt to restore democracy to its roots, they have returned to a public forum that richly served the nation's first Anglo settlers: the town hall forum. Using the format in presidential debate, Herbeck argues, is a sham. While appearing to connect with voters, politicians continue to provide pat answers to complex questions in 1- to 3-minute sound bites. The original concept of the *town hall* was a forum where citizens could join together to discuss/debate the issues most affecting them. Most important, the meeting was about *self*-governance. People met to listen and understand each other. But the ultimate purpose was to reach consensus on what to do next. Modern versions of the town hall, Herbeck contends, are merely political spectacles that mask the mediocre level of talk that passes as political argument, a "cynical product" of a candidate's "own strategic interests."

In the political realm, we are living in a world of expressive and monologic communication. Often, expressions in these realms are devoid of engagement, reciprocity, and dialogue. We have deceived ourselves and cheapened the value of genuine discourse if we look around and believe that what we hear is meaningful communication. Like so much other public talk, the illusion of discourse presents itself. Genuine political talk is difficult to find.

CHAPTER 1

Giant Sucking Sounds

Politics as Illusion

Rita Kirk Whillock
Southern Methodist University

Populus vult decipi, ergo decipiatur.

In his book *The Man Who Mistook His Wife for a Hat and Other Clinical Tales,* Oliver Sacks (1990) recounts the case histories of patients with severe neurological disorders. One case history is illustrative to this text. He entitles this case history "The President's Speech." According to Sacks, patients in the aphasia ward were brought to laughter during a speech by Ronald Reagan. The speech itself was not humorous, nor were the patients (to my liking) Yellow Dog Democrats. Instead, Sacks notes, they laughed because they understood the meaning all too well. Aphasics are extremely sensitive to bodily cues and vocal tones:

> To [each] grimace, to any falsity or impropriety in bodily appearance or posture, aphasics are preternaturally sensitive. And if they cannot see one—this is especially true of our blind aphasics—they have an infallible ear for every word nuance, the tone, the rhythm, the cadences, the music, the subtlest modulations, inflections, intonations, which can give—or remove—verisimilitude to or from a man's voice. (p. 82)

5

The paradox of the Reagan speech is that these patients were undeceived by the president and his empty words while the rest of us sat enwrapped in our willing suspension of disbelief. The patients who laughed at that speech mocked all of us who routinely suspend our innate judgment to allow ourselves to believe in the sincerity of such political pronouncements. Such suspension of judgment is not illogical or irrational. It is, however, self-serving. "Rational choice" theorists argue that people routinely make decisions based on their own cost-benefit analyses as they elect leaders (see, e.g., Davis, Hinich, & Ordeshook, 1970). They examine their pocketbooks, their value systems, their chances to keep or advance in the workplace, to determine whether they need to change current policies or to remain with the status quo. Similarly, dominant groups act in their own self-interest to preserve whatever benefits they derive from their privileged status. A politician's words of reassurance, even though they have long since lost their meaning or sincerity, are accepted as indicators that the status quo will be maintained.

Acts of self-interest are complemented by an indirect but effectual denial of privilege to dissimilar others when such action might change the balance of power or reduce benefits. For example, one act of denial is to preclude others from having a public platform for their ideas. This can be accomplished by two means: (a) dominating the public platform in a kind of virtual filibuster or (b) confining the divergent voice to channels that (at least almost) ensure the opposition will not be heard (perhaps even mocked for its failure to be in line with dominant thinking).

Over the last few decades, the media explosion has led us to believe, rightly, that the common person (ergo, a person without power or influence) has more access to channels of mass media than before. It has also encouraged us to believe, wrongly, that access alone matters. Computers have made it possible to merge thousands of names with direct mail solicitations to give the appearance that personalized communication is taking place—and that the nature of such direct mail coverage is akin to that of radio or television. It is not. The Internet has made access to thousands of cyborg personalities easy. Yet although it allows people to speak freely, it does not provide access to deliberative audiences, particularly those who might benefit most from having their ideas challenged in a thoughtful forum. Those who dominate the mainstream media channels do not engage the public in meaningful conversation, whereas media alternatives provide the illusion of a "public" voice with no one to hear it. Empty communication, then, is now a routine part of the political landscape. We accept the platitudes of politicians as readily as we bathe ourselves in the comfort of words that echo our own self-interest.

This chapter examines three conditions that have led to the death of discourse in politics. First, I argue that the era of political correctness has demonstrated that we have lost an ability to talk en masse about people with whom we have no contact or with whom we share no common problems. Once we accept this restriction on our public expression, an inadvertent chilling effect reduces the kind of critical judgment that rightfully belongs to the whole to decide—our national goals, our commitment to the precepts of the Constitution and the Bill of Rights, and the competing vision of would-be leaders. Our society has lost its ability to articulate a national (or grand) narrative for fear of not being inclusive or inadvertently alienating parts of the whole. Second, I argue that the mass media are responsible for our inability to distinguish audiences from publics. *Audiences* are demographic clusters that are significant only because of their market share or size, not because of the collective wisdom or their public voice. *Publics,* by contrast, are groups of people on whom success or failure of our institutions depends. Audiences are talked *to;* publics are talked *with.* Audiences are entertained; publics are engaged. Audiences live in the moment; publics have both memory and dreams. Audiences have opinions; publics have thoughts. Finally, I contend that *more* communication does not equate with *meaningful* communication. Having a voice does not guarantee power or political presence.

THE ALIENATION OF DISSENT: THE CONTRIBUTION
OF POLITICAL CORRECTNESS TO THE DEATH OF DISCOURSE

No clearer example can be offered for my argument that political dissent has been marginalized than the phenomenon known as *political correctness* (or P.C.). The fact that it is so widely used and understood that our culture has given it a name is notable.

Political correctness greatly contributes to the death of discourse. In this public style, language is generalized in order to please the many and to avoid alienating any constituency. To be P.C. means that you offend no one, that your communication is above public rebuke. Of course, this would not even be a factor in a nonmediated world. P.C. is driven by dissimilar people trying to talk in the presence of a mass audience. The mass media magnify talk, holding it up for scrutiny. But it is not scrutiny of thought, but language that results from its application. In a wicked twist of the old adage, people assume that "sticks and stones" can break your bones and that words can also harm you.

The harm of people having opinions that others do not want publicly expressed is manifested in many ways. One way is to sue in court for legal redress of the insult. Over the past few years, the rise in the number of lawsuits for defamation has been substantive (see Bezansom, Cranberg, & Soloski, 1987, p. 8). Rodney Smolla (1986) argues that this is a result of people realizing the power of words to harm another person's "emotional tranquility." As a result of this "general thinning of the American skin" (p. 16), people are suing the press and each other. The resultant "chilling effect" makes flagrant, expressive dialogue less likely. Except for those who are willing to be sued for risking discussion, public talk is being reduced to pablum.

Another way P.C. is enforced is through public outcries. As a code of public decorum, political correctness is used to bring attention to language abuse, even at the cost of suppressing passion, personal experience, or ignorance. To argue against political correctness is not to argue that the public should condone anti-P.C. pronouncements. As free speech scholar Steve Smith points out, sometimes the point is to flush out the bigots. The crux of the issue is about suppression of opposition views, not whether a broader public would accept them as valid.

The use of P.C. as de facto censorship means that the public is deprived of the opportunity to address significant, divisive, and sometimes destructive biases among large segments of the population. Merely closing people out of a national discussion does not mean that they go away, that problems are resolved, or that biases no longer exist. It merely means that those in power have chosen to ignore the problems until forced to deal with them.

Much of the debate over standards of political correctness centers on the use of stereotypes. The simple fact is that stereotypes are reflections of experiential bias. To deny their expression is to deny the existence of difference.

In Texas, a young mother was placed on trial for the brutal murder of her two young sons. The case was the center of a media focus for weeks both regionally and nationally. As the trial approached, prosecutors were given a daily pounding from family members who believed they had charged the wrong person. Prosecutors, convinced of their case, continued to take the high ground, answering media questions and attempting to explain their point of view. One evening, one prosecutor "lost it." As the cameras were rolling, the defendant's mother once again verbally attacked the prosecutor. Slow to anger, the prosecutor finally lashed out and used an ill-advised description of the family. He labeled them "trailer trash," an intriguing statement, given the fact that the family lived in a quite well-to-do neighborhood. The media uproar was deafening. Few people considered that he may have genuinely expressed his feelings, for such an expression would not be politically correct, particularly for an officer of the court. Even fewer people considered what the prosecution team was going through themselves. For weeks, prosecutors had to live with the pictures of two young boys stabbed to death, knowing that the crime occurred in the boys' own home with both parents present and that, as much as prosecutors would prefer to believe otherwise, the links pointed to the mother as murderer. Rather than confront the underlying premise—that the family was without social values that might preclude selfish or violent acts against others and their property—the focus was placed on the language used. The prosecutor later apologized for losing his cool. Yet maybe, just maybe, the public would be better served by someone who openly expressed outrage on behalf of the public for such a shocking crime.

The issue in this case, of course, is about stereotyping. It is true that many people who live in trailers are not "trashy." It is also true that some people who live in trailers are. To accept only the P.C. version in public discourse is to deny the experiences of those who claim to have seen this darker, less pleasant side of the populace. Because, in this case, the mother did not actually live in a trailer park but in a well-to-do neighborhood, perhaps other things were being said, things the public needed to think about, such as "money doesn't make a person virtuous" or "financial prominence doesn't signify innocence." But those messages were never absorbed or addressed. Stereotypes are often unfair generalizations. Yet, in the absence of dialogue, they remain—buried and suppressed, perhaps, but they remain.

ABC provides another example of how dialogue is squelched. In 1997, the network's entertainment division took a bold step to announce a controversial new episode of the television show *Ellen*. In it, viewers would witness the character's "coming out" as a lesbian. Such an announcement would usually generate public debate and discussion and might have done so except that two censoring events took place. The first came from the pulpit as a noted evangelist, labeling the actor/character Ellen "Degenerate," called for a boycott of the show's product sponsors unless the show was pulled. Rather than engage in a dialogue about his point of view or find means to explain to the public his religious conviction about the (im)morality of the act, he resorted to censorship attempts to remove the subject from public debate altogether.

The network did no better. Encouraged that a long-suppressed point of view was being given positive treatment through the show's story line, the nation's largest gay/lesbian lobbying group (the Human Rights Campaign) wanted to purchase advertising space during the show. The ad was intended to promote the Employment Non-Discrimination Act, which failed to pass

Congress in 1996 by one vote and is scheduled for consideration again this year. ABC, which along with parent company Disney is viewed positively for its treatment of its gay employees, rejected the ad because it violated its policy against "controversial issue advertising." Little wonder that the American public cannot discuss issues because they are denied an opportunity to examine what acceptance of others' points of view might have on society—either positively or negatively.

Political dialogue breaks down when we can no longer deal with the substance of what people say, but rather must deal with the periphery (the P.C. language, or in this case the political taboo). Perhaps society would be better off if people learned to empathize with others like Ellen who come to accept a sexuality different from their own. Conversely, society might be better off if we accepted clear standards of right or wrong like those who fervently believe that their religious teachings find gay/lesbian behaviors to be flagrant violations of basic religious tenets. In either case, the squelching of dialogue in the name of some politically correct standard denies both sides the opportunity to voice, and perhaps to persuade others to, their point of view.

To speak of the death of discourse, then, is to argue that negative consequences flow from its absence. As this last example illustrates, one consequence is polarization of the public into camps that do not talk with each other.

Rhetorical polarization occurs any time a rhetor advances claims based on the unlikely event that contradictory arguments will find an equally effective and oppositional platform. This gives rise to what Gitlin (1995) calls "identity politics." Rather than speak to deliberative groups, rhetors find niche publics to whom they can customize a message, unify the audience, and build a coalition, even if that occurs at the expense of a demonized out-group. Identity politics supplants the traditional political mantra of "the common good" in exchange for what is good for a particular group.

In its most basic form, *identity politics* is a strategy that aligns select groups of people by promoting differences between themselves and others. Once identity is established, the homogenous group closes ranks so tightly that, Gitlin (1995) argues, they virtually eliminate dissent in order to maintain the power created by their cohesion. The result is an isolationist rhetoric that precludes groups from finding some common ground to accomplish some greater act that would promote the common good.

For example, David Duke, Pat Robertson, and Patrick Buchanan effectively use identity politics. Not only do they achieve group cohesion among followers, but they also use it to insulate followers from those who hold divergent opinions. They achieve cohesion by focusing arguments around out-groups with whom they take issue (gays, pro-life advocates, or welfare mothers). Then they shield themselves from attack by arguing that societal pressures for less radical pronouncements on their part are attempts by the dominant culture—be that the "party" system, blacks, or liberals—to marginalize them. Critically, the arguments are not designed with persuasive intent outside the target (identity) group. The argument is only designed with one purpose: to establish close identity with one constituency even if that is accomplished by demonizing the opposition. As a result, such rhetors leave no rhetorical ground for compromise or deliberation.

Such divisive splits in the political arena have always existed but perhaps none so dynamic as the decisive changes that occurred as candidates learned how to make use of depersonalized but highly personal, voyeuristic communication in the 1980s (see Iyengar & Kinder, 1984, 1986). Candidates for president stopped talking about the philosophical divisions created by various policy approaches to national issues such as the war in Vietnam, how to address issues of poverty in this country, or civil rights. Instead, finding difference became more important than arriving at some consensus for public action. For example, presidential candidates began identifying opponents by "liberal" or "conservative" labels attached to positions on issues the president would be powerless to resolve—issues such as gun control, the death penalty, or prayer in the schools (see, e.g., Germond & Witcover, 1989, p. 50). Such divisions over issues beyond the policy scope of the presidency lead to chasms that could not be bridged through discourse. Peggy Noonan, in her book *What I Saw at the Revolution* (1990), summarizes what she learned from her years as a presidential speech writer. It applies to the argument here:

> There are, I think, two kinds of serious political activists: those who are impelled by love, and those who get their energy from hate. The ones moved by love—for America, for the poor, for freedom—often contribute to the debate. Those moved by hate—for liberals, for conservatives, for the rich, for America's sins—make the process ugly. They cannot engage in honorable debate because they cannot see the honor on the other side. (p. 357)

Politics is a raw, raucous sport to many. Those who have worked in political campaigns understand Noonan's point, but a specific example may provide specificity to Noonan's claim. Bill Carrick, campaign manager for Dick Gephardt, was particularly upset with Al Gore's strategy in the 1988

Democratic presidential primaries. Gore strategically decided to ignore Iowa in his bid for the presidency. It left Gephardt without the clear victory the campaign hoped to achieve over the field of Democratic contenders. Carrick told Tom Edsall of the *Washington Post:*

> I can't wait. It's bloodlust. Let me at him, I hate him. I hate all of them. I think they are the phoniest two-bit bastards that ever came down the pike, starting with Al Gore, moving through boy wonder ex-wordsmith, the mosquito that roared [a reference to Gore campaign manager Fred Martin]. (cited in Germond & Witcover, 1989, p. 266)

Failure to honor opinions of adversaries leads to a political warfare that bloodies the airwaves and leaves the public in malaise.

Such self-interest harms the body politic and, carried to the extreme, can have devastating results. Eventually, one group will come to power. When it does, it will leave no room for rhetorical dissent. History is replete with examples of what happens when silencing the opposition becomes a political objective of those in power. For example, in 1942, a group of German students attempted to mobilize public opposition to the Nazis. They called themselves the White Rose. In their first leaflet, they argued that "nothing is so unworthy of a civilized nation as allowing itself to be 'governed' without opposition by an irresponsible clique that has yielded to base instinct" (Scholl, 1983, p. 73). Those would not appear to be high-risk words of criticism in today's world. But in an era of extreme adherence to one popular point of view, taking exception to Nazi policies cost the students their lives. Although most people prefer to think of such incidents as historical or foreign or both, real atrocities still occur in this world. And, of course, they will occur again.

Perhaps we should consider the fact that rhetoric—and its suppression— has real consequences. Douglas Porpora, in his book *How Holocausts Happen* (1984), notes that

> the real lesson of the Holocaust is that it is not necessary for us to be extremely hateful for us to give power to extremely hateful people. All we need to do is overlook the evil in leaders we otherwise find appealing. (p. 39)

If we cannot discuss the opinions, proclamations, and decisions of public figures, we cannot begin to address the factors that would empower leaders more interested in the public good than in their rise to power as head of some select interest group.

ILLUSIONS OF DISCOURSE:
PUBLIC OPINION AND SPIN CONTROL

Certainly, the argument exists that public discussions of controversial issues are more prolific, thoughtful, and publicly available than ever before. In a public forum I attended, John Sununu and Warren Rudman argued that television talk shows on which informed politicians-turned-journalists square off on the issues is a great way of educating the public. Walter Lippmann's (1922) concept of the journalist as educator would seem to support such forums. In practice, however, what passes for educational discussion is not. Rather, it is, as James Fallows (1996) points out, an arena "in which ambitious politicians struggle for dominance, rather than a structure in which citizens can deal with worrisome collective problems" (p. 31). Programs filled with the quick exchange of verbal quips make for effective television only if the standard of judgment we use is entertainment.

Few people disagree that entertainment is the dominant standard for news ratings today. Hart (1994) attributes part of the responsibility for this lack of substance to the media themselves: "Television's job description is therefore clear: Find two colorful personalities for each side of each dialectic; let them nip at each other's heels, then call it disputation" (p. 70). Much of the discourse that passes for political information is nothing more than a distraction from the issues of governance.

Larry Sabato (1993) goes one step further, arguing that journalists also have a role in diminishing debate. He argues that "feeding frenzies" by the news media are *created*. Stories about politicians follow "preconceived images and stereotypes" that become the subtext for future stories.

> Journalists are always on the lookout for circumstances that fit the common perceptions and prejudices about a candidate, particularly his shortcomings. A major incident that validates the subtext (and therefore the press's own judgment) has a good chance of being magnified and becoming a feeding frenzy. (p. 71)

News stories that support journalists' interpretations of reality are magnified, whereas those that do not are underreported, if covered at all.

Research, then, supports the conclusion that public communication has become ritualized, a form of entertainment rather than a vehicle for exchange and debate. To continue to feed our lust for more entertainment, we crave more detail regardless of what it costs others. One of my colleagues at Southern Methodist University, Bill May, argues that this kind of entertainment is a result of stripping humanity from the communication situation. May argues that when one removes the human emotion of love from the sex act, all that is left is gratuitous sex. When one takes grief from death, one has random violence. Without the humanity, May argues, tabloid talk shows, sleazy sex scenes, and random violence are not satisfying. As a result, it takes more to satiate our appetite. It is unfulfilling.

The current trend of journalism would seem to support May's conclusion. For example, when former Speaker of the House Jim Wright underwent an intense ethical investigation regarding his book deal, he became a freak show: dehumanized, isolated, and hounded. Wright notes:

> I would never have comprehended the anguish visited by the "death watch" of the media. To have people surrounding our home with a real carnival atmosphere, shouting questions at you with a boom microphone and long-lens cameras, it makes one feel like a hunted animal driven to his lair. (quoted in Cohen, 1989, p. 2086)

In the end, coverage of the Wright scandal was not satisfying. Such event-oriented news does not enlighten the public on ideas, provide contextual cues about how more effective decisions could be made, or assist the public in finding greater meaning. Instead, we have a plethora of scandal stories—Whitewater, campaign finance, the Gingrich book deal— each covered like the Wright episode as a titillating sideline to the business of politics. Such stories appear to be more about feeding some emptiness than about informing the public.

Feeding frenzies are not limited to news organizations; they also exist on the policy front. Robert MacNeil, formerly with *MacNeil/Lehrer News Hour* on PBS, provides several examples of failed political actions resulting from the pastiche of public responses to images. He reports, for example, that President Reagan sent Marines into Lebanon because of the terrifying pictures of Palestinian massacres in refugee camps (MacNeil, 1994). The pictures of bombed U.S. barracks are equally vivid reminders that actions have consequences.

News coverage in the dominant mass media channels does not assist citizens in understanding. We have all heard the argument that news is entertainment. More important is that the stories almost always report the maneuvering to achieve policy victories without explaining the potential outcomes. Consequences are about who won or lost, not the resultant effects of policy decisions on the lives of citizens. As Schudson (1995) notes, "political reporters tend to be politics-wonks rather than policy-wonks, absorbed in 'inside baseball' analysis rather than fascinated by the question of how government should run the country" (p. 10).

In the context of public debate, the consequences are important. I recall sitting in rapt attention to the minute-by-minute developments during the Persian Gulf War: our troops and theirs, our leaders versus theirs. For weeks, troop buildups led informed citizens to the conclusion that war was imminent. But once it broke out, many were surprised. At the very time we should have been discussing appropriateness, we had other issues on our collective mind. The journalistic mantra "if it doesn't bleed, it doesn't lead" seemed appropriate to the prewar situation analysis. Once the war broke out, military strategists second-guessed the generals, and other than a host of human interest stories, few people talked about the why and virtually no one thought about what would happen next (when the war was over). I agree with Schudson's (1995) conclusion:

> [T]elevision executives live in a time-and-space capsule closely linked to research reports on market trends but very far from deeper currents of experience in the contemporary world. And since they do not yet know this, may never know this, may not want to know this, they may never tell us the stories about ourselves from which we could genuinely learn. (p. 123)

This is not to say that the fault for weak government rests solely with the media. This is not just an argument about journalistic intent; rather, the argument also stems from the fact that these mediums have inherent characteristics that distance people from one another, making the importance of consequences less intriguing because we have little interest in the plight of people with whom we hold no human bond.

Much of what passes as important public information is nothing more than plastic images of lifelike beings. Richard Sennett (1977) argues that television lured us away from public domains and drew society into the private. This move was accompanied by private swimming pools, cocooning at home to watch movies, and a host of other once-public activities. This move to privatization, he argues, has an impact on the political process because it also provides boundaries for what can be properly said or done in public:

> [I]t became logical for people to think of those who could actively display their emotions in public, whether as artists or politicians, as being men of special and superior personality. These men were to control, rather than interact with, the audience in front of whom they appeared. Gradually the audience lost faith

in itself to judge them; it became a spectator rather than a witness. The audience
thus lost a sense of itself as an active force, as a "public." (p. 261)

This blurring of boundaries between what the public needs to know in
order to make better decisions and what the public needs in order to
satisfy its hunger for entertainment is important. Lazarsfeld and Merton
(1948) argue that the media possess a "narcotizing dysfunction," dulling
the audience's ability to think altogether. In fact, Rod Hart (1995) argues
that the electronic media "conflate issues and images almost completely
and encourage us to do so as well. . . . Because television is a visual
medium, its pictures have a self-authenticating quality. . . . Television, in
short, encourages the arrogance of the eye" (p. 61). These images are not
benign.

Images have power because they influence opinion. Germond and Witcover (1989) contend that politicians have come to understand that the
"visual" is dominant:

> First, a good piece of film would be shown apparently without a great deal of
> questioning by either network producers or local news directors of its news
> value or the merits of the story. Second, a good piece of film would have far
> more impact on viewers—and voters—than the words that were being spoken
> while it was being shown. (p. 55)

Controlling the news, then, has become the dominant game for the successful political figure.

To protect themselves in this entertainment sphere, public figures have
become increasingly reliant on public relations consultants to guard their
images, monitor the environment for potential traps, and take proactive
stances to bolster their public images. Indeed, over the last few decades,
spinmeisters have come to dominate the political arena, and they are good
at it. They give us the illusion that our opinions are being monitored and
our concerns are being addressed. But is that really true? Public opinion
reporting is often specious at best. Even with clearer publication standards
for the reporting of reliable data, too much of what passes for polling is
nothing short of outright manipulation. Even polls that are scientifically
produced can be influenced by skilled manipulators. Today, it has become
"routine for campaign managers to buy advertising time on television in
advance of newspaper polls or their own, thus 'driving up the numbers' in
such polls" (Germond & Witcover, 1989, pp. 56-57). These inflated statistics are used for a variety of functions: to influence the undecided, to

convince contributors to give money, and to build campaign momentum. Success in these areas leads to another media buy, better numbers, and more momentum for repeating the process until the numbers turn downward, the money runs out, or the election is over.

Such a critique of policy-by-public-opinion is not new. An essay published in 1879 argues that public opinion "has become a slogan by which the complacent and intellectually lazy mass is supplied with a pretext for avoiding the labor of thinking for themselves" (Holtzendorff cited in Habermas, 1989, p. 240).

Public opinion in a media age is much more complicated and intriguing than just reporting polling data. Public opinion is also more malleable than ever. For the most part, people are learning to live "in the moment." With information accessed so easily, people do not need to recite memorized passages or to recall crucial information. They can merely look it up when they have need of it.

This absence of memory makes it easy to claim the ideas of others, to bring about an unconscious comfort at words spoken from an earlier time. Recent history is replete with examples. Joe Biden, in the 1988 presidential campaign, was blackened when reports came to light that he had virtually stolen the personal story of Neil Kinnock, leader of Britain's Labor Party. Compare these two stories:

Kinnock: Why am I the first Kinnock in a thousand generations to be able to get to university? Why is Glenys the first woman in her family in a thousand generations to be able to get to university? Was it because all our predecessors were thick?

Did they lack talent? Those people who could sing and play and recite and write poetry? Those people who could make wonderful, beautiful things with their hands? Those people who could dream dreams, see visions? Why didn't they get it? Was it because they were weak? Those people who could work 8 hours underground and then come up and play football? Weak?

Does anybody really think that they didn't get what we had because they didn't have the talent or the strength or the endurance to the commitment? Of course not. It was because there was no platform on which they could stand. (Kinnock television commercial)

Biden: I was thinking as I was coming over here. Why is it that Joe Biden is the first in his family ever to go to a university? Why is it that my wife, who is sitting out there in the audience, is the first in her family to ever go to college? Is it because our fathers and mothers were not bright? Is it because I'm the first

Biden in a thousand generations to get a college and a graduate degree that I was smarter than the rest?

Those same people who read poetry and wrote poetry and taught me how to sing verse? Is it because they didn't work hard? My ancestors, who worked in the coal mines of northeast Pennsylvania and would come up after 12 hours and play football for 4 hours?

No, it's not because they weren't as smart. It's not because they didn't work as hard. It's because they didn't have a platform on which to stand. (Biden speech at the Iowa State Fair debate, 1988)

Such "borrowing" of another person's identity was substantive reason for Biden's ouster from the presidential primary. To some people, Biden's punishment demonstrates that the system works. To others, it illustrates an isolated case of someone who went too far. Much of what passes as public information is placed there by media consultants. And much of the "identity borrowing" is a natural result of our loss of public memory.

How authentic is the information the public hears? James Reston (1986), a reporter for the *New York Times,* notes that although the public can still identify the speaker, we do not know whose words are being spoken. Managing the news is an old game in Washington, but what has changed is the pervasiveness of behind-the-scenes directors for on-screen political actors. Critic Wayne Booth (1974) argues that such manipulative practices reduce good reasons to logical calculations about the effect of rhetorical pronouncements. In the end, the issues often pit our values against our rational judgment. This, according to Booth, makes value debates nonrational and persuasion a method of manipulating the public, rather than of attempting mutual learning through discourse.

RHETORICAL PLACEBOS: THE ILLUSION OF HOPE

When asked what can be done to correct the system, many pundits turn to the exploding channels of communication as evidence that more and more "common" people are finding ways to make "real" connections. But the age of electronic communication does not mean that people are more eager to engage in substantive debate. Many people will continue to seek out those who agree with them, pausing to browse through others' thoughts only when they can be used as a source of amusement or ridicule.

And we are mistaken if we think the Internet is anymore "real" than other forms of communication. Indeed, one feature of cyber-citizens is that they are often unreal. Like the Biden example, the personae created on the Web may not resemble the actual person. So what does that matter in politics? Plenty. Studies indicate that people rank the "personal qualities" of political figures over "policy preferences" by four to one (see Greenstein, 1965; see also Conway, Stevens, & Smith, 1975). This helps explain the heavy domination of image advertising in politics. As cyborg versions of political candidates appear on the Web, we may end up having even less clarity about the personal qualities of the candidates. Thus, we are further removed from a firsthand ability to judge character issues accurately.

Hart (1995) argues that the game of analyzing political personalities is pivotal in politics because voters find it personally rewarding to do so:

(1) [B]ecause such examinations tap into our natural expertise about how people think, we stand little chance of being declared incompetent; (2) because politicians are changeful, there is always work to be done, a new psychological wrinkle to work out, and that is exciting; (3) because political rhetoric is so often quotidian, we can quickly feel superior to those who use it. (p. 64)

But how do we analyze a fictitious persona? And what is the point?

The Internet mocks the personal communication style of the letter. Personal letters and journals hold a special place in the literature of many alienated social groups (see, e.g., Castillo, 1986; Flores, 1996; Fulkerson, 1979). As one writer argues, it permits us "to record what others erase when I speak" (Anzaldua cited in Palczewski, 1996, p. 3). At face value, the Internet would appear to be a communication vehicle similar in nature to such personal communiques. Yet the differences are notable. The Internet has created a place for people to experiment with their own identities, often creating numerous facades. Such "cyborg personalities" may or may not be real, thus diminishing the authenticity of voice that is paramount in personal letters or journals. Writer Gloria Anzaldua's admonition to writers is particularly insightful when applied to Internet communication: The danger is "not fusing our personal experience and world view with the social reality we live in, with our inner life, our history, our economics, and our vision" (Anzaldua cited in Palczewski, 1996, p. 2).

Also, a false identification of the public permeates the Internet. We sometimes forget that most Internet projects are *technical* projects. They "don't involve the community; have 'professionals' guide the project; and don't think politically" (Schuller, 1996, p. 1). The result is that "most 'official' city sites extend the one-way public information model into cyberspace" (McMillan & Campbell, 1996). Touting the success of its

"Democracy Online" experiment during the 1994 elections, the California Voter Foundation (CVF) claimed that 14,000 log-ins occurred between October 4 and Election Day and that 36,000 documents were retrieved (CVF press release, 1995). No mention is made in the report about communication exchange. The sole nature of the success is in the public's ability to retrieve information. More important, perhaps, the study does not indicate that any *new* users retrieved any information—that is, those who would not have retrieved the information from other sources had the Internet not been available. To claim, then, that this new medium is enhancing the decision-making process or facilitating public communication is simply erroneous.

As stated earlier, the Internet is merely a communication vehicle. The only way communication can change is for users to use it differently. In some notable instances, such communication has been used effectively to facilitate political ends. Li (1990) explains how Chinese students successfully coalesced as a unified public by using the Internet as the dominant means of organizing behind political action. But cyber-democracy is limited by inequities that are inherent in the system.

One of those inequities stems from participation bias. Only those people who are computer literate have *participatory* access to this medium. Even if the new technological developments permit lurkers to use their television sets to monitor Web sites, without computer literacy they are unable to participate. Another factor is the bias in network access. Early studies on the use of the Internet show that users tend to be young, male, educated, and affluent (see, e.g., Media Studies Center, 1996). Again, for those who argue that the Internet is the salvo for democratic thought, thought is limited to a narrow segment of the population that has access.

Another inequity stems from the inherent contradiction of a system that allows anyone (with means to access the Internet) to join various groups. At first glance, it would appear that this would increase membership and facilitate discussion. That does not routinely occur. As Rothenberg (1992) points out, solitary benefits and participation are key factors in membership retention. Most Internet joiners find few benefits, and even fewer of them are active participants. The majority are "lurkers" who join for brief periods of time before dropping out. Although it is easier for people to sample organizations, the value of membership decreases when there are few substantive benefits for remaining (see, e.g., Moe, 1980). In fact, many new joiners are overwhelmed by the communication that takes place. Similarly, politicians cannot begin to respond individually to the load of new communication that developing technology requires of them. Newt Gingrich is reported to have received some 13,000 e-mail messages in the first 6 weeks of the 104th Congress (Bonchek, 1995). We must concede that, at least in the early stages of the Internet's development, people have been encouraged to speak in ways that are preempted in other channels of communication. On-line communications *may* allow people once again to engage in political dialogue. Michael Riley (1996), executive producer of "AllPolitics" and senior correspondent for *Time* magazine in Washington, noted,

> I think what you are seeing is politics has become a . . . monologue. People are disconnected, disenfranchised, alienated, fearful. Demagoguery is an easy game to play. There is no voice. You basically sit on the sofa and you watch ads or the debates. But [interactive formats] give people a chance to change that monologue into a dialogue, to reconnect.

Yet technology is merely a tool. It can be used well or poorly. Mastery of the tool precedes its use for higher purposes. Howard Rheingold (1996), author of *The Millennium Whole Earth Catalog,* rightly argues that "most processes for guiding public policy or influencing electoral politics involve communication—meeting people, developing ideas and arguments, persuading people to adopt your views, enlisting support, negotiating compromises, organizing actions." These *can* be enhanced with the right type of user knowledge in computer-assisted communications. When we realize that the Internet is only *one* tool and that, though fascinating, it is only an interesting distraction from the real purposes of communication, we begin to appreciate that it is an instrument of communication and not the substance of it.

This tool itself does not foster better communications. That is not to say that people who use the tool cannot. Hart (1995) claims that "we will have to recall things we have long known but have chosen to forget: that good ideas need protection; that governance is complicated; that only an informed citizenry can prosper; that all people are imperfect" (pp. 75-76). This will require people to overcome the anti-intellectual statements that encourage citizens to trust others, rather than involve themselves in the messy business of decision making. It will work *only* if people see themselves as agents of change, not as spectators.

This last point creates my cynicism about the Internet as a communication salvo. Although it has certainly stimulated more communication, it has also developed a population equivalent to couch potatoes called "lurkers." Although the messages are more prolific, they also use greater word economy with fewer explanations or detailed argument development. And because words alone cannot convey proper interpretations of meaning, ineffective "emoticons" have been developed to assist the reader in understanding author intent.

My strongest criticism of the Internet as a political change agent is that it encourages users to talk as if someone were listening. Political talk in a democracy is of dubious value unless some higher goal is to be achieved. For several years, I have been a critic of what I have termed "media navel-gazing." The media have become accustomed to hearing their own commentary about events, rather than reporting the news. Sunday morning political shows are filled with such roundtable babble. Similarly, the Internet is becoming a haven for groups that rattle rhetorical sabers at those who are not listening. The Internet has aided in the proliferation of small like-minded interest groups that, while talking to themselves, assume that others are being influenced.

The ease of proliferation of on-line interest groups has created additional problems. In essence, it has created a virtual Tower of Babel. The Internet has enabled hundreds of groups to form around common issues. But these groups rarely talk with one another, share common platforms, or actively join together to achieve a greater purpose. In this way, they have diluted the effect of a mass dedicated to political change.

For example, hate groups on the Internet have been on the increase. Schneider (1995) claims that the Internet has pushed the number of "hardcore supporters" from 1,000 to 4,000 in a period of 8 years (p. A12). Yet no evidence supports the claim that these supporters are more active, unified, or threatening. In fact, hate alone does not unify them. Isolated groups are unified only by their hatred of specific objects of disdain. Additionally, the depth and extent of their hatred is vastly different. Quite frankly, without some direct, unifying threat, so much divides the groups in a struggle for leadership and power that they are more isolated than unified. This does not mean that such groups are less threatening. In fact, the threat may escalate by calls to action as such groups become increasingly aware that, even with new technologies, they are not able to find a *public* platform for voicing their angst.

This diffuse effect is not limited to hate groups or harmed individuals but is also active with community networks designed to encourage local political activism. As Doug Schuller (1996), founder of the Seattle Communicate Network, notes, "The powerless are becoming increasingly isolated. Their opinions are infrequently sought; their concerns are often not even acknowledged." He reasons that this occurs, at least in part, because although software engineers are quite good at making the technology work, "they don't know how to build community."

CONCLUSION

The dominant ideological voice echoed by leaders using centralized mass media is being rejected in the new media age. That voice, though loud and clear, has never permitted room for alternative versions of experience. As Vattimo (1992) argues, "history speaks only of events involving those who count, the nobles, the sovereigns, or the middle classes once they became powerful. The poor, and those aspects of life considered 'base,' do not 'make history' " (p. 3). Now these underrepresented populations that have demanded and been denied access are finding a means of expression in the new media. Here, they offer multiple histories, project diverse images, and advance disparate visions for the future.

What is different between these stories and those of the past? Finding commonalities used to be considered the goal of political advocates. Today, the need to bridge cultures is decreasing. People fight for dominance at the expense of others or are content to insulate themselves by establishing rhetorical distance from dissimilar others.

Certainly, one casualty of this multivoice is a changing view of progress. Progress, as once viewed, is no longer *the* measure of human development because the benchmarks for that advancement were determined only by those with dominant voice. Progress to them is only a term that marked the advancement of Western ideologies (see, e.g., Vattimo, 1992). Now that competing visions and ends are explored, finding common goals is increasingly difficult.

The pursuit of common goals is an important attribute of a stable government. Many political leaders do not know what the ends of government are anymore. Today, no measures for effective government are universally agreed upon. This plethora of voices, this proliferation of *Weltanschauungen,* has erased the "grand narratives" that have held larger political organizations together.

Why? Because national (or grand) narratives were never designed to provide equal representation of voices. As our nation got started, people took risks to come and settle here because they wanted freedom from state-imposed strictures on how they should live. In small communities, they found common ground with others like themselves. The Puritans, the

Quakers, the Pilgrims, and numerous other like-minded groups began colonies with the notion that they could live their lives differently from what the state demanded. With few restrictions, given the distance from the motherland, they could form their own government, apply their own standards of conduct, and impose their own set of laws governing behavior. As these smaller colonies grew and found a need to join for protection, the government on which they were united was given only the most cursory power, the majority of it left for the states. Today, our nation has left its roots. We have come almost full circle. The state is imposing strictures that govern the kinds of specific moral precepts that our forbearers rebelled against.

The founders of this republic were able to construct a satisfying democratic formula for governing populations that act as autonomous fiefdoms that believed and relished in the communal differences. Former Speaker of the House Tip O'Neil was correct when he noted that "all politics is local." Politics is territorially based: We vote in districts where we live. Whether we choose to acknowledge it or not, we are intrinsically linked with our neighbors. Yet increasingly, our public talk demands that we make public decisions about issues we are ill-suited to address—issues about which we have no feeling and little interest. We have a fight for dominance of federal policy each time a new hot issue emerges. As once-isolated groups gain broad attention, as multiple goals and images are advanced, national leaders enact oscillating policies. Rather than adhere to a narrow range of issues that should rightfully govern all groups, they respond to the public sentiment du jour and enact intrusive policies that foster division. This is already evident in the problems we have been developing as a long-range national agenda that advances the best interests of "the whole." Because "we" cannot agree on how to talk about ourselves, our national policy is weakened. Former Secretary of State Warren Christopher warns that these fickle and consuming public images cannot become "the North Star of American foreign policy" (Christopher cited in MacNeil, 1994). If they do, contradictory policy shifts will occur. Eventually, people in other countries will see us as fickle allies, and those at home will become disenchanted (if they have not already) by government's lack of progress, by officials' inability to lead, and by stagnation.

When I speak of the death of discourse, I do not encourage a pessimistic vision that argues people should speak in one voice, that powerful people should once again dominate the mass media, or that the public be damned. Yet, for a national government to be successful over a sustained period of time, at least some decisions are made in linear progression. One aspect of the death of discourse to which I refer here is a death of linear thinking, planning, and policy implementation. McLuhan and Powers (1989) argue that the electronic media encourage an "all-at-onceness" that supplants traditional linear thought. The pastiche of images encourages impression and absorption and may even entertain us, but it is not processed with any goal in mind. Neil Postman (1985) contends that "the fundamental assumption of that world is not coherence, but discontinuity" (p. 110). That characteristic is wonderful if the aim is to encourage free thought, invention, and discovery. It is terrific for empowerment, self-fulfillment, and egocentrism. But it is deadly to the art of politics.

That is why scholars and analysts contend that political figures must vacillate between two modes today: the campaign mode and the governing mode. Increasingly, the perpetual campaign is disabling our leaders. They can no longer govern because they have lost sight of the long-term, linear progression necessary for growth in favor of quick-fix, immediate-response policies. Sustained governmental policies require the development of coherent arguments. These arguments are inherently debatable and flawed because we realize that the facts and experiences on which they are based are selective, not completely representative of the population of facts and experiences. That is why our national government was designed to move slowly. The speed of legislation passing the House is slowed in the Senate, where leaders have 6 years to build a record for reelection. Governments are supposed to move slowly to avoid the whims of public passion. Once adopted, legislators move the government forward to some measurable end. In the current milieu of governing by public opinion, policies change according to which group screams the loudest, pays the freight, or controls the images. We are no longer mediating toward centrist policies, but rather are being governed by extremity.

The expanding media, though seemingly providing more vehicles for communicating, is essentially stripping us of the public space needed to debate national issues. Such public space is necessary: "cohabitation of a territorial space" is a requirement for community building (Gumpert, 1987, p. 78). In his work on the rhetorical impact of city designs on communication exchange, Richard Sennett (1990) contends that we have created "bland neutralizing spaces, spaces which remove the threat of social contact" from others (p. xii). Virtual communities continue to isolate us even more. And even though we may argue that such media create communities that are not territorially defined, we must remember that political domains *are* territorially defined. From local governing bodies (city councils and school boards) to nations with borders, we must consider that governing is tied to boundaries. Our connections with virtual others in nonplace communities (see Gumpert, 1987) stand in opposition to the community-building communication needed to enact governing policies that regulate our day-to-day environment in the place where we live.

The notion of territory, of space, is fundamental to our understanding of the death of discourse. Studies have shown that citizens are less informed than ever before (see, e.g., Neuman, 1986) despite the fact that more news is available to us through television, radio, print sources, and the Internet than ever before. Others have discovered that, when watching the news, viewers tend to assume roles of entertainment consumers, rather than of citizens (Paletz & Entman, 1981). News, then, is a fictional melodrama played out with interesting but distant actors (Feuer, 1988). All of this distancing, this lack of knowledge, stems from the public's inability to see a connection with their own lives. As Beniger (1987) argues, we have developed into a society of pseudo-communities, "a reversal of a centuries-old trend from organic community—based on interpersonal relation-ships—to impersonal association integrated by mass means" (p. 369). The net result is a lack of connectedness that harms the body politic.

Can anything be done to reverse this trend? Yes. We must first recognize that territory matters. As long as we have voting districts that are geographi-cally determined, we must find ways of communicating with those people who physically reside in our communities. That requires communication scholars to address the issues of community building and to contribute to the development of communication vehicles that permit a new connected-ness. Second, we must find ways of teaching people how to relish personal freedom while learning to talk with others who choose different paths. That does not assume that people agree with each other, avoid difficult topics, or even accept another's choice as valid. It does mean that we must learn how to debate issues, to move slowly through the plethora of arguments that are at issue when our paths cross in order to find accommodation, and to make informed judgments on matters of public interest. Just as our founders realized that we have more differences than commonalties, we must adhere to structures based on a few principles that constitute common ground. Third, we must recognize that communication that succeeds is personal. What we say, the messages we reinforce, must be considered important and not just strategic. We must consider consequences, not just effects. When we come to terms with communication as a personal vehicle of expression, we understand that personhood is at the center of discourse. The death of discourse is a death of personhood. It can only be revived by reestablishing its importance in our daily communicative experience.

REFERENCES

Beniger, J. (1987). Personalization of mass media and the growth of pseudo-community. *Communication Research, 14*(3), 352-371.

Bezansom, J., Cranberg, G., & Soloski, J. (1987). *Libel law and the press: Myth and reality.* New York: Free Press.

Bonchek, M. S. (1995, April 6). *Grassroots in cyberspace: Using computer networks to facilitate political participation.* Paper presented at the 53rd Annual Meeting of the Midwest Political Science Association, Chicago. [On-line]. Available: http://www.pin.org/library/grs_root.htm

Booth, W. C. (1974). *Modern dogma and the rhetoric of assent.* Chicago: University of Chicago Press.

California Voter Foundation (CVF). (1995, March 3). Press release [On-line].

Castillo, A. (1986). *The Mixquiahuala letters.* Tempe, AZ: Bilingual Press.

Cohen, R. E. (1989, August 19). Fall from power. *National Journal, 21,* 2086.

Conway, M., Stevens, A. J., & Smith, R. (1975). The relationship between media use and children's civic awareness. *Journalism Quarterly, 52,* 531-538.

Davis, O., Hinich, M., & Ordeshook, P. (1970). An expository development of a mathematical model of the electoral process. *American Political Science Review, 64,* 426-448.

Fallows, J. (1996). *Breaking the news: How the media undermine American democracy.* New York: Pantheon.

Feuer, J. (1988). Good morning in America. In J. Carey (Ed.), *Media, myths, and narratives: Television and the press.* Newbury Park, CA: Sage.

Flores, L. A. (1996, May). Creating discursive space through a rhetoric of difference: Chicana feminists craft a homeland. *Quarterly Journal of Speech, 82,* 133-182.

Fulkerson, R. P. (1979). The public letter as a rhetorical form: Structure, logic, and style in King's "Letter From a Birmingham Jail." *Quarterly Journal of Speech, 65,* 121-136.

Germond, J. W., & Witcover, J. (1989). *Whose broad stripes and bright stars? The trivial pursuit of the presidency 1988.* New York: Warner.

Gitlin, T. (1995). *The twilight of common dreams: Why America is wracked by culture wars.* New York: Metropolitan Books.

Greenstein, F. (1965). Popular images of the president. *American Journal of Psychiatry, 122,* 523-529.

Gumpert, G. (1987). *Talking tombstones and other tales of the media age.* New York: Oxford University Press.

Habermas, J. (1989). *The structural transformation of the public sphere: An inquiry into a category of bourgeois society* (T. Burger, Trans.). Cambridge: MIT Press.

Hart, R. P. (1994). *Seducing America: How television charms the modern voter.* New York: Oxford University Press.

Iyengar, S., & Kinder, D. (1984). The evening news and presidential evaluations. *Journal of Personality and Social Psychology, 46,* 778-787.

Iyengar, S., & Kinder, D. (1986). More than meets the eye: TV news, priming, and public evaluations of the president. *Public Communication and Behavior, 1,* 135-171.

Lazarsfeld, P., & Merton, R. (1948). Mass communication, popular taste, and organized social action. In W. Schramm (Ed.), *Mass communications* (pp. 492-503). Urbana: University of Illinois Press.

Li, T. (1990). Computer-mediated communications and the Chinese studies in the U.S. *Information Society, 7,* 125-137.

Lippmann, W. (1922). *Public opinion.* New York: Free Press.

MacNeil, R. (1994, Spring). The flickering images that drive presidents. *Media Studies Journal, 8*(2), 145-154.

McLuhan, M., & Powers, B. (1989). *The global village.* Oxford, UK: Oxford University Press.

McMillan, S., & Campbell, K. B. (1996). On-line cities: Are they building a virtual public sphere or expanding consumption communities? [On-line]. Available: http://darkwing.uordegon.edu/sjm/cityweb/

Media Studies Center. (1996, October 8). *Digital democracy: New media coverage of the 1996 campaign.* New York: Author.

Moe, T. M. (1980). *The organization of interests: Incentives and the internal dynamics of political interest groups.* Chicago: University of Chicago Press.

Neuman, W. R. (1986). *The paradox of mass politics: Knowledge and opinion in the American electorate.* Cambridge, MA: Harvard University Press.

Noonan, P. (1990). *What I saw at the revolution: A political life in the Reagan era.* New York: Ivy.

Palczewski, C. H. (1996, Fall). Bodies, borders, and letters: Gloria Anzaldua's "Speaking in tongues: A letter to Third World women writers." *Southern Communication Journal, 62,* 1-16.

Paletz, D. L., & Entman, R. M. (1981). *Media, power, politics.* New York: Free Press.

Porpora, D. V. (1984). *How holocausts happen: The United States in Central America.* Philadelphia: Temple University Press.

Postman, N. (1985). *Amusing ourselves to death.* Harrisonburg, VA: R. R. Donnelley.

Reston, J. (1986, April 9). Online politics. *New York Times,* p. A27.

Rheingold, H. (1996). Electronic democracy tool kit. [On-line]. Available: http://www.well.com/user/hlr/electronicdemoc.html

Riley, M. (1996, November 4). *Digital democracy: New media coverage of the 1996 campaign.* Media Studies Center. Available: http://www.mediastudies.org/democracy/html

Rothenberg, L. (1992). *Linking citizens to government: Interest group politics and Common Cause.* Cambridge, UK: Cambridge University Press.

Sabato, L. (1993). *Feeding frenzy: How attack journalism has transformed American politics.* New York: Free Press.

Sacks, O. (1990). *The man who mistook his wife for a hat and other clinical tales.* New York: HarperPerennial.

Schneider, K. (1995, March 13). Hate groups use tools of the electronic trade. *New York Times,* p. A12.

Scholl, I. (1983). *The first leaflet: The White Rose* (A. R. Schultz, Trans.). Middleton, CT: Wesleyan University Press.

Schudson, M. (1995). *The power of news.* Cambridge, MA: Harvard University Press.

Schuller, D. (1996, January). How to kill community networks. *Network Observer, 3,* p. 1 [On-line]. Available: http://www.pin.org/library/killtech.htm

Sennett, R. (1977). *The fall of public man.* New York: Knopf.

Sennett, R. (1990). *The conscience of the eye: The design and social life of cities.* New York: Knopf.

Smolla, R. (1986). *Suing the press.* New York: Oxford University Press.

Vattimo, G. (1992). *The transparent society.* Baltimore: Johns Hopkins University Press.

CHAPTER 2

Call and Response

Sports, Talk Radio, and the Death of Democracy

David Theo Goldberg
Arizona State University School of Justice Studies

DOG DAYZ

Midweek morning rush hour. Car radio tuned to the talking head haute culture of NPR morning news, the highway of informed democracy. Volume turned up hard enough to be heard above the air-conditioning humdrum, drowning out the dissonance of a disinformed public as it washes out the surround-sound traffic noise. The self-encasement that keeps democracy safe, (public) radio as privat(ized) consumption. Alone in and with my-world-in-22-minutes, as rubber rocks the road.

Static, then silence. The digital display blinks blank. Panic stations. This is *not* a test of the Emergency Broadcasting System. The mediated thoughts that fill my mind about current events dissolve along with the radio signal. The radio, my mind and word-world, democracy, at once at risk. Noise swirls about as cars swish by, horns honk, jets vaporize overhead, men

AUTHOR'S NOTE: I thank my colleagues Gray Cavender and David Altheide for their helpful suggestions in thinking about sport and talk radio, and my research assistant Sam Michalowski for knowing the score.

curse, sirens scream, rock and roll of all the insults thumps in from someone else's car audio. There's something wrong with my radio, goddammit. Fiddling frantically with the dial doesn't help any. I inadvertently knock the AM button. The drone that before had split the silence of an informed public radio audience is displaced by the shrill shrieking of local talk. My dial is fixed on AM! Top of the morning to the meat market of ideas in America, Democracy Inc.

A psychoanalyst friend once insightfully suggested to me, as I prepared to drive from Philadelphia to Phoenix, that I would have no better sense of place, of the vast differences in (between) America, than to listen to AM radio on the road. Local is to radio what states rights are to federalism. On more waves than one, I was about to discover how right my doctor of the unconscious was.

Lost on the AM airwaves, I sampled each station. Talk radio: political, religious, do-it-yourself psychology, more local politics, Randy Weaver talks with the local Viper militia, more local religion, CBS oldies nostalgia (postmodernism lives even—especially—on local radio), more griping, more religion.

RADIO ON

And then . . . then sports talk. Talking about sports. Twenty-four hours. If the spanking new stadia that mark cities are the new cathedrals (a town doesn't get to be a city, isn't marked on the map, without one, as I've argued elsewhere), sports radio is the bully pulpit, the MTV of/for sports. Call and response in the church of athletic self-opinion. MTV sells as it entertains, markets as it broadcasts. So, too, sports talk radio. It announces, informs, pontificates, moralizes, politicizes, commercializes, and commodifies—as it entertains. It should come as no surprise, then, that MTV Sports should be a popular prime-time Monday evening program hosted by none other than Scott Ferrall, the Dennis Rodman of sports talk radio. Ferrall is the quintessential Gen-Xer who speaks a mile a minute with a raspy gargling in an ironic "I-don't-give-a-fuck" in-your-face self-promoting style. In a nod to the ratings effects of surface social consciousness, he growls, "Get involved, get deep, go up the mountain to Lake Tahoe to support the snowboarders' benefit for breast cancer. It'll make you feel good." No doubt, you've got a four-wheel drive and a Working Assets car phone calling card to take you to a freedom winter mountaintop. This is a feel-good social consciousness, pleasure as im-politic(s).

Sports talk radio, as talk radio generally, is all about entertainment. Yesteryear's sports radio was principally concerned with play-by-play, player and team stats, the season's progress. Radio days: Take me out to the ball game even if I can't actually go. This function has been taken over in any case by ESPN. For sports talk radio, the romance with numbers counts only superficially if at all. Today, sports talk radio concerns itself overwhelmingly, if not exclusively, as an arena for voicing opinion—about sports, of course, but about sports as a surrogate for almost anything. Sports talk radio is both symbol and expression of the "democratizing" of opinion, equal opportunity beliefs, evidence or its lack notwithstanding. Shout, shout, let it all out, these are the things we're thinking (and not thinking) about. If I can vent more entertainingly than the next guy, if I can shout louder and longer (and what better training than being a sports fan), I'm king not for a day but for my 15 seconds of self-elevated and self-promoting fame. Jim Rome, Mad Dog Russo, and Scott Ferrall have made their reputations on that stage, the kings of sports talk rap. Howard Stern meets The Last Poets, Rush reaching out to touch Geraldo. Good callers give good phone, imitating the style (if not the substance) of their hosts. Even if the unfed baby is screaming for food in the background. "It's a jungle out there, man." First-time callers be warned: Say something disagreeable, and you're radio-actively flushed down the toilet, thrown through shattering glass, subjected to a drug test, even shot. Click, you're off the air, baby. Life's over. Your 15-second soapbox just got swept away. Democratic consumption calls for public sphere police officers.

Talk radio is marked by class. Public radio in the talking head formats represents the intellectually inclined, upmarket, and somewhat more liberally oriented audience. Here, Diane Reams (in political reverse) is to public radio what Cornel West or Noam Chomsky are to C-Span, the exception that proves the rule. By contrast, AM talk radio reaches (out to) a more conservative, white male clientele. In 1960, only two radio stations—KABC in Los Angeles and KMOX in St. Louis—were devoted to talk formats. Through the 1960s, AM turned increasingly to talk as the explosion of rock and roll enabled the transmission muscle of FM to dominate music stations. Talk radio stations mushroomed in the 1980s, prompted by a confluence of inexpensive satellite capabilities, deregulation, sophisticated niche marketing, and dramatic localism spurred by growing antistatist sentiments. In a single decade, talk radio stations quadrupled remarkably to 800. This represents a new talk station every 4 or 5 days! That's a whole lot of jawing going on.

By 1996, more than 4,000 talk shows were on 1,200 stations and networks, a more than tenfold increase in less than two decades. Today, talk radio "captures" one fifth of the male audience over age 18, mainly middle and working class. In 1994, 20 million people were rushing each week to laugh along with Limbaugh on 659 stations. Talk radio listeners and participants are largely men who, in the midterm elections of 1994 (and probably still), tended (significantly more so than women listeners) to vote Republican, disaffected Reagan-Rush acolytes. Between 5% and 10% of the African American audience tune in to talk radio, mostly to shows offered on the 189 black-owned stations. Interestingly enough, white and black men listen to talk radio in roughly the same proportions (about 20% of each group), although listening to talk radio has no demonstrable bearing on African American male voting patterns in the ways it has on white male voting patterns (Coleman, 1996). Talk radio, to refashion William Rusher's (1995) characterization only slightly, has become a white male "conservative precinct" (Bolce, DeMaio, & Muzzio, 1996; Hutchby, 1992; Page & Tannenbaum, 1996).

CLASS OF THE '90s

Sports talk radio likewise is all about class formation, even as it represents itself as classless—as class blind or class transcendent. How could it escape class formation in a market where 7-year contracts run from $50m to $120m, where a 21-year-old golfer earns $40m on a promise before winning a professional tournament from a company able to pay him only because its product is made by those it barely pays at all. And yet, the audience for sports talk radio ranges from the un- or under- or lowly-employed at one end of contemporary class structure to the beeper/cellular phone/beamer generation at the other. By the mid-1990s, there were 100 24-hour sports talk stations: all sports talk, all the time. There are sports talk stations that serve sports franchises, cheerleading owners' commitments, apologists for "what it takes" for a franchise to get a city to subsidize its activities (a new stadium or arena, downtown revitalization, sales tax subsidy, selling the public on a trade of popular players). KMVP in Phoenix, the new CBS affiliate, for instance, is user friendly to Jerry Colangelo, mega sports overlord of the Phoenix Suns (basketball), the

Phoenix Coyotes (hockey, formerly the Winnipeg Jets), the Arizona Diamondbacks (the expansion baseball team), and the Arizona Rattlers (Arena
football team).[1] Not only do these radio stations broadcast franchise games,
but the likes of Al McCoy ("voice" of the Suns) and Greg Schulte ("voice"
of the Diamondbacks) run regular daytime byline commentaries, homeboy
Peter Vecseys or Frank Giffords. Radio callers here tend to be the cellular
phone clientele, wishful clients or hopeful subcontractors, community
partners or sky box inhabitants of their "home" teams.

Downmarket, by contrast, one finds (I think more interestingly) sports
radio talking to and for, about and with, the little guy, sewing him into the
seamless web of American consumptive practice, giving him a place he can
call his own while dropping a buck in its name. The bleacher bums
(Whoopi's whooping *Eddie,* the dawg pound masochists, collars and all),
pooling resources for pay-per-view simulcasts where tickets for the game
are out of reach. More vocally opinionated, more locally knowledgeable
than the coach about the team's woes, longer suffering than anyone should
be and still prepared to pay for it. The quintessential Cubs or Cleveland
Browns fan. Upscale audio, down to earth radio; man in the car talking to
himself on his car phone (never a moment alone), man in the street ranting
at anyone who will listen (forced by circumstance to be alone); "good guy"
radio, "bad dude" radio. Brent Musberger and Mad Dog.

Pamela Haag, nevertheless (or precisely consequently), thinks there is
something inherently democratizing about sports talk radio, for she thinks
it fashions civil talk in public space as an alternative to "hate radio," as well
as giving local color to the all but hegemonic "corporate voice" of media
representation: playful offense in the face of both hate speech and humor-
less homogenized commercialized blandness. Local living color rather than
nationally syndicated sameness, civil disagreement rather than anarchic
militia disobedience, playful projection rather than put-upon politics. Giving in to the thin romance of the local in the face of the homogeneity of the
multinational, Haag concludes that sports talk radio fulfills people's desires
to be "thrown together in unexpected, impassioned, even random social
relations and communities."[2] They do? No segregation in this vision. Folks
want "to mix with people they have nothing (but sports) in common with.
They want to be *from* somewhere again, to be part of a heterogeneous tribe
rather than a narrowly defined political cabal" (Haag, 1996, p. 467). Across
class, irrespective of race, against the grain of gender. That's a different
sports talk radio than the one I'm stuck with.

Haag's romantic longing suggests a telling point, although not quite the
one she has in mind to project. Sports *is* productive of a sort of *uni*formity,

and sports talk radio helps fashion it. Uniforms encourage, enable, establish sameness, identity, and identification. They throw together almost indistinguishably the large and small, fat and thin, dark and fair, large-chested and lanky, fat cats and working stiffs, high rollers and the tightfisted. The magnification of sports in our culture thus has massive ramifications for democracy, although otherwise than in the idealized sense Haag would have it. Public sphere exchange is mediated through the trading off of commitments to sports franchises, endless debates about who's better than whom, who should be MVP, who "belongs" in the Hall of Fame. In the end, it adds up now to little more than the commitment to purchase marketed merchandise, to root for the same team no matter how exploitative of fan sentimentality. The professional sports franchises in cities, owned by mega-capital conglomerate interests, establish their indispensability to civic life by fabricating the consciousness that they are "*your* Chicago Bulls/Phoenix Suns/New York Knicks/etc." This enacts at once a team loyalty exhibited through the purchase of a team T-shirt or baseball cap. We're all dancing to the same tune here, watching the same cheerleading dancers high-stepping, dressed *identi*cally, shouting in unison, "Let's go . . .!" "De-fense!" We're closer here to the mass psychology of fascism with a human face than to a democratic public sphere.

Sports talk radio plays a central role in producing this uniformity—a uniformity in style of expression, of opinion, of team support. Giving away team T-shirts and caps, tickets and corporate promotions. Getting fans to line up behind team players and chemistry, product development and consumption, trades and waivers, benchings and discipline, rationalization and exoneration through individualized charities that cover (up) for corporate profits. Something is abstractly ethno-nationalistic about the enterprise. Supporting one's team today has taken the place of what it was once like supporting one's country, right or wrong. Sports talk radio is the propaganda machine of the new fan-aticism.

The demographic and commercial makeup of professional sports in America has always reflected, as it has reified, prevailing social relations. Think of Jesse Owens or Joe Louis in 1936, the Negro League and the Women's League, Jackie Robinson and President Truman's desegregation of the military, free agency and deregulation, affirmative action and Al Campanis. Why should sports be any (in)different now? And why should sports talk radio make a social difference, rather than represent prevailing social relations? Sports reflects the divide between rich and poor; the stylized and improvisational; the incessant commercialized shifting of the fashionable required by commodified professionalism in the face of the necessary repetition of the everyday; the physically demanding, aggressive violence of daily life hidden behind the veneer of an exhilarating, breathtaking aesthetic beauty; the rule-bound, repetitive, task-oriented nature of so much in late modern life in the face of the entrepreneurial need to push the limits, break the bounds, defy regularity, the norm(al), the law(s of nature). Made for and imitative of, yet imitated by, television. Sport imitates life, which ironically has come to follow the lead of sports fashion.

We are encouraged by sports and sports talk to remember the winners and stars, and we forget all too quickly the role players and losers (this latter word itself drips pejoratively off the tongues of sports radio hosts: In a world where winner takes all, we couldn't be caught losing, now, could we?). The star phenomenon individualizes sport, hiding the collective efforts of producing competitiveness (even in the case of radically individualized giants like Muhammad Ali, or Carl Lewis, Michael Johnson or Michael Jordan, FloJo or Martina), elevating the pleasures of success while deriding the pains of their preparation, dismissing all too quickly the disappointments of their failures, blind to the hidden costs of life in retirement as the smile of the professional spotlight fades too often to a grimace of a life faced with physical suffering. Muhammad Ali has been resurrected in the public eye only now that his politics are deemed no longer relevant.

MEN/TO/RING BOYZ, AIRING RACE

Talk on sports radio ranges across the political, more than occasionally explicitly about race in sports, always implicitly about race in America. And it invariably represents men's interests. For example, the local sports talk downmarket station runs a weekly segment, "What's Your Beef?" encouraging callers to gripe, not just about sports and sports character concerns, but about "anything" and "anyone" in one's life one might want to chew or stew upon. This furnishes, in other words, a forum for letting off steam, for venting venom(ously). It effectively opens a channel for the performativity of angry white males (who are overwhelmingly its performers). "The worst thing a woman can have is lip hair." "Women should not be allowed to broadcast men's sports." "Women's professional basketball, what a joke. You wouldn't catch me dead watching it." Sports talk radio provides a covert political stage for those who think of themselves as nonpolitical or (what in the age of self-proclaimed political correctness amounts to the same thing) as politically disenfranchised. Like Limbaugh, though more discretely, sports talk radio enables white men to express themselves white and male.

David Roediger (1996) remarks, in an interesting read of Rush Limbaugh's cultural resonance in America, that "banality can carry much more social power than genius where white consciousness is concerned" (p. 42). Whiteness silently produces and reproduces itself behind the vocality of loudmouthed, flaccid ranting. Sports talk similarly enacts its whiteness through the banal, no longer through the micro details of sports statistics (in itself banal enough, though relatively harmless) but via the disputational and contentious, the licensed arrogance of self-opinionated expression where anything goes so long as one is heard to say it forcefully and angrily enough. Sports radio discussion overwhelmingly infantilized concerns raised about Fuzzy Zoeller's disparately arrogant references to Tiger Woods as "that little boy" likely to serve "fried chicken and collard greens" at the "green jacket dinner" in the wake of Woods's record-breaking win at the Augusta Masters, dismissing them as choices of the politically correct unable (once again) to take a joke. No surprise that no mention was made of the Internet appearance soon after of the call to boycott K-mart because, by dropping Zoeller as its spokesman in the wake of his remarks about Woods, the chain had chosen to cater to a "black clientele," thereby ignoring the interests of whites. By contrast, two local hosts on the sports station that for a while ran a daily segment of Howard Stern's morning show spent an hour talking about the virtues for men of tight-fitting but uncomfortable women's lingerie. Sports talk is to radio what the Wide World of Wrestling is to television. These are marriages made at the polls of the lowest common denominator of whitemaleness.

Men invest in mediated sports as a down payment on the (reproduced) pervasiveness of male domination. It is obviously not that all men are better than all women in sports, only that the best male athletes on the established physical criteria outstrip the best women. And this is the point: Men's investment in spectator sports accordingly becomes investment in their own projected superiority through the superiority of the best athletes (who "just happen to be" men) (Messner, 1989). Sports talk radio facilitates this (masculine) self-elevation, the ideological reproduction of hegemony— risk- and cost-free but for the price of the toll call.

A caller the other day to Jim Rome's "In the Jungle" trashed what he called "the Trailgangsters"—referring to the off court criminal troubles of the Portland Trailblazers—for "all they can beat up is women." Notice the rhetorical force of *all* here, which effeminizes "the Trailgangsters" even as it demonizes them for physically assaulting women (as one of the team members was, in fact, accused). Another caller to another program positively gushed, "My estimation of Marv Albert [NBC basketball play-by-play analyst accused of assaulting a woman in a hotel room, biting her repeatedly, forcing her to commit fellatio, and then sodomizing her] just went up." The caller indicated in his remarks that he had hitherto assumed Albert sexually inept, a conclusion he had derived with impeccable logic from the "fact" of Albert's supposed (self-evident, it seems) toupee. Apparently, Albert hadn't heeded the exhortation, in this caller's estimate, of the ads run regularly on all sports talk radio stations to seek out (the presidency of) The Men's Hair Club. The charge of sexual abuse, its innuendo, is payment sufficient for white men to offset the sin of (covering up) baldness (black men apparently don't need to, as they "clearly" have no hair to speak of, as evidenced by the likes of Michael Jordan and Charles Barkley).

Behind the projection of masculinity here obviously lurks race. Many of the best, the most high-profile athletes in the most high-profile sports are—or at least are considered to be—people of color, as the euphemism would have it, whereas the players—hosts and callers alike—in sports talk radio are almost invariably white men. (The one very notable exception among sports talk hosts is the Fabulous Sports Babe, Nanci Donnellan, the dominatrix of sports talk; she who knows more and kicks butt harder than her competitors.) Here we find risk-free identification with the superiority of black men in sports—the action-at-a-distance of being born-to-it assumption—while rhetorically reenacting technologically and technophonically that segregating divide of black folk residentially, educationally, socioeconomically, and culturally marking America throughout the 20th century.

Sports talk has become a leading forum for expressing "whitemaleness." Whitemaleness traditionally has taken itself as the arbiter of rationality, of intelligence, reduced impotently to reflecting on and about what signifies overwhelmingly as physical activity. Sports talk manifests a peculiar version of this. Isaiah Thomas complained at the beginning of the 1990s about white basketball commentators gushing on about "the genius" of white players, whereas black talent was characterized merely as physically gifted. Everyone "knows" that "white men can't jump," so they must cut it through superior intelligence and work ethic. In this context, sports talk radio mediates the racialized gaze on the (black) body in and through sports. A colleague, a self-declared radical feminist, once blurted out in my company, "Oh, Shawn Kemp, he's gorgeous, from the neck down." Sports talk radio enables white men to imagine the black body in a sense without being in its presence, unthreatened by it racially or homoerotically, unchallenged by the sexuality projected onto it imaginatively by the racialized fantasies of ("their") white women. In that sense, Dennis Rodman's cross-dressing is radical, certainly more risky—as it is more risqué—than the safety of the reflexive metatalk about it on sports talk radio by the likes of Scott Ferrall. Rodman's performance in acting out or up expresses the audacity of speaking back, for which he inevitably gets endlessly spoken about—paraded and oddly parroted—by radio talkers and stalkers.

INTERPELLATED SELVES, INVISIBLE SUBJECTS

Sports has become not only big business but also the arbiter of fashion, and fashion increasingly has been set/led by black stylin'. The baggy shorts craze that has swept youthful America leapt first from the street of black youths into high fashion projected by the antics of Michigan Wolverines' Fab Five and kid rappers Kris Kross. Sports crosses over commercially with rap in the bank account of the Shaq Attack. The market meets the street, where "the street" floats signifyin'ly between the sign for the stock market ("Wall St.") and the culture of hip hop, the former an investment in being "up," the latter in being "down." Whitemaleness finds a place for self-expression through fandom, the market of youthful parents and their doted kids with disposable cash in hand and the mentorship of fan-aticism, through consumptive apparel. I recently sat next to a father and his 8-year-old son at a Phoenix Suns game. The child, sporting the mandatory Kevin Johnson vest, quietly sipped on a soft drink and munched tacos through much of the game, until late in the fourth quarter when, buoyed by his father's increasingly aggressive support for the team, he began screaming in tune with his dad. Here in the flesh, I thought, I was witnessing sports (talk radio's) interpellating power at work. Sports radio fashions a clientele, filling the unconscious with desires less and less of its own making. It molds subjects as seekers of spectatorial excitement, instantaneous gratification, consumers of newly fashioned and packaged merchandise, releasing expressions of commitment the force of which leave the cool reflectiveness of a thoughtful democracy in the public sphere quite chilled (out). Sport is the perfect medium for this fanatical consumptive power. It is all about winners and losers, excitability and excitement, releasing nervous energy that is at once manic yet for the most part socially controllable. It is unpredictable within predictable parameters, sensuously stimulating, open almost constantly to new configuration, therefore perfectly conducive to fashionable commodification and commodifiable fashion.

Beyond this, sport and sports talk radio have proved conducive also—a medium well fitted—to the "advancement" of the new racism over the past two decades: racist expression coded as race neutrality, racialized exclusions as color blindness, racist discrimination as market choices, as commodity preferences. If I fanatically support a team that is all black, how can I be racist in trashing welfare state policies? Indeed, my freedom to support that team is identical to my preference against welfare for anybody. It "just happens to be" that the racially marginalized lose out by welfare divestment. Racial neutrality is sustained only by historical amnesia, political erasure, and moral ignorance. The public disinvestment in the welfare state means I have more disposable cash in hand to spend on my team's merchandise, should I so choose. It's a win-win situation, only by virtue of rendering the losers invisible. We never hear their voices on democratically arranged sports talk radio.

Anne McClintock (1995, pp. 31-36) demonstrates the late 19th-century shift that emerged in dominant forms of racist expression from scientific racism to commodity racism. *Commodity racism* manifests in consumer spectacles: advertizing, expositions, museum exhibitions. It could be added that today commodity racism finds its principal expression in and through the hyperconsumptive spectacle of sports. Sports sneakers like Nike promote their market superiority through the physical prowess of their overwhelmingly black sports superstars. The megasalaries associated with the racialized bodies of sports heroes hide from view the exploitative conditions marking racialized bodies elsewhere that precisely make such spectacular salaries possible. At the height of the controversy over Nike's exploitative labor practices in Indonesia and Vietnam, sports talk callers to a person dissed the concern: "Those countries should do something about it if they are so concerned, but they're getting good jobs. . . . It's not happening in America, so who cares." We might call this, without too much conceptual twisting, "commodity neo-colonialism." At the same time, the whiteness of sports talk radio is reflected in the music it advertises: Clapton, the Eagles, Country, as its class commitments are reflected in commercials for the likes of Sears and Home Depot.

Racialized commodity neo-colonialism hides in good part behind the feel-good color blindness of sports talk hosts: "We don't care whether someone is white, black, yellow, pink, or green." Color may not matter, but race surely does. So Scott Ferrall growls menacingly that Patrick Ewing's nostrils are wide enough for a basketball to fit. Sufficiently conscious that he has silently invoked the "r" word in a way that might get his radio balloon popped, he quickly adds, "This is not a race thing, it's a nose thing." Must be the nose thing that allows him to play so well, huh. Perhaps he can take in more air, thus allowing him to elevate more easily in the drive to the rim. I now understand that it's the aerodynamics of the nose, not the Nikes, that explain how black men get to jump so high. This is not so far a cry from the restaurant remarks about slavery and thigh bones that got Jimmy the Greek fired from CBS Sports.

FAN-ATIC COMMUNITIES

Talk radio creates new communities, or at the least the artifice of old communities anew. *Sports* talk radio re-creates the artifice of a whitemale community of like-minded, like-thinking souls, gated circles of virtual friends whose virtuality is reflected by the abstractness, the irreality of the friendships and the ephemerality, the ethereality, of the community. But irreality and ethereality notwithstanding, it reproduces the artifice, the sense of whitemaleness, by offering if only informally an apparatus of ideological interpellation, the hailing to be part of a subjectivity larger than oneself, a member of a body (politic) enactive of (self-)elevation and (social) mobility via racialized and (en)gendered exclusions.

This is, if only by indirection, the death of civil discourse, of a discourse of civility, as social control through fan-aticism takes over. It is prescient in this context to note that there is more on-field/on-court/on-ice violence in American sport than there is among fans. And noteworthy as well, the altogether white sport of ice hockey has shown such growth in fan and sports radio support. Against this icy uncool background, I end by emphasizing that "I love this game" reduces all too quickly to "Life is a game. Play hard." Life is sport, as (my) sport is life (on the whole, "I'd rather be . . ."). Winner takes all. No fear. As long as the Dow is climbing, my team's winning, my mutual funds are soaring. I can retire to . . . the living room to watch the next world final whatever. Drinking Miller Lite or Bud, eating nachos or tacos, my newest model Nikes thumping the couch, the fantasy of my leased Lexis or Nissan in the garage, the car audio and cellular phone safely out of reach of all those nonwhite vultures I see on *Cops* (when I'm watching sport of another kind), who if they didn't make it into professional sports are prowling my streets looking to commit a crime. And the homeless are not camped outside my suburban home, not selling their newspaper on my highway to work, not raiding my garbage can, not living off the taxes I'm no longer paying. Talk radio makes me just do it, at least in those intervals when television isn't gripping me.

Ahh, Our America. A commercial time-out for the dream (on) team. I believe I can fly, I believe I can touch the sky. Lite me up another. Life is good. Don't worry, be happy. I love what you do for me. Enjoy the ride.

As the game fades noisily to black. Welcome to the real terrordome.

NOTES

1. KMVP recently took over sports from KTAR, now a 24-hour talk radio format, hiring many of the latter's sports personnel, no doubt, with the blessing of the father figure. KMVP has stations in major sports markets nationwide, the sports talk version of AutoNation, Wayne Huizenga's "blockbuster" new "discount" auto franchise. Huizenga owns the Miami Dolphins (football), the Florida Marlins (baseball), and the Florida Panthers (hockey) teams in three of the four major league professional sports covering the country's third largest television market. Colangelo and Huizenga are to sports perhaps what Turner and Murdoch are to broadcasting. They represent the new entrepreneurship in the rapidly expanding southern/southwestern demographic markets of Arizona and Florida, respectively. They offer to late modernity what Ford once made available to the immigrant *driven* expansion into the Midwest, or Mayer and Selznick to the movie industry, capturing the popular imagination of their times.

2. Cerullo, Ruane, and Chayko (1992) make out a similar line of argument regarding talk radio more generally—namely, that it offers "technological ties that bind," "time efficient ways to enjoy social interaction," a perfect form of community for the times. Similarly, Bolce, DeMaio, and Muzzio (1996) suggest the emergence of a "hyper-" version of "cyberdemocracy": "Talk radio can create instantaneous communities of coexistent interest and passion over continental distances."

REFERENCES

Bolce, L., DeMaio, G., & Muzzio, D. (1996). Dial-in-democracy: Talk radio and the 1994 election. *Political Science Quarterly, 111*(3), 457-481.

Cerullo, K., Ruane, J., & Chayko, M. (1992). Technological ties that bind: Media-generated primary groups. *Communication Research, 19,* 102-129.

Coleman, T. (1996). Black talk. *Emerge, 8*(2), 50-57.

Haag, P. (1996). "50,000 watt sports bar": Talk radio and the ethic of the fan. *South Atlantic Quarterly, 95*(2), 453-470.

Hutchby, I. (1992). The pursuit of controversy: Routine skepticism in talk on "talk radio." *Sociology, 26*(4), 673-694.

McClintock, A. (1995). *Imperial leather: Race, gender, and sexuality in the colonial contest.* New York: Routledge.

Messner, M. (1989). Masculinities and athletic careers. *Gender & Society, 3,* 71-88.

Page, B., & Tannenbaum, J. (1996). Populistic deliberation and talk radio. *Journal of Communication, 46*(2), 33-54.

Roediger, D. (1996). White looks: Hairy apes, true stories, and Limbaugh's laughs. *Minnesota Review, 47.*

Rusher, W. (1995). The importance of talk radio. *Newspaper Enterprise Association, 3.*

CHAPTER 3

Democratic Delusions

The Town Meeting in an Electronic Age

Dale Herbeck
Boston College

Many thoughtful commentators have lamented over the death of public argument in American politics (see, e.g., Collins & Skover, 1996; Entman, 1989; Kellner, 1990; Postman, 1985; Sabato, 1991). Even as the quantity of political speech has increased, the quality of argument in the public sphere has grown noticeably more impoverished. Nowhere is this paradox more evident than in presidential campaigns. The length of these campaigns has increased in recent years, yet there seems to be less and less discussion of the issues. Spending on these campaigns has reached record highs, but the amount of meaningful information provided to voters to assess the candidates has decreased. Opinion polls have become more common, and reporting on poll results has become a substitute for substantive coverage of the campaigns. Candidates are seemingly always in the media, but the length of each exposure has decreased as sound bites have grown shorter and shorter. No personal narrative is too tragic, no personal matter too private, when candidates are appealing for votes.

Given the absence of meaningful discourse in contemporary presidential campaigns, debates between candidates for the highest national office seem to provide a unique opportunity for public argument. Debates offer an extended opportunity for the candidates to communicate with millions of eligible voters for an extended period of time. Highlighting the potential implicit in presidential debates, Kathleen Hall Jamieson and David Birdsell (1988) have suggested that "debates offer the longest, most intense views of the candidates available to the electorate. Uninterrupted by ads, uncontaminated by the devices programmers use to ensnare and hold prime-time attention, the debates offer sustained and serious encounters with candidates" (p. 126).

Unfortunately, the potential implicit in debates among the presidential candidates has gone largely unrealized. Instead of affording observers a rich discussion of the issues and the candidates' respective positions, presidential debates have become shallow political spectacles, media events virtually devoid of intellectual substance or merit (Zarefsky, 1992). Unfortunately, all too many explanations have been posed for why debates have failed to realize our expectations. Representatives of the political parties have skillfully negotiated formats that allow the candidates routinely to avoid answering important questions and to evade meaningful discussion. For their part, candidates have learned to recite memorized or scripted passages, to display appropriate emotions and act "presidential," and artfully to avoid discussion of troublesome topics. The media have played an equally dubious role, often reducing a 90-minute debate to a memorable clip appearing later on the news, using questionable polls and devices to declare winners and losers instantly, and trivializing the substance of debate with insipid commentary.

Despite this record of futility, interest in political debates has remained high in recent years[1] because of the penultimate nature of the spectacle and innovative formats. One of the most heralded changes has been to model presidential debates after a New England town meeting. The first of these so-called town hall debates between presidential candidates occurred in 1992, when President George Bush, Bill Clinton, and Ross Perot used a format that allowed citizens to question the candidates directly. The result was a lively debate, and given the success of the format, it is not surprising that 4 years later one of the two debates between President Clinton and Bob Dole used the town hall format.

Through such town halls, presidential campaigns have attempted to create a means to reach through the media and directly connect with the voters. All across America, candidates for lesser offices have recognized the powerful political appeal implicit in such meetings and adopted similar strategies. Although such forums seem to offer the possibility of meaningful interaction, in this chapter I argue that the town hall debate is a democratic fiction, an appeal to a cherished political institution designed to mask the mediocrity of contemporary political discourse. To prove this contention, the 1992 town hall debate among Bush, Clinton, and Perot is offered as an illustration. In the pages that follow, I consider the decision to adopt a town hall format, characterize the traditional New England town meeting that is the basis of the modern town hall, and conclude by arguing that the first town hall debate between presidential nominees was more of a political spectacle than an exercise in democratic self-government. Working from this experience, I briefly consider the possibility of an "electronic town square," a powerful democratic image invoked by President Clinton in his 1996 State of the Union Address.

THE CHANGING FACE OF PRESIDENTIAL ELECTIONS

Debates between competing candidates have become a major event in presidential election campaigns. In 1960, 1976, 1980, 1984, 1988, 1992, and 1996, the leading presidential candidates met in televised debates before the general election. Although a variety of formats have been used for these exchanges, the most common until recently featured the candidates responding to questions posed by a panel of journalists: A journalist's question is directed to one of the candidates, then the opposing candidate is given the opportunity to respond, after which time may be allotted for a rebuttal.

From the outset of the debates, argumentation scholars have known that the panel format forces the candidate to choose between answering the questions asked by a panelist and debating the opposing candidates (see Bitzer & Reuter, 1980, p. 197). These scholars have also recognized that the panelists are not objective intermediaries, but rather have rightly observed that panelists necessarily play an adversarial role with the candidates in presidential debates. Reflecting on the debates between President Gerald Ford and challenger Jimmy Carter in 1976, Lloyd Bitzer and Theodore Reuter (1980) found an

adversarial tone and content in many of the questions. Panelists frequently did more than ask questions: they argued with the candidates and sought to refute them; they set forth charges and accusations and they provided unfavorable characterizations of candidates and their actions or policies. (p. 41)

Responding to the 1988 debates between George Bush and Michael Dukakis, J. Michael Hogan (1989) has claimed:

> Just as modern campaign "reporting" goes far beyond reporting what candidates say and do, the "questioning" of candidates in the debates goes far beyond *asking questions* that elicit information about the candidates' beliefs and proposals. Not once in the 270 minutes of the 1988 debates did a journalist simply ask a candidate: "What is your position on such and such an issue?" Instead, each and every question was preceded by a mini-speech—always argumentative and often belligerent—either expressing the "media personality's" pessimistic assessment of some state of affairs or, in some fashion, refuting or belittling the candidate. (p. 221)

Commenting on the same series of debates, Michael Weiler (1989) went so far as to conclude, "Through lengthy declarative prefaces to questions, repetition of questions, hyperbole, and other devices, the press may become as much debater as facilitator of debate" (p. 219).

Criticism of the panel format has not been restricted to academicians or academic journals. At a practical level, anyone can see that having four journalists interrogate two or more candidates, with each candidate having the right of reply or rebuttal, will produce shallow discussion unlikely to provide much insight into what each candidate would actually do to cope with the nation's most pressing problems. Looking beyond the logistical problems posed by a panel of journalists, critics have also criticized the actual questions asked by the panelists. More than a few commentators have lamented that the journalists on the panels tend to trip over their egos in their eagerness to ask their own questions—leaving gaps and evasions in the previous answer without a follow-up. Even campaign officials and political consultants have questioned whether political debates involving panels of journalists truly produce any useful information (see Reed, 1996). Although criticism of the panel format has been widespread for years, it took the 1992 campaign to break with tradition and adopt a new format.

The 1992 campaign was unique, as two of the candidates, Democratic challenger Bill Clinton and Independent candidate Ross Perot, both displayed a willingness to use innovative means to reach the voters. Bill Clinton in particular made strategic use of the media in his successful campaign.[2] Immediately before the New Hampshire primary, for example, Clinton responded to widespread allegations of marital infidelity by appearing on *60 Minutes* with his wife, Hillary. When questions subsequently arose about how he had avoided serving in the Vietnam War,

Clinton responded through a televised town hall meeting in New Hampshire. Still later in the campaign, Clinton appeared in dark glasses with his saxophone on *The Arsenio Hall Show*. Although the viewing audience for the actual show was minuscule, Clinton received extensive coverage in the mainstream media for his rendition of "Heartbreak Hotel."

In his independent campaign for the presidency, Ross Perot also used nontraditional techniques to appeal for support. Although his populist campaign themes were markedly different from those of Clinton, Perot was equally willing to explore opportunities previously spurned by presidential candidates. In February, during an interview on "Larry King Live," Perot intimated that he might be persuaded to run for president if there was enough citizen support to have his name placed on the ballot in all 50 states. After formally declaring his candidacy, Perot made frequent use of half-hour infomercials on television to explain his policy positions and to solicit support. Finally, like Clinton, Perot was always willing to appear on television talk shows and to participate in town hall meetings.

As the campaign reached its climax, the Commission on Presidential Debates proposed four debates—three presidential contests and a single contest between the vice presidential candidates. The bipartisan commission, which had been created to negotiate the logistics of the debates, recommended a single-moderator format. This format, the commission believed, would promote more substantive answers by allowing follow-up questions from the moderator while simultaneously creating the possibility of direct confrontation between the candidates. The Clinton campaign readily agreed to the scheme proposed by the commission, but the Bush campaign was unwilling to accept this plan. Apparently believing that agreeing to debate too early would freeze any momentum toward Bush while also fearing that the format would work to Clinton's advantage, the Bush campaign summarily rejected the commission's recommendations. The inability to agree on a format forced the cancellation of the first debate, and for a time it appeared that no presidential debates would take place in 1992. Finally, after months of posturing, the Bush and Clinton campaigns agreed to a series of debates featuring a variety of formats and invited Ross Perot to participate. Given the competing interests, it is not surprising that the presidential debates held in 1992 reflected a series of compromises. One compromise was the second debate, scheduled for Richmond, Virginia, which featured a town hall format. Under this format, an audience composed of undecided voters would symbolically represent the body politic as they engaged the candidates in a discussion of the issues. The format was unique, and it is doubtful that the Richmond town hall would have occurred were it not for the unusual juxtaposition of politicians, campaigns, and events (see Depoe & Short-Thompson, 1994, pp. 86-87).

THE NEW ENGLAND TOWN
MEETING AND SELF-GOVERNMENT

The town meeting has a long tradition in American politics. In his ruminations on life in early America, Alexis de Tocqueville (1835/1969) was impressed by the New England town meeting (see pp. 71-81). He observed that, from the first days when settlers colonized New England, the colonists had practiced democratic self-government on issues of local concern through town meetings. He was, of course, not alone in marveling at the town meeting as an institution. One hundred thirty years later, in his influential work *Political Freedom,* Alexander Meiklejohn (1960) observed that the New England town meeting "is commonly, and rightly, regarded as a model by which free political procedures may be measured. It is self-government in its simplest form" (p. 24). Writing about the myriad forces that shaped life in America, historian Carl Degler (1970) posits, "In practice the town meeting was one of the most democratic features of seventeenth-century life" (pp. 25-26).

Although these lofty characterizations are somewhat misleading (relatively few citizens were qualified voters eligible to participate), the New England town meeting was a meeting of equals who shared power through communal decision making. What made, and still makes, the town meeting a political ideal is its unique instantiation of democracy. "Similar to the ancient Greek city-states where oratory was central to the function of society," Janette Kenner Muir (1994) observes, "the town meeting provided the opportunity for every voting member to speak in defense of his or her own actions or to argue for change in policies" (p. 342). "Each has a right and a duty," Meiklejohn (1960) argued, "to think his own thoughts, to express them, and to listen to the arguments of others" (p. 24).

The town meeting has become a democratic ideal because it reminds people of the origins of America. All qualified voters residing in a community could come together in a meeting house at a particular time to discuss a matter of public import—a new school, road repairs or capital improvements, health or public safety. A moderator or chair would be appointed to impose the most basic rules of order. Even though rules were adopted to structure the discussion, all those present were entitled to express their opinion. Reasoned debate progressed between free and equal participants working together to solve a problem. Although the participants played the role of partisans, their partisanship was necessarily restrained by the recognition that they were acting together for the public good. If consensus was impossible, after allowing a reasonable amount of time for discussion, a vote was taken to determine the will of the majority.

Although the town meeting remains a democratic ideal, it is impossible to return to the America of yesterday. The town meeting is still practiced in some communities, but it has receded in importance as government has become progressively larger and more professionalized. In a physical sense, most communities are now so large that it would be impossible to either assemble or conduct an organized dialogue. The growth of our nation, among other forces, has required our nation to move from a participatory to a representative democracy. But in a spiritual sense, the possibility of community implicit in a town meeting has been forever shattered by the fragmentation of modern life. Herein lies the rhetorical power of the town hall forum. By suggesting the possibility of a national town meeting, the town hall format appeals to the past while simultaneously offering the illusion of democratic self-government.

THE 1992 TOWN HALL DEBATE: DEMOCRATIC RITUAL OR POLITICAL SPECTACLE?

The second presidential debate in 1992 was held on October 15 at the University of Richmond in Richmond, Virginia. The debate was unique, as it was loosely modeled after a New England town meeting in which candidates responded to questions from the audience. To facilitate interaction, the traditional podiums were removed and each candidate was provided with a tall stool. Candidates were permitted to move about the stage when responding to questions. Carole Simpson of *ABC News* played the role of moderator, roaming though the audience to solicit questions from 209 undecided voters empaneled by an independent polling organization. Each question was directed to a particular candidate, but the other candidates were also given the opportunity to respond. Simpson was allowed to clarify and follow up on questions asked by the audience. No order of response was mandated, nor was the debate balanced to guarantee equal time to all three participants. The debate concluded with a 2-minute closing statement from each candidate.

It was clear from the outset that the town hall debate would be different from previous presidential debates. In her opening remarks, Carole Simpson prognosticated that "tonight's program is unlike any presidential debate in history—we're making history here now, and it's pretty exciting."[3] Questions from the citizens that evening were noteworthy, partly because for the first time citizens were involved in a presidential debate, and partly because the citizens insisted that the candidates focus on substantive issues. One of the first questioners complained, "The amount of time the candidates have spent in this campaign trashing their opponents' character and their programs is depressingly large. Why can't your discussions and proposals reflect the genuine complexity and the difficulty of the issues to try to build a consensus around the best aspects of all proposals?" The very next questioner asked, "Can we focus on the issues and not the personalities and the mud?"

The questions dealt almost exclusively with domestic issues; a single query was made about America's role as a superpower. To the surprise of many commentators, the citizen questioners ignored the character issues associated with Clinton's draft record and his antiwar activities in Europe that had been such a large part of the first debate. Although the debate did produce a notable exchange between the candidates about Clinton's character, the most poignant moment of the debate occurred when a young black woman asked, "How has the national debt personally affected each of your lives? And if it hasn't, how can you honestly find a cure for the economic problems of the common people if you have no experience in what's ailing them?"

Answers to this question varied, but they are worth studying because they reveal a great deal about both the town hall format and how the media portrayed the debate. Ross Perot, the first to enter the fray, responded as follows:

It caused me to disrupt my private life and my business to get involved in this activity. That's how much I care about it. And believe me, if you knew my family and if you knew the private life I have, you would agree in a minute that that's a whole lot more fun than getting involved in politics. But I have lived the American dream. I came from a very modest background. Nobody's been luckier than I've been, all the way across the spectrum, and the greatest riches of all are my wife and children. That's true of any family. But I want all the children—I want these young people up here to be able to start with nothing but an idea like I did and build a business. But they've got to have a strong basic economy and if you're in debt, it's like having a ball and chain around you. I just figure, as lucky as I've been, I owe it to them and I owe it to the future generations and on a very personal basis, I owe it to my children and grandchildren.

After Perot, the question fell to President Bush. "Well, I think the national debt affects everybody," Bush began. The questioner interrupted, "You personally." Flustered, Bush tried again, "Obviously, it has a lot to do with interest rates." This time, moderator Simpson interrupted, "She's saying, you personally." The questioner quickly interjected, "You, on a personal basis—how has it affected you?" before Simpson could ask, "Has it affected you personally?" Clearly flustered, Bush replied, "I'm sure it has. I love my grandchildren. . . . I want to think that they're going to be able to afford an education. I think that that's an important part of being a parent. If the question—maybe I—get it wrong. Are you suggesting that if somebody has means that the national debt doesn't affect them?" The questioner tried to clarify, suggesting, "I know people who cannot afford to pay the mortgage on their homes, their car payment. I have personal problems with the national debt. But how has it affected you, and if you have no experience in it, how can you help us, if you don't know what we're feeling?" Bush tried one final time:

Well, listen, you ought to be in the White House for a day and hear what I hear and see what I see and read the mail I read and touch the people that I touch from time to time. I was in the Lomax AME Church. It's a black church just outside of Washington, D.C. And I read in the bulletin about teenage pregnancies, about the difficulties that families are having to make ends meet. I talk to parents. I mean, you've got to care. Everybody cares if people aren't doing well. But I don't think it's fair to say, you haven't had cancer. Therefore, you don't know what's it like. I don't think it's fair to say, you know, whatever it is, that if you haven't been hit by it personally. But everybody's affected by the debt because of the tremendous interest that goes into paying on that debt everything's more expensive. Everything comes out of your pocket and my pocket. So it's that. But I think in terms of the recession, of course, you feel it when you're president of the U.S. And that's why I'm trying to do something about it by stimulating the export, vesting more, better education systems. Thank you. I'm glad you clarified it.

When presented with the opportunity to answer the same question, Clinton pounced. As he began to respond, he moved toward the front of the stage while simultaneously engaging the questioner, "Tell me how it's affected you again." Before the questioner could internalize the query and respond, Clinton intuitively asked, "You know people who've lost their jobs and lost their homes?" Not allowing time for a response, Clinton instead offered his own answer:

> Well, I've been governor of a small state for 12 years. I'll tell you how it's affected me. Every year, Congress and the president sign laws that make us do more things and give us less money to do it with. I see people in my state, middle-class people—their taxes have gone up in Washington and their services have gone down while the wealthy have gotten tax cuts. I have seen what's happened in this last 4 years when—in my state, when people lose their jobs there's a good chance I'll know them by their names. When a factory closes, I know the people who ran it. When the businesses go bankrupt, I know them. And I've been out here for 13 months meeting in meetings just like this ever since October, with people like you all over America, people that have lost their jobs, lost their livelihood, lost their health insurance. What I want you to understand is the national debt is not the only cause of that. It is because America has not invested in its people. It is because we have not grown. It is because we've had 12 years of trickle down economics. We've gone from 1st to 12th in the world in wages. We've had 4 years where we've produced no private sector jobs. Most people are working harder for less money than they were making 10 years ago. It is because we are in the grip of a failed economic theory. And this decision you're about to make better be about what kind of economic theory you want, not just people saying I'm going to go fix it but what are we going to do? I think what we have to do is invest in American jobs, American education, control American health care costs and bring the American people together again.

Response to the town hall format was enthusiastic. Reporting on a research project involving groups of voters assembled to view the debate together, John Meyer and Diana Carlin (1994) found, "The focus group members' reactions to this debate format were strongly positive; it was seen as more relaxed and more democratic, and allowed for more openness, honesty, and personality exposure for the candidates" (p. 78). Although focus group members offered a variety of explanations for why they preferred the town hall format to the panel of journalists, it was clear that they preferred the format by a substantial margin. Some members of the focus group thought the questions were less predictable, others believed they could identify with the questioners, and finally, many claimed the candidates had to respond to the concerns of the audiences (those asking questions and those watching the exchange on their televisions) more directly (see Depoe & Short-Thompson, 1994, pp. 96-97).

Although there was some criticism (see especially Krauthammer, 1992), in general, reaction to the town hall format in the media was equally enthusiastic. Commentators observed that the Richmond debate had the candidates on literally the same level as the electorate and suggested that ordinary citizens, much more effectively than journalists, could force the candidates to address the issues and avoid negative attacks (see, e.g., Kloer, 1992). In accounts pregnant with irony, commentators praised the debate for its substance even as they worked to reduce the debate into a short series of video highlights (Baer, 1992).

THE DEATH OF DISCOURSE: THE MYTH OF THE TOWN MEETING

To liken town hall debates between presidential candidates to a traditional New England town meeting is akin to analogizing watching an athletic contest on television to actually participating in the contest. Although it is true that the candidates submitted themselves to the public by consenting to the debate, their participation in the town hall was more symbolic than substantive. Instead of using the debate as an opportunity to engage those present on the issues, all three candidates used the town hall as a forum for reiterating campaign themes to the tens of millions viewing the debate on television. Simply put, the town hall format was a cynical product of the candidates' calculation of their own strategic interest. As a result, the town hall was structured to discourage argument and media coverage of the debate, further reducing the importance of what the candidates said in Richmond.

The Format

A careful review of the transcript of the debate suggests that the town hall format prevented the citizens from arguing with the candidates. Carole Simpson, playing the role of moderator, circulated through the audience, selecting citizens to ask questions. Each questioner had the opportunity to ask a single question, whereas each candidate claimed the right to respond to all questions. Because audience members had no opportunity to ask follow-up questions, true interaction between the candidates and the questioners was impossible. The debate had none of the public argument characteristic of the traditional New England town meeting because the format devised by the candidates prevented any possibility of dialogue. Even though all the citizens had a chance to ask questions, no one was able to engage the candidates on a particular issue.

Further, the town hall format encouraged a cursory treatment of the widest possible breadth of topics at the expense of in-depth analysis. Instead of focusing on a single topic in the tradition of the New England town meeting, the Richmond format allowed questions on any subject of interest to the questioners. Although this created the impression that no topics were precluded, the practical result was a town hall that featured questions about access to foreign markets, the national deficit, physical infrastructure, crime in cities, term limits, health care, the national debt, Social Security, America's role in the new world order, creating jobs, and the prospect of an African American and female ticket winning the presidency. Given the number of issues addressed in 90 minutes, it is not surprising that the treatment of any specific issue was extremely superficial.

Watching a mediated town hall is not akin to participating in a town meeting. Even though citizens were present in the audience, they did not have the opportunity to argue with the candidates. At the same time, the number of issues addressed necessarily kept the discussion superficial, and the format prevented the citizens from focusing on a particular theme. The Richmond debate may have been good television, but it is surely a misnomer to liken it to the New England town meeting.

The Broadcast Media

Although the debate was not a New England town meeting, media coverage of the debate helped transform what transpired in Richmond into a spectacle. Before the debate, the new format was hyped as a dramatic confrontation between the candidates and the voters. On the eve of the event, democratic appeals and rousing music were used to set the stage. Although television carried the unedited debate to the viewers, the moment the debate ended, commentators switched from observers to participants as they offered judgments regarding the outcome and the likely impact the debate would have on the election.

There may have been much to criticize, but many commentators were quick to highlight the fact that President Bush was unable to answer the question about the personal impact of the national debt, when in fact Bush had responded to the question. Bush was correct; in a personal sense, the national debt had not affected him. Further, Bush was able to invoke the cancer analogy to challenge the premise of the question. The fact that he was not personally affected by the national debt did not mean he was either unaware of the economic hardship being suffered or unqualified to solve the problem.

At the same time the media criticized Bush's answer, Clinton was praised for his emotive response. Commentators noted that Clinton had convinced the audience that he could feel the pain. Yet although Arkansas is a small state, it defies credibility to believe that Clinton knew the names of all the individuals who lost their jobs or who had lost their businesses to bankruptcy. Clinton's response was a flagrant appeal to emotion, but he was rewarded by a medium that privileges such warm pleas over cold facts.

In addition to interpreting the town hall, broadcast accounts immediately assessed the outcome of the debate. On the basis of an instant poll conducted immediately after the debate, for example, *CBS News* reported that 53% of the respondents thought Clinton had won, more than double the 25% who chose Bush, with Perot trailing closely behind at 21% (Page & Shaw, 1992). This outcome, of course, was integrated into coverage of the larger election story. According to these accounts, Bush was trailing badly and he had squandered a late opportunity to close the gap, throw the knockout punch, or hit a home run.[4]

Neil Postman (1985) suggests, "Entertainment is the supraideology of all discourse on television" (p. 87). Given coverage of the town hall debate by the broadcast media, Postman's cynicism is well justified. The Richmond debate was not a town meeting; it was a political spectacle. In retrospect, it is clear that the candidates created a town hall format uniquely suited for television. They came to a historic American city, they sat on stools, and they promised to interact with the voters. To make the format entertaining, the candidates developed sophisticated techniques for moving on the stage, appearing empathic, and reaching out to the viewers. The broadcast media cooperated in this enterprise, treating the debate as a major political event. By the time the story reached the evening news, it had been reduced to a brief series of predigested sound bites. As the event receded from the news, it congealed in the public memory as a story told by the broadcast media.

The Print Media

Whereas the broadcast media contextualized the debate, the print media further trivialized the discussion of substantive issues raised during the town hall. Instead of commenting on a particular issue addressed in the debate, the dominant themes in the media were visual or stylistic. Consider, for example, the following characterizations of the town hall debate in Richmond that appeared in some of the leading national newspapers the following day:

Los Angeles Times—
   It was perhaps inevitable, in this odd election year, that George Bush, Bill Clinton and Ross Perot would at least meet knee-to-knee on a set modeled after an afternoon talk show. (Jehl, 1992, p. A25)[5]

   That was no debate Thursday night between the presidential candidates. That was the triumph of the talk show format over substantive political discourse. Oprah Winfrey and Phil Donahue should sue for the hijacking of their format. (Thomas, 1992, p. 3B)[6]

Washington Post—
   Last night's presidential debate was aired live from Richmond, Va., but sometimes seemed dead on its feet. A modified talk-show format was imposed, with a studio audience asking the questions. The result was a kind of political "Donahue" or "Oprah Winfrey" show, but with much of the energy drained out. (Shales, 1992, p. D1)[7]

New York Times—
   The format of the second presidential debate last night may have resembled the sort of daytime talk shows where the guest was confessional and personal on all human idiosyncrasies. (Dowd, 1992, p. A1)[8]

Houston Chronicle—
   The "Phil Donahue Debate" with a "real people" format has now made its debut in this marathon made-for-TV presidential campaign. What next? The Oprah Outtakes? The Geraldo Get-Together? Maury and the Men Who Would Be President? (Hodges, 1992, p. A16)[9]

Such characterizations functioned to trivialize the town hall as a political event. Whereas the town hall format was clearly intended to invoke the democratic image of the New England town meeting, the commentary offered by the media shattered the analogy by analogizing the debate to the most common form of entertainment. If the debate was less than the analogy, the media coverage of the debate only magnified the disappointment.

Along with denigrating the town hall format, media accounts also marginalized the participants. Although all agreed that Clinton's performance had been exemplary, accounts of the debate praised him for his acumen as an entertainer and not for the quality of his discourse or policy initiatives. Clinton was favorably compared with Ronald Reagan (Ely, 1992), a talk show host (Siegel, 1992; Waldman, 1992), and a performer ("In Debates," 1992). Throughout print accounts, Clinton was praised for being a good entertainer, not for the originality or substance of his responses (Page & Shaw, 1992, p. 5; Shulman, 1992). Commentators were impressed by his ability to work the crowd like Donahue, for moving toward the audience when he answered questions, and for his skillful use of eye contact with questioners. These characterizations may be accurate, but taken together they had the unfortunate effect of reducing the town hall meeting to a political beauty pageant.

Whereas these accounts praised Clinton, print accounts of the debate highlighted visual elements to discount the performance of George Bush. In particular, commentators suggested that Bush seemed distant, unable to connect emotively with the audience (Jubera, 1992; Page & Shaw, 1992, p. 5). Worse yet, during the debate Bush made the inadvertent mistake of looking at his watch. These unfortunate glances, captured by the camera and used in stories to summarize the debate, took on their own political significance. An article in the *Houston Chronicle* claimed, "Restrained from the low blow and not as adept as Clinton at the up-close-and-personal, Bush fumbled. Three times he glanced at his watch. Was he bored? Was he fitful? Or was he just out of his element?"[10] (Rodriguez, 1992, p. 29). The *Boston Globe* concurred: "At 9:50 p.m. last night, George Bush looked at his wristwatch. Was time on his mind because it is running out? Did he have a date to pitch horseshoes? Another theory based on his behavior is that he is trying to roll time backwards to the original George Bush"[11] (Nolan, 1992, p. 1). These glances, coupled with his lack of empathy when speaking of the nation's economic woes, were all the evidence necessary to prove conclusively that George Bush was an indifferent leader who had clearly lost the battle of Richmond for the soul of America.

Although the media had praised Ross Perot for his pithy one-liners ("If there's a fairer way, I'm all ears") in the first presidential debate in 1992, accounts of his town hall performance were less charitable. Within days, Perot's act had grown old, and commentators now complained this his performance was old and tired.[12] Just as Bush had been chided for glancing at his watch, Perot was faulted for his inability to occupy his stool completely. An article in the *Washington Post* observed, "Even the crabby Munchkin, Ross Perot, who got several laughs with his one-liners at Sunday night's opener, seemed enervated and spent . . . Perot may have avoided actually sitting on his stool because, if he did sit on it, his feet wouldn't touch the ground"[13] (Shales, 1992, p. D1). Given these characterizations, it is not surprising that anyone who read print accounts of the debate would agree with the broadcast pronouncements that Clinton was the obvious winner.

In defense of the media, it might be argued that these accounts accurately represent what transpired in Richmond. Although this claim may hold some truth, a growing body of quantitative evidence suggests that impressions are shaped more by commentary than by actual performance in the debates (Jamieson & Birdsell, 1988, p. 171). Each presidential debate has been summarized, reduced to a defining story, and remembered by the media. According to these chronicles, the 1960 debate between Richard Nixon and John F. Kennedy is notable for images of a youthful Kennedy confronting a sweaty Nixon whose face bore a suspicious five o'clock shadow. President Gerald Ford is still remembered for emphatically stating in a 1976 debate with Jimmy Carter that there was no Soviet domination of Eastern Europe. President Jimmy Carter will likewise be remembered from the 1980 debate against Ronald Reagan for admitting that he discussed nuclear doctrine with his daughter, Amy. The same Ronald Reagan lives in debate infamy for an incoherent trip down a California highway in his 1984 debate with Walter Mondale. Michael Dukakis, the Democrats' candidate in 1988, is notable for his clinical and detached response to Bernard Shaw's emotionally charged question about the hypothetical rape of his wife.

In retrospect, it is apparent that Bill Clinton capitalized on the town hall format because it fit his style and his message. This town hall format also reinforced the implicit campaign theme that Clinton was in touch with the common people, whereas Bush had lost touch. At the same time, it is also clear that the Richmond town hall bears little relation to the New England town meeting. The town hall debate was not an exercise in self-government, but rather a political spectacle. The candidates created the format because it fit their political interest, and the format made true argument impossible. Media accounts of the debate, though celebrating the democratic tradition, functioned to trivialize what little discourse actually occurred in Richmond.

THE FUTURE OF THE PAST: THE ELECTRONIC TOWN MEETING

In his 1996 State of the Union Address, President Bill Clinton offered the vision of an America connected by a national computer network. According to Clinton, "As the Internet becomes our new town square, a computer in every home—a teacher of all subjects, a connection to all cultures—this will no longer be a dream, but a necessity."[14] Should such a vision ever become a reality, it would be possible to have an ongoing town meeting. Anyone connected with the Internet could, theoretically, engage in dialogue about local, state, and national issues (Leopold, 1996).

Those who have paused to consider the relationship between democracy and politics seem to agree that the Internet will provide the opportunity for direct—as opposed to representative—democracy. Janette Kenner Muir (1994), for example, has observed, "As electronic media further develop, so does the capacity to reach many more people, and in turn, to increase public participation" (p. 343). According to proponents, herein likes the unique opportunity of the electronic town hall. Because the Internet can accommodate a multitude of users, it should be possible for thousands of citizens to interact simultaneously with each other, government agencies, and elected officials.

The mediated town hall debate in 1992 was a campaign event, and as such it was firmly rooted in a representative understanding of democracy. What happened in Richmond was part of an election process that asked the voters to think about politics, to assess the competing candidates, and then to render a decision. Once the vote was cast, the body politic dissolved, the voters returned home, and those candidates who were elected to govern functioned as the citizens' representatives. Between elections, these elected leaders interact with their constituents on an irregular basis. Aside from the referendum on issues provided by public opinion polls and personal communication, the people's representatives have limited opportunities to consult the citizenry on questions of public policy.

In marked contrast, the electronic town hall offers the promise of both perpetual and instantaneous dialogue between those governing and those being governed. The Internet creates the possibility of direct democracy by linking the government directly with individual citizens. It seems to create a unique "public space,"[15] a forum that creates the possibility of substantive dialogue on all questions of public concern. Communication in such space requires genuine interaction, not the pandering common in campaign rhetoric or political spots. The result of such exchanges, proponents of the electronic town hall argue, would be a public argument that tests ideas and produces consensus on policy. If this vision becomes a reality, the "electronic town square" will become one defining element of American democracy.

At the same time that it offers such revolutionary potential, the possibility of an electronic town hall might prove to be the ultimate of political illusions. Because the technology creates the opportunity for direct interaction, those participating in the dialogue may come to believe that their electronic speech is heard, that their opinion is valued. A more cynical response would remember what happened at the town hall debate at Richmond. Although Bush, Clinton, and Perot did come before the voters, their participation was more strategic than democratic. Further, a close inspection of the debate reveals no real interaction between the candidates and the citizen questioners. The candidates' answers were stylized responses, carefully crafted appeals intended to produce votes disguised as answers to the questions being asked. The media further reduced the town hall by filtering out the content while highlighting the visual elements in stories about the debate.

Although some have warned that the Internet might create a form of "hyperactive democracy," with candidates constantly calibrating political positions and legislative votes to react to the smallest or latest shift in public opinion, a more likely scenario suggests that the candidates will co-opt the electronic town hall into another opportunity to broadcast their messages to voters. Given the experience with the town hall debate in 1992, it is clear that politics shapes the forum more than the forum shapes the politics.

As the presidential election in the year 2000 approaches, the leading presidential contenders will loudly announce that they intend to use the Internet to interact directly with the voters. Because genuine interaction between the candidates and millions of computer users is impossible, the campaigns will strategically offer the candidates at well-publicized times to answer questions. Aside from these occasional forums, voter inquiries at the town hall will be "processed" to create the appearance of interaction. Each citizen will receive a prompt and courteous reply, the relevant assurances and information will be provided, and the citizen's e-mail address will be added to the appropriate file for future mailings.

As politicians grow more proficient at using the new medium, campaigns will be able to use the Internet to give the illusion of direct democracy. There is every reason to expect, on the basis of past experience, that politicians will use the electronic town hall to respond to inquiries from the voters. Much as they did in Richmond, the candidates will come before the voters and offer the appropriate responses. The mainstream media, angered by their exclusion, will respond with predictably condescending language about happenings in the electronic town square. The result will be a political spectacle, a campaign event carefully staged to create the illusion of democratic self-government.

It might be argued that this progression is inevitable as the political parties assimilate a new form of technology. There is a danger in the electronic town hall, however, because it implies that voters are using the Internet to direct their elected public officials, when in reality, the elected public officials will be using the Internet to create the illusion of participation and manage their constituents. The proof of this can be seen, ever so clearly, in the legacy of the town hall debate of 1992. Although the Richmond debate invoked the imagery of the New England town meeting, the result was a desecration of a long-standing democratic tradition. Unless we are vigilant, the electronic town square of the future may prove to be the ultimate democratic delusion.

NOTES

1. According to data gathered by the A. C. Nielson Company, an estimated 70 million viewers in 18 million households watched the Richmond town hall. This figure translates into a 41.2 rating or a 58% share of the audience ("Candidates on Trial," 1991).

2. For a more elaborate discussion of Clinton's use of the media, see Whillock (1994).

3. All quotations from the debate are taken from the transcript prepared by the Commission on Presidential Debates, which is available at http://www.debates96.org/.

4. For a more elaborate discussion of naming, see Blankenship (1990).

5. Jehl (1992). ©1992, Los Angeles Times Publishing Company. Reprinted by permission.

6. Thomas (1992). ©1992, Los Angeles Times Publishing Company. Reprinted by permission.

7. Shales (1992). ©1992, The Washington Post. Reprinted by permission.

8. Dowd (1992). ©1992, New York Times Company. Reprinted by permission.

9. Hodges (1992). ©1992, Houston Chronicle Publishing Company. Reprinted by permission.

10. Rodriguez (1992). ©1992, Houston Chronicle Publishing Company. Reprinted by permission.

11. Nolan (1992). ©1992, Boston Globe Publishing Company. Reprinted by permission.

12. See "The Campaign Nears" (1992), Roush (1992), and Lichfield (1992).

13. Shales (1992). © 1992, The Washington Post. Reprinted with permission.

14. The full text of Clinton's speech is available at http://www2.whitehouse.gov/WH/New/other/stateunion-top.html.

15. For a more elaborate discussion of public space, see Zarefsky (1992, p. 412).

REFERENCES

Baer, S. (1992, October 18). Press and public differ in view of debates. *Chicago Sun-Times,* p. 40.

Bitzer, L., & Reuter, T. (1980). *Carter vs. Ford: The counterfeit debates of 1976.* Madison: University of Wisconsin Press.

Blankenship, J. (1990). Naming and name calling as acts of definition: Politician campaigns and the 1988 presidential debates. In R. Trapp & J. Schuetz (Eds.), *Perspectives on argumentation: Essays in honor of Wayne Brockriede* (pp. 162-174). Prospect Heights, IL: Waveland.

The campaign nears decision by default; Three debates leave Bush almost out of time to work the miracle he needs. (1992, October 26). *Time,* p. 20.

Candidates on trial as vote nears. (1991, October 16). *Chicago Tribune,* p. C1.

Collins, R. K. L., & Skover, D. M. (1996). *The death of discourse.* Boulder, CO: Westview.

In debates, the presidency meets a TV-style new age. (1992, October 16). *Atlanta Journal and Constitution,* p. 12.

Degler, C. N. (1970). *Out of our past: The forces that shaped modern America.* New York: Harper & Row.

Depoe, S. P., & Short-Thompson, C. (1994). Let the people speak: The emergence of public space in the Richmond presidential debate. In D. B. Carlin & M. S. McKinney (Eds.), *The 1992 presidential debates in focus* (pp. 85-98). New York: Praeger.

Dowd, M. (1992, October 16). A no-nonsense sort of talk show. *New York Times,* p. A1.

Ely, J. (1992, October 18). Can Bush still get the voters to listen? *Houston Chronicle,* p. 2.

Entman, R. M. (1989). *Democracy without citizens: Media and the decay of American politics.* New York: Oxford University Press.

Hodges, A. (1992, October 16). The second debate: Talk show format hurts the seriousness of event. *Houston Chronicle,* p. A16.

Hogan, J. M. (1989, Spring). Media nihilism and the presidential debates. *Journal of the American Forensic Association, 25,* 221.

Jamieson, K. H., & Birdsell, D. S. (1988). *Presidential debates: The challenge of creating an informed electorate.* New York: Oxford University Press.

Jehl, D. (1992, October 16). The presidential debates; Round two; Donahue-style meeting for would-be leaders. *Los Angeles Times,* p. A25.

Jubera, D. (1992, October 16). Oprah debate levels candidates. *Atlanta Journal and Constitution,* p. A7.

Kellner, D. (1990). *Television and the crisis of democracy.* Boulder, CO: Westview.

Kloer, P. (1992, October 20). One television debate score: Thursday's was the best of the bunch. *Atlanta Journal and Constitution,* p. D7.

Krauthammer, C. (1992, October 23). Little lessons of the campaign. *Washington Post,* p. A21.

Leopold, G. (1996, April 29). Electronic town hall stirs dialogue. *Electronic Engineering Times,* p. 42.

Lichfield, J. (1992, October 17). The U.S. presidential elections: "Wishy-washy" Bush loses again. *The Independent,* p. 11.

Meiklejohn, A. (1960). *Political freedom: The constitutional powers of the people.* Westport, CT: Greenwood.

Meyer, J., & Carlin, D. B. (1994). The impact of formats on voter reaction. In D. B. Carlin & M. S. McKinney (Eds.), *The 1992 presidential debates in focus* (pp. 69-83). New York: Praeger.

Muir, J. K. (1994). Clinton goes to town hall. In S. A. Smith (Ed.), *Bill Clinton on stump, state, and stage: The rhetorical road to the White House.* Fayetteville: University of Arkansas Press.

Nolan, M. F. (1992, October 16). Time closing in on him, Bush turns onto high road. *Boston Globe,* p. 1.

Page, S., & Shaw, G. (1992, October 16). The voters strike back; Town-hall debate forces candidates to stick to issues. *Newsday,* p. 5.

Postman, N. (1985). *Amusing ourselves to death: Public discourse in the age of show business.* New York: Viking.

Reed, M. (1996, October 16). Of debatable use: Presidential campaign forums need revamping, panelists say. *Los Angeles Times,* p. A3.

Rodriguez, L. (1992, October 17). The people won debate Thursday. *Houston Chronicle,* p. 29.

Roush, M. (1992, October 16). The voters set tone of debate, and it was about time they did. *USA Today,* p. 5.

Sabato, L. J. (1991). *Feeding frenzy: How attack journalism transformed American politics.* New York: Free Press.

Shales, T. (1992, October 16). The debate goes on . . . and on and on. *Washington Post,* p. D1.

Shulman, S. (1992, October 18). The debates: Free lessons in public speaking. *Atlanta Journal and Constitution,* p. H2.

Siegel, E. (1992, October 16). People's questions made for good TV. *Boston Globe,* p. 18.

Thomas, C. (1992, October 18). Talents of Phil, Oprah missing from debate. *St. Louis Post-Dispatch,* p. 3B.

de Tocqueville, A. (1969). *Democracy in America* (J. P. Mayer, Ed.). Garden City, NY: Anchor. (Original work published 1835)

Waldman, M. S. (1992, October 16). Demand for a new political stagecraft. *Newsday,* p. 23.

Weiler, M. (1989, Spring). The 1988 electoral debates and debate theory. *Journal of the American Forensic Association, 25,* 219.

Whillock, R. K. (1994). Easy access to sloppy truths: The '92 presidential media campaign. In S. A. Smith (Ed.), *Bill Clinton on stump, state, and stage: The rhetorical road to the White House* (pp. 292-314). Fayetteville: University of Arkansas Press.

Zarefsky, D. (1992, December). Spectator politics and the revival of public argument. *Communication Monographs, 59,* 411-414.

PART II

Censored and Silenced: Acts of Resistance and Populism

One recurring criticism or complaint about the postmodern linguistic landscape is the surfeit of talk about talk and the dearth of substantial or real scholarly inquiry. But to configure talk or discourse as itself an unworthy topic of discussion is yet another exclusionary tactic in a cultural environment that has become increasingly exclusionary, prescriptive, and politicized. Also, to cite talk about talk—or talk about the lack of talk, which is the subject of this book—is to argue not too subtly against theory, against public means or areas of discourse, and against the possible social values expressive of, and facilitated by, talk/discourse/exchange. To limit the subject areas, to prescribe what is permissible, is to censor what can be said, who can say it, and where and how it can be said.

The tactic of charging that talk about talk is nonsense attempts to negate the expression of those who would attempt to call into question current means of discourse and access to those means. Such efforts of exclusion about what is permissible and of worth is, in effect, a denial of voice, of community, and of identity. It is also a repressive trivialization of the crucial attempt to deconstruct existing power structures that set the rules of expression: who can talk, what can be talked about, and how and when it must be talked about.

Those denying the validity of the viewpoint of those who would question what passes as acceptable dialogic arenas, players, and rules of the game will find Part II, "Censored and Silenced: Acts of Resistance and Populism," to be yet another academic preoccupation with fine points and marginal questions and subject matters. Yet, as the survey of subjects in this part will show—graffiti, subversive images, and whiteness—the problems, questions, and answers covered here are elements crucial to perpetuating and refining a free, open, and healthy society, a major characteristic of which must be free and open discourse representative of all members of the society.

Within this discussion, keywords arise: *multicultural, image, resistance, identity, silence, mainstream, margin, representation,* and *censorship.* And these words dispute or affirm corruptions and definitions of public discourse in a free society, asking us to rethink the very definition of what is "public" and what is "discourse."

In Chapter 4, Les Back, Michael Keith, and John Solomos cite graffiti as "perhaps the exemplary mode of outlaw communication" and, in doing so, allow us to consider it beyond the various dismissive labels characterizing it as a sort of mindless vandalism and to see it instead as having a variety of uses and being indicative of a range of effects: as a form of popular protest, a people's art, and also implicated in brutal forms of symbolic violence, genocide, and racism. Graffiti and their meanings are intimately tied to, if not dependent on, context. As the authors remind us, "graffiti . . . in a literal sense, [is] semantically dependent on the space that precedes the text." And this is a key point, one that suggests we see graffiti's presence as an urban graphology whose very existence and persistence points to "an emergent struggle over inclusion, of citizenship, entitlement, and belonging." As an alternative narrative—and as the authors remind us, all graffiti attempt to tell alternative narratives about places and their meanings—graffiti argue for the limits of public discourse and demand that attention be paid to outlaw voices threatening to be heard.

In Chapter 5, Carol Becker argues that some images "perpetuate illusions, distance people from reality, and create further mystification" and that because they "fill the public space and obliterate real discourse and debate, their effects are lethal to the health of society." In making such an assertion, she at once asserts that art is a negative as well as positive force and forces us to come to terms with the social role of image making, moving art from a merely aesthetic and removed realm to an active participant in the creation of the social dimension of public space. In opposition to mystifying images that have a detrimental effect on the social body, she offers the salvo of images that have the power to pierce reality and "heighten the understanding of societal conditions." Such a critical discourse—the discourse of subversive images examining issues of race, class, gender, emotional disease—provides us with a therapeutic, because emancipatory practice "relies on invention and surprise."

In Chapter 6, Peter McLaren asks us to recognize whiteness as a "racialized practice of power and privilege" although it is rarely seen as such because its presence is both ubiquitous and invisible. But the very transparency of whiteness tends to universalize it as an identity that supersedes and transcends ethnicity; and this characteristic removal of whiteness as a racialized social practice effectively removes from the public realm discussions of the "epistemological, phenomenological, metaphysical, political, or ethical implications of racialized social practices in our everyday experiences as racialized subjects." We exist within a media environment that transcodes racial differences as cultural differences. Accordingly, the globalization of commodity culture tends to view cultural differences as lifestyle differences. Only by resisting whiteness—defined as an "invisible marker for conceptualizing normative arrangements of citizenship practices"—can we engage in a real (and constructive) dialogue to come to terms with the processes by and through which a racialized identity constitutes itself.

All of these authors suggest and confirm the need to rethink the margins: what they are and how they can influence and redirect the mainstream, not necessarily absorbed into it, but rather enriching and increasing it while at the same time standing intact and apart from it.

CHAPTER 4

Reading the Writing on the Wall

Graffiti in the Racialized City

Les Back
Goldsmiths College, London

Michael Keith
Goldsmiths College, London

John Solomos
South Bank University, London

Graffiti is perhaps the exemplary mode of outlaw communication. By definition it is intrusive, emblematic, and opportunistic. Derived from the Italian *graffiare,* meaning "to scratch," graffiti as a genre has been understood variously as a form of popular protest, a people's art, and also implicated in brutal forms of symbolic violence, genocide, and racism.[1] Much of the concern about the proliferation of subway graffiti in the United States was a reaction to the unwanted infringement into the public imagination of the anonymous face of inner-city racial otherness. In a very different fashion, in recent years the spraying of racist and neo-fascist

AUTHORS' NOTE: The research on which this chapter is based is supported by a grant from the Harry Frank Guggenheim Foundation for the project "The Cultural Mechanisms of Racist Expression: A Study of Racism and Anti-Semitism in Graffiti, Pamphlets, Style, and Body Symbolism." We are grateful to the foundation for its support.

graffiti over the premises of minority shopkeepers in France or Jewish graveyards in Britain provided a haunting reminder of the endurance of a proactive and expressive white power politics. Yet, graffiti is more than just a haunting emblem of public fears and anxieties. It is crucially implicated in cultures of urban expression, both as a means to inscribe a "decentralised and decentered insubordination" (Ferrell, 1993, p. 197) and because it challenges the very status of language, dialogue, and discourse within the public sphere.

The debate about graffiti both in the United States and Europe has focused on viewing wall writing as a form of "visual pollution." This was compounded by the indecipherability of the esoteric hip hop signatures (tags) or more elaborate cartoonlike paintings on subway cars. Equally, racist forms of graffiti have deployed mysterious stylistic elements alongside crass forms of racial rhetoric and abuse. Common to all types of graffiti is that they are written on what is taken publicly to be an illegitimate canvas. Graffiti is always an intrusion, and in this sense it is premeditatedly—but purposefully—*out of place*. So, understanding urban writing is ultimately about appreciating the symbolism of the surface on which it is inscribed. The way graffiti is interpreted, then, in a literal sense, is semantically dependent on the space that precedes the text. As Patrick Hagopian (1988) points out,

> The question of whether graffiti constitutes an "enhancement" or "defacement" seems . . . to depend on whose property is being written on, and who is doing the writing and who judges the results. . . . Thus, the question of whose world will be "written over" and whose writing will prevail, is never a pure aesthetic question. (p. 109)

What we want to suggest is a complex interplay between the surface and the inscription. The planes of the metropolis do not determine the writing, but equally the inscription cannot completely govern the meaning of the abraded concrete or metal canvas. Rather, at stake in these forms of urban graphology is an emergent struggle over inclusion, of citizenship, entitlement, and belonging.

In a sense, what we would like to examine is whether any ground is present between the naive celebration of transgression and the fear of the populist inscription. We believe that it is possible to find such a ground if we begin to think about:

- graffiti as a technology of expression
- writing as invariably aimed at an audience

- articulation as invariably and simultaneously both aesthetic and political, crystallizing complex desires, dreams, and claims
- inscribing as a moment of articulation that is not necessarily discursive but always narrative in its power

Anthropologists and other commentators have stressed the importance of the seemingly banal character of wall writing with regard to the way it reveals the hidden codes of a particular culture (Dundes, 1966; Henderson, 1981; Perry, 1976; Rees, 1979; Reynolds, 1975). We are particularly concerned to look at how graffiti is implicated in the sphere of the urban politics of difference, identity, and racism—in particular, how is the practice of urban wall writing connected with the expressive cultural mechanisms of racism and antiracism? Before coming back to these questions, we first look at how graffiti has entered the wider debate over urban culture and the nature of the public sphere within cities.

Wall writing has a long history that dates back to ancient times (Lindsay, 1960; Reisner, 1974), and what makes it interesting in the context of this book is the diverse ways it has been interpreted. Some epigraphologists have connected the emergence of graffiti with the expansion of literacy and popular protests (Abel & Buckley, 1977; Cockcroft, 1977). Others have viewed wall writing as personal expression and spontaneous acts of symbolic subversion in the tradition of *détournement*.[2] Equally, a literature argues that, in repressive societies, graffiti is an underground means of communication for those who are excluded from the public sphere (Bushnell, 1990; Cresswell, 1996; Ferrell, 1993). The very ambiguous nature of this archaic mode of communication makes it interesting in the information age. Why should this most basic communicative technology have survived amid the throng of multimedia late modernity? Is graffiti an alternative discourse, or is it an example of the end of discourse itself? Before coming back to these questions, we first look at how graffiti has entered the wider debate over urban culture and the nature of the public sphere within cities.

SIGNS OF DANGER: GRAFFITI, URBAN CULTURE, AND THE PUBLIC SPHERE

Public space is variously the terrain in which civil society is performed, the social space over which "proper" political regulation is deployed, and the arena in which particular kinds of sociality are developed. If the first two uses of the term imply a consensual set of values, the third most certainly does not, and in this chapter we examine the way one form of intrusion into the public spaces of the city might make us think about the relationship between society and space.

In a celebrated article, the right-wing American criminologist James Q. Wilson identifies graffiti as the defining moment of incipient community breakdown (Wilson & Kelling, 1982). The inscriptions of those who deface the received order of the spaces of the city challenge and disrupt order and the neighborhood as the spatial realization of pure *gemeinschaft*. Left unchallenged, graffiti is both symptomatic of threat and a signal that prompts further moral decline. Out of such environmentally deterministic rhetoric and a particular concern with graffiti, the notion of "zero tolerance" was born. Similarly, Nathan Glazer (1974) has written on the fear engendered by the graffiti as a subway rider in New York: "While I do not find myself consciously making the connection between the graffiti-markers and the criminals who occasionally rob, rape, assault, and murder passengers, the sense that all are part of one world of uncontrollable predators seems inescapable" (p. 4). Glazer, the champion of the passenger—who seems implicitly coded as white—presents the other side of James Q. Wilson's vision of attrition and social breakdown. Glazer's discussion might also be read as liberal democracy itself struggling to come to terms with the unknowable and the seemingly uncontrollable. Glazer wrestles over and over again with his question: Why can't graffiti be controlled? But it is clear that graffiti simply can't be tamed by his version of sociological pragmatism because the logics and impulses that compel people to write are outside a liberal democratic imagination. Although never really speaking the language of race, such frustration seems to invoke metaphorically the gap between the democratic ideals of American citizenship and the fact of social exclusion and racial inequities within the public sphere.

The issue of reconciliation within the public sphere is one central theme of the work of the urbanist Richard Sennett, for whom graffiti also signifies an important symptom of urban life. Over a wide range of important works, Sennett has developed a series of theses on the relationship between particular forms of social life and the spaces of the cities in which they are realized. Drawing heavily on many of the themes from Wirth and Simmel, Sennett, in *The Uses of Disorder* (1973), *The Hidden Injuries of Class* (1972), *The Fall of Public Man* (1976), *The Conscience of the Eye* (1991), and the most recent collection of essays *Flesh and Stone* (1994), has developed a sustained engagement with notions of city life that addresses a massive agenda not readily simplified. At the heart of all of his work, however, is his construction of urbanism that attempts to cherish the city as the privileged medium for the reconciliation of *difference* and *strangeness* so essential to the construction of both a realized polity and an imagined sociality.

In Richard Sennett's vision of the city, particularly that expressed in his most behaviorist text *The Conscience of the Eye* (1991), something about the design of cities structures social life. At times, with debts to Skinner barely hidden, we are told that some spaces "work" by facilitating the sociality of the public sphere through ways others do not. Rockefeller Center, Battery Park City, and the artifacts of the Miesian legacy create anomie, but the coffeehouse and the piazza open up the individual through "streets full of time" in which fragmentation of self and encounters with difference can coexist. Drawing on the work of the Chicago school, he suggests that this is not the result of the city permitting difference, but rather a product of the concentration of difference:

> [U]rban differences seemed to [Robert] Park and Louis Wirth provocations of otherness, surprise and stimulation. Yet these sociologists had a brilliant, counter-intuitive insight; provocation occurs in the very loosening of strong connections between people in a city. . . . Thus, Park in his later writings, like his younger colleague Wirth, moved away from the conceiving of the city as a place that permits differences, and towards understanding the city as a place that encourages the concentration of difference. Its moral order is the lack of moral order that exercises hegemony over the city as a whole. (pp. 126-127)

The sense of modern fragmentation of the self is understood as positive, a celebratory facet of urbanism because the fragmented self is more responsive. Enlightenment, unity, and coherence are thus not the means to self-development; rather, fragmented urban experience that opens itself and collides with differences of both flesh and stone offers new possibilities for personhood and public life.

There is much in Sennett's argument to commend it, not least the ethos that celebrates the meeting of difference at the expense of the *destructive gemeinschaft*. Nevertheless, his suspicion of the planning imperative to sanitize space is surely overstated. In such a cosmology, graffiti is necessarily symptomatic of a failure to reconcile social life and urban design, in some ways echoing the reactionary sociology of James Q. Wilson. For Sennett, who cites Glazer's (1974) essay on graffiti, New York graffiti is little more than an announcement of the unified subject. The impasto of painted IDs fails to communicate "any message save one: *feci,* 'I made this,' this mark is me. . . . An 'I' declared" (Sennett, 1991, p. 207). It is the very concreteness of graffiti, both literally and as sign of identity, that Sennett opposes.[3]

Yet, Sennett is wrong to reduce the technology of the sign writer and the tagger to the single message. In marked contrast, alternative historians of graffiti have traced the redemptive force of this transgressive moment, the power of graffiti to accrete far greater symbolic power through its presence in particular places. A range of sociologists, linguists, and photographers have suggested that Chicano and African American young people have used subway graffiti as a mechanism for self-expression and resistance in the context of their social marginalization and disenfranchisement (Cesaretti, 1975; Cooper & Chalfant, 1980). The nuances of these forms of expression and allusion constitute a hidden semiological realm and a kind of alternative public sphere that operates beyond the understanding of both liberal and radical commentators. This is summed up by Wicked Gary, a Brooklyn writer:

> If you needed to know anything that happened on the subway, you could ask a graffiti artist. . . . That was our playground, that was our work and . . . we were involved. Schedules of trains, schedules of tunnels, we had information on everything. It was a whole other system of communication and interaction from the normal system that we deal with like the English language and money and stuff like that. We had our own language, our own technology, terminology. The words we had meant things to us that nobody else could identify. (cited in Castleman, 1982, pp. 86-87)

This amounts to much more than Sennett's view of graffiti as a throng of identity marks; indeed, there may well be things at stake in the process of naming that transcend a narrow declarative individualism.

In a sense, we are trying to identify here a degree of uneasiness we feel about two very different takes on behavior in the public sphere. Certain forms of reactionary contemporary populism see the public sphere primarily in terms of risk minimization and the rights of individual security. Writers such as Glazer and Wilson may be influential but are principally symptomatic of such positions. In contrast, Sennett's intellectual project is far distant from such conservative ideology. Whatever else the book is, *The Conscience of the Eye* (and other work) self-consciously celebrates a certain form of urbanism in the attempt to create a city ideal tied with an imagery of the proper behavior of strangers, one to another in a public realm of the present day. We want to suggest one flaw common to both of these slightly caricatured positions: They underestimate the degree to which the spaces of the public sphere are malleable surfaces rather than passive containers of forms of sociality. The forms of communication invoked through graffiti writers' transformation of such spaces is just one dimension through which this malleability is illustrated. We also want to suggest that graffiti writing invokes a technology of communication that is neither entirely logocentric nor merely symbolic, but instead creates a regime of communication that refigures the public sphere just as it is defined by the surfaces of inscription on which this and other forms of wall writing occur.

In this context, it is interesting to think back to the early 1980s, in which the aesthetics of the writers on the wall were momentarily the subject of great artistic acclaim, to think more about the relationship between allusion and aesthetics. In particular, it is interesting to look with the wisdom of hindsight at the work of Haring and Basquiat, the most famous of this time, neither authentically street writers, both graffiti artists. Popularized by poet and commentator Rene Ricard,[4] Basquiat and Haring were celebrated as the most innovative artists of their generation. In Haring's work, "the installation could compete with the urban environment, the space and content from which the drawings were evolving. And because these drawings were also appearing in subways, they became urban guerrilla art, like that of the graffitists" (Sussman, 1997, p. 10).

In New York, the graffiti painters, the East Village artists, and the political coalition groups were brought together in major exhibitions, including the 1980 Times Square Show, in which *Village Voice* commentator Richard Goldstein (1993) described "a concordance of styles . . . often referred to as visual punk" (p. 55). In part, it seems apposite that the theme that resonates through such work is the urbanist articulation of subsequent juxtapositions of high and low culture. The appropriation of city spaces as alternative "spaces of representation" was as much a part of the populism as the aesthetic of graffiti art itself. In this sense, it appears apposite that it should be in Times Square, an invocation of the dissolute that such a transgressive moment should initiate the 1980s just as much as the newly disciplined and sanitized Times Square sets a marker for the public spaces of the Business Improvement Districts in the late 1990s, in which there is to be zero tolerance of any deviant presence.

As Hebdidge (1993) has persuasively argued, it is as misleading to seek in the inscriptions of the graffiti artist the authentic voice of the street as it is to understate the possibilities of an alternative aesthetic based on a set of expressive practices that do not render themselves easily mapped by conventional calculus of aesthetic value.

The idea that Jean Michel Basquiat was an "idiot savant" who merely poured out his heart in the white heat of his genius and put it on his display for all and sundry is palpably misguided. It is as ludicrous and patronizing as the implication that he didn't speak with the authentic "voice of the street" because his daddy lived in a three story brownstone in Boerum Hill. (p. 64)

But equally, the debates that rage around the "value" of aesthetics illustrate just one key problem with the easy relegation of the writing on the wall. Basquiat's frame of reference was expressed through the visual ideology of the graffiti writer; the crown, the constant erasures of tags, the allusion to alternative expressive cultures of music, body, and comic (magazine) are all testament to their own aesthetic, which in Basquiat's case "did us all a service by uncovering and recapitulating the history of his own construction as a black American male" (Hebdidge, 1993, p. 65). It is not that such a repertoire, so acutely deployed, diminishes Basquiat or renders him commensurable with the taggers of the everyday, but neither does his genius disconnect himself from them. The commensurability of the repertoire instead confirms that the writing on the walls always subsumes an aesthetic of its own, a desire, a beauty, an ugliness, an eroticism, but never just an expression of a particular "I" or a function of a specific space.

More recently, the streets and walls in urban America have provided a canvas for memorial graffiti. These frequently elaborate and colorful murals often have at their center a name, usually of a young person who has died, usually violently. This form is a hybrid and updated version of the simple roadside crosses often erected at sites of automobile accidents in predominantly Catholic countries where it is believed that sudden death before receipt of last rites means the spirit of the victim is caught in purgatory. A marker serves as a reminder to passersby to pray for the person's soul and thus enable passage to heaven. Similarly, spray-can memorials in urban America serve as a communal remembrance of the premature loss of life engendered by "the systematic poverty and pervasive racism that promote the rampant flow of drugs and guns into inner city communities" (Cooper & Sciorra, 1994, p. 7). Painted crosses are combined with hip hop calligraphy to produce very moving murals that remember young lives cut short by the epidemic black-on-black and brown-on-brown violence. Their genealogy is thus complex. It draws on the basic repertoire of wall writing—the technology of the means of communication—and makes an appeal that is profane in its ritual of aestheticized transgression of space. It also speaks to a public, constructs an audience of strangers, in a sacred appeal that has much deeper antecedents. The graffiti itself becomes a rally point, a new place that lies behind the name, where people return to face pain, loss, and suffering in public.

Marshall Berman (1987) draws attention to the redemptive nature of such association. For him, public space becomes a site for reconciliation where modern men and women have to work to put their split, fragmented, and alienated selves together. Drawing on the work of Michael Walzer, Berman argues for a radicalized notion of open-minded space in which city dwellers can confront and integrate their divided selves. He goes on:

> It would be open, above all, to encounters between people of different classes, races, ages, religions, ideologies, cultures, and stances towards life. It would be planned to attract all these different populations, to enable them to look each other in the face, to listen, maybe to talk. . . . Open public space is a place where people can actively engage the suffering of this world together, and, as they do it, transform themselves into a public. (pp. 484-485)

Memorial graffiti offer a moment in which these processes of transformation can occur, but this is nevertheless momentary and incomplete. They are perhaps best represented as sutures over the divisions that Berman so articulately described.[5] Perhaps, as Sennett argues so powerfully, the very nature of fragmentation of self offers the potential for the confrontation with the stranger to be settled in less violent terms. It is interesting that both of these figures seek a more polyphonous and ethnically plural public culture but they also both share a kind of latent environmental determinism, in that particular places can offer or foster such outcomes. The graffiti writers—including those like Basquiat and Haring, who operated inside and outside the gallery—demonstrate that this process is always emergent, the product of an indeterminate relationship between particular urban arenas and surfaces and the spaces of identity.

We suggest that neither a reactionary nor a naively celebratory understanding of wall writing and graffiti is particularly helpful in reaching an understanding of life in the cities of late modernity. In particular, as part of an attempt to think about the modalities of expression through which various forms of intolerance are communicated, we believe that racist and nationalist graffiti and wall writing highlight both the paradoxes of the communicative rationalities they invoke and the necessity to develop a more nuanced understanding of the relationship between places and identities than most representations of the public spaces of contemporary urbanism would imply.

"SPACES OF IDENTITY AND THE IDENTITY OF SPACES": AN ITERATIVE UNDERSTANDING OF GRAFFITI, COMMUNITY, AND CONFLICT

It is not just the case that the inner cities provide surfaces of inscription through which identity is itself mediated. Graffiti are reducible neither to articulations of a priori natural areas nor to projections of territorial claims. We are trying to argue that they have to be placed within a narrative structure, a process of telling the identity of places. In this sense, graffiti mark an emergent and phantasmal territory. Paradoxically, in the contest to control the spaces of the urban, a shared reality creates a contested but nevertheless shared territory. The status and stakes of communication, be they by conventional or outlaw means, become crucial. As Borja and Castells (1997) argue: "Without a system for social and cultural integration that respects the differences while also establishing codes for communication between the various cultures, local tribalism will be the other side of the coin of global universalism" (p. 4).[6] We want to develop this argument in the English inner city and suburban contexts, respectively. From our research, it seems clear that the outer-city suburban context is where open racist graffiti are most commonly expressed, whereas the profoundly multicultural metropolitan interiors exhibit more complexly inflected moments of hate writing. Here, we want to explore the relationship between the communicative technologies of graffiti and the emergence of local tribalisms.

We focus initially on the graffiti of the East End of London, which has historically been the reception area for new migrations into the capital. French Huguenots settled here fleeing religious persecution along with East European Jews. Latterly, West Indian and South Asian migrants— most notably, Bengalis—have made East London their home. This area has equally been a center for right-wing political organizing. In the 1930s, a march by Oswald Mosley's fascist Blackshirts prompted the famous battle of Cable Street, in which Mosley's men clashed violently with antifascist opponents. More recently, in 1993, a British National Party candidate was successfully elected on a "Rights for Whites" platform as a local councillor in the district of Millwall. We want to focus on a series of examples of graffiti writing in this district by way of bringing into focus the emergent and complex struggles over entitlement, exclusion, and belonging that are taking place within present-day London. The first focuses on a park where a young Bengali man was racially attacked and killed.

Graffiti, Memory, and Erasure: Altab Ali Park

In 1978, Altab Ali was murdered in one of the more extreme of the grim catalogue of racist assaults that characterized East London at the time.[7] Altab Ali was attacked in St. Mary's Gardens, the site of the church of St. Mary Matfelon, known locally at the time as "Itchy" Park, after the tramps and vagrants who so often slept there, a coinage celebrated in the Small Faces 1960s record "Itchacooo Park." Altab Ali's murder provoked a mass mobilization of the Bengali community locally. It came to represent a watershed in the self-organization in the community as the protests against the murder, initially fronted by antiracist activists and worthies from outside the area, politicized a generation of young Bengali activists. Demonstrations and sit-ins on Brick Lane, just a few hundred yards from the site of the murder, were aimed to drive out (purify) the area of far right National Front activists, who at that time used Brick Lane as both a point of congregation and a focus of fascist activity, not least against the stall-holders and restauranteurs from ethnic minorities who were common in the street.

Partly in commemoration of his death and partly in respect to the mobilization, St. Mary's Gardens were officially renamed by the local council Altab Ali Park in 1979. A memorial gate was erected in the churchyard, and signs displayed the new name of the park. The sign was immediately subjected to defacement. This is perhaps less than surprising. More significant, however, the name continues to be erased. In 1997, almost 20 years after the murder, the sign that confirms the name of the park continued to be painted over with black spray paint (see Figures 4.1 and 4.2). On no fewer than seven occasions in that single year, the municipal authorities painted in the name of the park, only for the black paint to cover it up. No attempt was made to inscribe alternative names or ostensibly to reclaim the park in the name of particular political groupings. Moreover, the repeated processes of defacement have rarely been accompanied by specific political graffiti. Instead, a slightly surreal choreography develops between a local authority and perhaps a very small number of individuals. In each case, the "graffito"—if it can be called such—involves only the erasure of presence.

Characteristically, in some analytic treatments (Ley & Cybriwsky, 1974), such actions are cast as territorial statements of an ethologically threatened individual or group. Yet the repetitive nature of the process over such a long period of time might be taken to imply something slightly different. There are many histories here, each with a validity of its own,

Figure 4.1

many of them almost forgotten. From an open-air pulpit, preachers fa-
mously once harangued passing pedestrians. An old water fountain has left
a hole in the wall of the park, which is said to be a sight line for one of the
psychogeographical lay lines of London, and at one end of the park, directly
on this line, an imam holds theological discussions each summer. It is also
the site where Richard Brandon, the executioner of Charles I who was paid
£30 for his regicide, is buried. But Altab Ali's death was equally violent
and took place on his way home from shift work in a nearby sweatshop.
The event lives on in popular memory with a resonance that municipal
renaming acknowledged as much as bestowed.

   But attempts to exclude this particular set of memories continue. Arguably, the erasure is as much a refusal of recognition as an assertion of
territorial primacy. It renders invisible a particular telling of the story of
the park, subtly different from merely asserting alternative ownership. This
is a narrative moment that is not discursive or even emblematic; it is a
matter of overwriting and suppressing the polyphonous traces and chro-
nologies that are latent within this public space.

Figure 4.2

The stories through which the landscapes of the city are rendered legible are commonly contested, and in Altab Ali Park this contest has, in 1998, coalesced around proposals to site a Bangladeshi martyrs' memorial in the park. The original Shahid Minar was a memorial erected by medical students in Dacca Medical College in 1952 to commemorate their peers who had died the preceding year in the effort to establish Bengali as a recognized language. In the years after independence in 1947, the Pakistani state attempted to impose Urdu universally across both West and East Pakistan as part of the "nation building" process and was concerned at the perceived corruption of the Bengali language by Sanskrit words and phrases. The contest over the putative Arabization of the Bengali language contained within it the microcosm of confrontation between contrasting essences of identity between a shared Islam that was the *raison d'être* for the state of Pakistan (West and East) in 1947 and the secular nationalism that emerged as a Bangladeshi independence movement. Replicas of the original Shahid Minar have been constructed globally as commemorative marks by the Bengali Diaspora, including one in the northern British town of Oldham, and February 21 is observed in Bengali communities across the world as National Language Day.

The choice of Altab Ali Park for the East London copy of the Shahid Minar is not insignificant. In this sense, the martyrs' memorial in East London would link Altab Ali with the nationalist struggle and reinforce one particular telling of this space. Consequently, opposition comes both from those Bengali voices that reject secular nationalism (as opposed to Islamic universalism) as the basis of British-based diasporic politics and from expressions of white racist populism that resent this appropriation of the history of the park. Such disputes exist within a frame of reference that approximates the notion of what we are trying to describe as an alternative public sphere.

This is precisely what we mean to identify when we stress an iterative understanding of both graffiti and the relations of conflict. It is not a simple matter of graffiti constituting the effect of conflict. Much more is at stake here. It is rather that the iterative cycles, the to and fro of naming and erasure, shape an emergent and contested landscape in which the geography of identity and the identity of particular places is manifest, if continually in flux.

Allusion and Semiotic Integration: Chicksand Street

The next site we wish to describe is the Spitalfields area in the west of Tower Hamlets, immediately adjacent to the financial district in London. Coterminous with some of the most intense forms of concentrated poverty in the country, in this area are found some of the highest levels of residential segregation in 1990s Britain, with several estates and blocks more than 90% Bengali. It is one of the oldest sites of Bengali settlement and has witnessed, over the last 30 years, many clashes between racist groups and local communities, as well as between far right activists and the predominantly white articulations of the antiracist movement. However, it is now also popularly thought of as an area that, in terms of racial danger, is much "safer" than other parts of the East End precisely because of the generations of self-defense activism. In particular, we want to describe briefly one part of Spitalfields.

The area between Chicksand Street and Brick Lane is dominated by a sunken five-a-side football (soccer) pitch and an area of piazza-like open space in which people can watch the football, meet people, "hang out," or just engage in the deepest routines of "doing nothing" (Corrigan, 1976).

The cluttered array of wall writings tells many stories. Dozens of individuals have tagged the walls. A constant writing and overwriting of the names of the local gangs are sometimes superimposed, sometimes juxtaposed alongside such marks, the "we" alongside the more specific "I." A local street sign was (in the early 1990s) covered in white paint and the street name replaced with the word *Banglatown* (Figure 4.3). London districts are given post codes—which are the British equivalent of the U.S. ZIP code—to signal whether they are in the North, South, East, or West of the city; they are also given a number (e.g., SE23, N4). The post code for this part of London is E1, and so the horizontals of the letter have been joined in several cases to read B1 (Bangla 1 or Bengali 1). Thus, the metropolitan way of designating this territory is fused with a diasporic reference so that Banglatown enters London and, through its insertion, playfully disrupts the established grammar of locality.

But most interesting of all in the period from the early 1990s onward, one wall alongside the football pitch has been covered with highly decorative, carefully wrought invocations of an Islamic order. A stylized "Islam," more than 6 feet in height, is characterized by a calligraphy that resembles adjacent tags that owe their origins to New York subway graffiti discussed earlier (see Figure 4.4). The decoration is captioned by the phrase "Enjoin the Good and Forbid the Evil," and alongside it for a few years was another massive inscription proclaiming "Jihad those who fight for the cause of Allah." But these inscriptions are, like so many other graffiti, challenged locally, not so much by open patterns of racist abuse as by alternative notions of narrative space. Above the "Islam" tracing, it is possible to make out the inscription in another hand "The Neutral Zone Woz Here," cautiously ironic, whereas the Jihad graffito was erased from the wall in late 1997. Likewise in 1997, a series of posters in support of the Islamic group Hiz b'T Taheer (HT) prompted much controversy locally when they declared such statements as "Peace With Israel Is Haram" and carried pictures of the Middle East peace process and characters active in it with such captions as "Whoever gives away a handspan of Muslim land, Allah will grant them an equal handspan of hellfire" (Figure 4.5)

Posters and flyers, as well as graffiti, were left principally across the Bengali areas of the borough, with characteristically assertive messages, along with messages of support for the group Al Muhajiroun, listing their worldwide Web page (see Back, Keith, & Solomos, 1996). Yet, such inscriptions were frequently challenged. The Bangladesh struggle for independence was a civil war fought against a theocratic state, and the messages of the graffiti and posters were commonly challenged. In particular,

Figure 4.3

whereas the tags and the gang graffiti near Chicksand Street were left untouched, somebody erased with whitewash the "Jihad" from the wall, and many of the HT posters were also defaced. Ironically, the anti-Semitic tone of many of these messages was echoed in the winter of 1997-98 with a resurgence of far right activity in almost exactly the same area. On Cable Street, a site that witnessed clashes between the far right and the antifascist movement in the 1930s, the mural commemorating the confrontation was defaced in a way that, although not ostensibly directed at the majority Bengali population in the immediate vicinity, was directed again at a mythical Jewish presence that, in demographic terms, is now almost a historical memory and a residue of some of the older generation.

But what is to be made of this Babel-like set of messages, this admixture of words and symbols? We want to suggest that such writings repay a sustained analysis precisely because of what they reveal about the contestation and construction of imperfect and unruly forms of public debate. The forms of expression are not consciously discursive precisely because the

Figure 4.4

concatenation of intertextuality defies any meaningful "fields" of discourse. The depth of the provenance of some of the semiotics is undoubtedly commonly unknown. But also the breadth of the fields of reference on which these systems draw are routinely sophisticated and elaborate, combining local elements collaterally with global allusions. For both of these reasons, we believe that the cultural forms that wall writing and graffiti represent are frequently much more complex and warrant far closer scrutiny than is normally the case.

Graffiti as a genre has been long associated with the articulation of race, territory and youth groups, and subcultures in urban contexts (Moore, 1978). Particularly important is the work by psychologists Lomas and Weltman (1966) in Los Angeles and research by social geographers Ley and Cybriwsky (1974) in Philadelphia. Contained within this work are some clues about how one might conceptualize the relationship among graffiti, identity, and racism. Lomas and Weltman found in their research that the graffiti of youth groups was connected with claiming territory and

Figure 4.5

that gang graffiti became more frequent the closer one got to the home range of a particular group. Beyond this, they noted that graffiti was a key way of expressing class and ethnic markers:

> By considering the cultural milieu in which the wall writer operates we find messages reflect shared attitudes and values as well as ethnocentric variations on main cultural themes. Thus a comparative study of contemporary graffiti is to a great extent a cross-cultural investigation of class and ethnic differences. (Lomas, 1973, p. 71)

The problem with this way of thinking about graffiti is that it is ultimately reduced to the expressive effect of geographically defined social and cultural groups and identities. In this sense, we would argue that the visual ideologies draw on an iterative relationship between places and identities and the viewer and the viewed. Such a relationship disrupts and conflates Lefebvre's (1991) distinction between spaces of representation and representation of spaces. The graffiti are instead rendered visible through the particular nature of the modality of expression. Specifically, the characteristics we want to draw attention to here are as follows:

- The breadth of allusion
- The aesthetic appeal and symbolization of the wall writing
- The integration of the reader within a community of signs

Paradoxically, the imperative to communicate demands as much as assumes a shared set of cultural references: The will to distance and to purify is undermined by precisely this shared field of allusion. This returns us to the issue of communication that was raised earlier: The communication of hatred or opposition in and of itself involves the integration of the hate object into a community of allusion and symbolization. Otherwise, there would simply be no point to these communicative acts at all. To harass or challenge the presence of the Other, the writer needs to share a communicative technology with her or him. This involves the exchange of a decentered and promiscuous field of allusion, a symbolic language, and as we shall see later, even the mutual crossing of particular emblems.

To Whom Are You Talking? "Fragments Shored Against the Ruins"

It is not simply that graffiti constitute a secret language tied semantically to specific messages that need to be decoded. We reject any notion that, implicitly or explicitly, their meaning is to be found in the pathologies of the producers and the topographies of the spaces in which they are realized. In contrast, we would suggest that a focus on the audience for the messages of the wall writing undermines such simplicity. Put simply, the scribe invariably has an audience.

What difference does it make if we think of wall writing as a narrative genre that invokes the ethics and aesthetics of a particular scopic regime (Jay, 1992)? First, it makes us think about the precise form of visualization at work in such scripting. Graffiti is rarely an attempt to produce a realistic or naturalistic representation of a social or political reality; it neither replicates nor describes. Instead, it tells by visualizing: the I that is here, the we that tagged this place, the presences that must be erased, and the erasure that must be overwritten. Second, it clarifies the fact that the spaces are rendered visible in an iterative relationship with the scribes. This displays the link between space and identity in a different register from some of the more ethologically deterministic understandings of public spaces that work and those that do not. Even the bleakest spaces of desolate inner-city estates are humanized by particular moments of expressive culture. Third, it problematizes the easy taxonomies of racist and antiracist forms of wall writing. We return to this point later, but put simply, politically opposed groups may share a communicative repertoire that constitutes little more than the mirror opposite of the opponent. Fourth, it places a focus on the nature of allusion deployed in the process of graffiti writing. As we have argued, the allusions of the graffiti of intolerance in some ways undermine themselves through their own imperative to communicate. In this sense, the field of reference may not be discursive but is almost invariably intertextual. Tagging, writing, and "bombing" all share the need to develop a particular moment of communicative rationality.

If the notion that people "putting themselves together in public" through the modalities of graffiti writing is implicitly overoptimistic, it is not to underestimate the power of the forms of intolerance that are so often mobilized but instead to foreground process over outcome. This foregrounding of function over form highlights the construction of self and the articulation of place that is at the heart of the inscription of graffiti on the racialized walls of the city. We want to develop this line of argument through a discussion of openly and explicitly racist graffiti. Although the examples we have discussed above relate to the ethnically plural inner-city locations, we want to look at the contexts in which racist graffiti are used as part of quotidian harassment and the maintenance and embodiment of racially exclusive territories.

BOMB THE SUBURBS: WRITING ON (THE WALLS OF) THE RACIALIZED CITY

A Chicago-based graffiti artist called Upski, aka William Wimsatt, has turned the preoccupation for locating graffiti within the inner city on its head. Provocatively, he has called for the inner-city legion of taggers and writers to turn their aerosols on the suburbs: "I say bomb[8] the suburbs because the suburbs have been bombing us for at least forty years. They have waged an economic, political, and cultural war on life in the city. The city has responded by declaring war on itself" (Wimsatt, 1994, p. 10). This is an interesting inversion of the ways the concern over graffiti has been spatialized. But in the context of racist graffiti in Britain, the suburbs have for some time been a canvas for graffiti, except in this case the targets have been black and minority residents who have ventured into the once exclusive white preserves (Hesse, 1993; Hesse, Dhanwant, Bennett, & Lone, 1990).

The suburbs of England's main cities occupy an ambiguous place in the national imagination. Their rose-bushed gardens and domestic splendor serve as an emblem of propriety, respectability, and ordinary success, a kind of cultural totem for a nation that seems under threat from the cultural diversity of its metropolitan interiors. In these areas, too, suburban public housing estates were constructed to receive the white workers who were being offered a privileged residential place outside the inner city (see Rex & Moore, 1967; Rex & Tomlinson, 1979). In recent times, these places have also provided the context for extreme outbreaks of racist violence as these neighborhoods have became homes for visible minorities from various backgrounds.

Here, we want to focus on examples of racist graffiti in a suburban district of Birmingham to examine the sometimes complex ways they are used to communicate intolerance and harassment.[9] Birmingham is located in the former industrial heartland of the Midlands. It is the second largest city in England and has a population of about one million. Approximately 25% of this population is drawn from various minority communities—in particular, former migrants from the Asian subcontinent (Pakistan, India, and Bangladesh) and from the Caribbean (Jamaica, in particular) and small numbers of Africans, Cypriots, and Chinese. As in other major cities, minority populations are in large part concentrated in the inner districts. Racist graffiti are most common in the outlying suburban districts.

The surfaces onto which racist graffiti are inscribed betray this preoccupation with asserting claims over the cityscape. Graffiti are often painted on routeways like bus stops, lampposts, paths, and even roads. They mark an attempt to assert utopian notions of white racial identity. Yet, they may also act as "Keep Out" signs aimed to halt the flow of difference within urban areas. These two functions are invariably related but are not always identical. Graffiti are also used to harass minority shopkeepers and residents through the defacement of their property. In this sense, racist graffiti always possess a mode of address or a vector of abuse. Both a visual repertoire of symbolization and a linguistic grammar of words and phrases are clearly evident, both of which imply quite straightforwardly that the writing on the wall is there to be read. This preoccupation with audience we have taken to be a key aspect of the communicative technology of graffiti. It is produced through a combination of the chosen canvas and the form of graffiti.

Recently, in a suburban, predominantly white working-class district of Birmingham that we have researched, an Indian shopkeeper was subjected continuously to abusive racist graffiti on the doors, windows, and virtually every possible surface of his shop. This harassment included neo-fascist slogans and abbreviations (NF—National Front, and BNP—British National Party) alongside scatological profanities and references to local conflicts. Each graffito was sprayed on the surface of the shop itself and intended to address and hector the shopkeeper. Initially, this harassment was perpetrated by local white young men who used reference to right-wing political groups in an instrumental and opportunistic fashion. The conflict attracted the interest of local far-right activists, however, who then descended on this locale and painted another series of graffiti. What seemed significant about the second wave of graffiti was that the mode of address or vector changed. Rather than focused harassment of the shopkeeper, the graffiti were directed at the neighborhood. Figure 4.6 shows a graffito that was painted on the path in front of the shop—"England for Whites." The lettering is directed out toward the community at large and intended to be read as a "rights for whites" slogan. Prior to this, racist graffiti were addressed in the opposite direction, with emblems and abbreviations like NF and APL (Anti-Paki League; see Figure 4.7) painted on the same area of pavement but intended to be read from the vantage point of the shopkeeper's window. Here, these loaded abbreviations constituted a kind of challenge, a form of posturing through dangerous symbols intended to intimidate and invoke fear. Unlike the earlier graffiti, the "England for Whites" slogan did not refer to or address the Indian shopkeeper in a direct way, although the very fact that it was painted in front of the shop implied that his presence in this district was viewed by the writers as illegitimate and unwanted.

Local reaction to this appeal for "white solidarity" was revealing. Most local residents resented the opportunistic tactics of the right-wing graffiti writers and poured scorn on their tactics. This was in large part a resistance to the entryism from right-wing political groupings because they were from outside the neighborhood. The tactics of the far right could be condemned

Figure 4.6

while local styles of racism continued to be expressed against the Indian shopkeeper. This example shows clearly that one needs to be cautious about reading the territorial claims made through graffiti as merely a reflection or organic expression of the aspirations of particular geographically distributed communities. The "England for Whites" graffito was the projection of a particular claim to this locality as a "white space." Some people

Figure 4.7

within the local community subscribed to this view but resented its impo-
sition from a group of politically motivated outsiders. Other antiracist
white residents rejected both the political agenda of the National Front

graffiti writers and the definition of the neighborhood as an exclusively white territory. Racist graffiti tried to mask or conceal the diversity of interests that existed within this predominantly white neighborhood. It attempted to stylize the community in a particular way, which both undermined the status of local ethnic minority residents and sent a clear message to black citizens from other areas to "keep out." In this sense, it narrates the imagination of community through a process of systematic erasure. Consequently, it is necessary to view graffiti as a signifying system that is not only inscribed onto the social and physical fabric of the city but also part of the process by which the social objects of community and identity shape the reconstruction the city itself in a different image.

Graffiti as a form is more than merely a vehicle for the expression of territorial identities and a tool in racial harassment. It also constitutes a semantic and linguistic system similar to that discussed earlier in relation to New York Subway graffiti. As with all languages, one has to learn how to read and write within the codes of graffiti culture. More than this, graffiti often adopts forms of encryption that define a community of sometimes antagonistic readers and writers. A common form of encryption is to use numerals to substitute for letters. For example, 88 is commonly used in racist graffiti, with the numeral 8 symbolizing *H,* the eighth letter of the alphabet, and together this graffito signifies "Heil Hitler" (see Bushnell, 1990). Another example is C18, which is the identity of a small and violent grouping linked with the British National Party. The C18 tag is a widely used emblem in racist graffiti; decoded, the symbol means *C* for combat, and the numbers signify the initials of Adolf Hitler (1 stands for *A,* and 8 the eighth letter in the alphabet, *H*). The reader has to learn these codes, although in some cases it is known that a particular graffito (e.g., C18) is associated with racist politics without necessarily being aware of the coded symbolization.

Another abbreviation used by British racists is APL. This example demonstrates the inventive dimension of racist expression and its use of parody and allusion. The graffito means "Anti-Paki League," a political pastiche of the Anti-Nazi League, popularly referred to as the ANL. This widely documented antiracist movement achieved high levels of activity in the late 1970s and early 1980s (Gilroy, 1987). The notion "Paki" is used by racists as a stigmatized shorthand for all of Britain's south Asian communities regardless of whether they have links with Pakistan. This graffito substitutes "Nazi" with "Paki" and thus turns an antiracist abbreviation into a racist epithet. This substitution acknowledges a political opponent while ridiculing antiracism through pastiche. Also important here

Figure 4.8

is that "APL" does not refer to an organized collectivity or racist group; it only has meaning in the context of the expression of racist hostility through graffiti. Opposing graffiti writers often share a knowledge of their respective sets of linguistic signs. In this case, the process of linguistic appropriation is a matter of self-conscious parody of opponents' writing.

Although graffiti writers might be placed in an antagonistic relationship, they constitute a linguistic community united in its opposition to a wider normative community. Graffiti writing itself constitutes a kind of unruly alternative public sphere in which political argument and verbal debate are substituted with a kind of nondiscursive battle between opposing groups armed with spray cans and marker pens. British racist and antiracist graffiti writers monitor each other in an intense fashion, learning the others' symbolic languages. Graffiti politics is as much a semiotic/interpretative process as it is a struggle for a public presence through the quantity of inscription. As a result, racist and antiracist writing often entails overwriting, or erasing, the opponents' graffiti. Where the canvas is the property of a black or ethnic minority resident, the walls may be written over time and time again by both right-wing and left-wing graffiti.

Another target of graffiti artists was a newsagent shop (see Figure 4.8) owned by a south Asian family in the outer London district of Barking, a suburb of the East London districts discussed earlier. Here, the shutters of the shop provided the canvas for three separate waves of graffiti. Initially, a local group of right-wing graffiti writers sprayed "C18" on each of the three shutter panels and two Celtic crosses. In response, a group of antiracist writers affiliated with Anti-Fascist Action (AFA) and Youth Against Racism in Europe (YRE) wrote their own slogans "AFA," "YRE," and "BNP = SCUM" over the racist graffiti. Then a second group of competing antiracist activists from the Anti-Nazi League (ANL) overwrote both sets of graffiti with a series of claims and axioms: "C18 = NAZIS," "BLACK & WHITE UNITE AND FIGHT," "ANL," and "SMASH THE NAZIS—NO NAZIS IN BARKING." Alarmingly, this political struggle over lettering took place on the victims' property without their consent. The racially harassed shopkeeper's premises merely became the space onto which competing political groupings projected their pretensions to anti-racist efficacy.

Examples like this one suggest a dependent and reciprocal relationship between racist movements and antiracist organizations. One might ask to what extent these avowedly antagonistic groups need each other in order to sustain themselves over time. We don't have space to answer this question here, but what is interesting is that graffiti politics brings this question into focus. It seems clear that, within the writing wars being waged in British cities and elsewhere in Europe, each side of the political divide is locked into an antagonistic but reciprocal relationship. The effectiveness of challenging racism through these means is limited because of the mutually reinforcing nature of graffiti politics. This also raises some important questions about the quality of communication or dialogue being performed within graffiti. No discursive argument is exchanged through these means; rather, what is traded is a series of slogans and emblems.

Graffiti of this type constitutes a kind of symbolic salute to the political ideologies announced in its inscription. It is impossible to argue with a salute; such acts declare their presence in a moment of nano communication. Indeed, we would argue that Richard Sennett's ideas about the limits of declarative inscription would be better applied to this type of graffiti.

Perhaps, a more sophisticated way to counter racist graffiti is to subject them to a *détournement* that subverts the identities embodied within them. It is interesting that the respective ideologies of the Right and the Left are fixed through the process of assertion. The racist, or for that matter antiracist, "we" is at one stroke defined and reified, precluding any further discourse beyond graffiti. Such urban writing is both the sign and the boundary of politically opposed groups, but it is also the epitaph to discursive argument and debate.

The relevance of these issues need to be evaluated in view of the rise in neo-fascist activity in Europe and the growing intensity of popular racism. If these movements are to be effectively countered, it is essential to develop a sophisticated appraisal of the protean nature of racist cultures and their networks of circulation. George Mosse (1985), perhaps the preeminent scholar of fascist culture, has commented that a key part of the power of racism is the way it helps account for specific social relations in a simple manner through a visual ideology. Viewed from this perspective, graffiti can be seen as one key ocular mechanism of racist expression.

It is necessary to be able to decode graffiti not only to interpret contemporary forms of racism but also to evaluate the political strategies that have been mobilized against them. The real danger is that antiracist politics is fast becoming little more than the mirror opposite of its professed foe, whose very existence is locked into an ever more functional dependency on the activities of the opponent. One of the most alarming things emerging from our research is that graffiti politics seems separate from the experience of the victims of racism. No wonder, then, that the victims themselves are sometimes reticent to remove racist graffiti.

One shopkeeper told us:

> I stopped taking it off at one time, I left it there. In the daytime, when the shutters are up, there's nothing you can see. It's at night when you're closing [that you see the graffiti]. . . . I think to myself, "Let the people who live here see what their children are doing," let them have to look at it. I have been here too long to be shocked anymore.

Here, the homes and shops of the victims have been reduced to little more than a canvas for the expression of competing slogans and political desires. But powerfully, this sentiment inverts the narrative force of the graffiti; the tale of ethnic erasure becomes a testament of shame as the putative victim refocuses the writing to address a different audience.

CONCLUSION

The forms of wall writing we have examined are clearly driven by contrasting political impulses. It is not our aim, or even our desire, to suggest that these modes of urban expression can be tamed within a totalizing model of graffiti writing. Yet, while stressing variety and the importance of context and situatedness in reading graffiti, it is also necessary to identify the key elements contained within this form as a mode of expression. Throughout the chapter, we have used loosely the notion of a communicative technology to refer to the elementary apparatus of wall writing. Here, we want to draw together these ideas with regard to how they relate to the issues of public life, communication, and dialogue.

The only thing that unites the New York tagger with the neo-Nazi propagandist is that their inscriptions are outlawed equally. But, the prohibitions on each of these forms of graffiti are articulated through very different moral imperatives. Graffiti is also a symptom of the failure or the limits of permissible or legitimate communication within the public sphere. Yet, what is interesting about graffiti in all its diverse forms is that it challenges us to think about the relationship between people and places. We have stressed throughout this chapter that graffiti is a profoundly iterative form of urban expression. The types of social identity that emerge are produced by the people in a particular place as much as the place in them. More than this, graffiti is not merely the sign or the effect of an underlying ethological community; rather, it is the embodied social landscape. As a result, graffiti draws attention to how communities are manifested and articulated in a necessarily incomplete, uneven, and contingent fashion. Thus, we would argue that graffiti as a communicative technology is crucially implicated in an emergent spatial politics of entitlement and belonging within the city.

One key feature of graffiti is that it combines multiple modes of signification. So, in a Sassurean sense, graffiti is more parole than langue. It includes a visual repertoire of emblems and symbols with an often syncretic linguistic structure that deploys standard forms of language to articulate slogans and snatches of discourse. These forms of communication deploy encryption to encode the intended meaning. This can take a lexigraphic form in which letters symbolize whole words (e.g., NF for National Front) or numerals denote letters that in turn symbolize words (e.g., 88 for Heil Hitler). Seemingly opposed groups of writers may, in this situation, share symbolic resources. This traffic between graffiti writers may be opaque and unselfconscious. Bengali taggers known as the Danger Zone Posse (DZP) from the Whitechapel district of East London have, in recent times, assimilated elements from racist graffiti. Apart from the three-letter acronym style that is evocative of BNP graffiti, this group has also assimilated the target-like symbol of the Celtic cross commonly deployed by racist writers. The point here is that graffiti writing is a polysemic and open linguistic form at the level of both lexicon and genre.

Graffiti works through allusion rather than the explicit discourse of the mainstream. We suggest that allusion operates in one sense both externally and internally here. By *internal allusion,* we mean coded communication that is interpreted by a distinct community of writers and readers. Here, we are particularly thinking about New York hip hop graffiti, which we argued is read in very different ways, depending on whether it is viewed from the inside (by the writers themselves and their constituency) or from the outside (by liberal or even radical commentators like Wilson, Glazer, and even Sennett). In this sense, these outlaw forms of communication are precious because they both transform the mainstream through writing over it, yet at the same time exclude the mainstream from their—the graffiti writers'—discourse. By *external allusion,* we mean the strategic use of signs to provoke a particular audience, be it an individual or a social group. A good example of this is the ways Palestinian Intifada graffiti use the swastika alongside the Star of David often connected with an equal sign. The swastika invokes the experience of the Jewish Holocaust both to implicate Zionism in fascism and simply to offend through the sheer symbolic weight of its presence.[10] Oliver and Steinberg (1993) describe a young Palestinian who, "grabbing our notebook, scrawled a swastika across a page and exclaimed, 'See this? It drives the Jews crazy.'" (p. 5). This distinction is to some degree artificial because many forms of graffiti combine to different degrees internal and external elements of allusion, depending on the nature of the audience(s).

All graffiti are narrative in that they attempt to tell alternative stories about places. These stories, at their most basic, signal the failure of the public sphere to incorporate them. In this respect, we suggest that graffiti can be viewed as an unruly alternative public sphere that, though allowing forbidden inscription, contains contradictions of its own. The patrolled and circumscribed nature of graffiti culture militates against it being open and inclusive. So, the self-regulating endogenous nature of graffiti expression limits its own potential to spawn a true alternative. It may well be a mistake to yearn for a utopian and inclusive public sphere that engenders authentic communication. The achievement of such an inclusive urban culture seems inevitably tenuous. Perhaps this is why graffiti has endured as the most archaic form of written communication. In this sense, we need to be able to read the writing on the wall, for in these opaque and arcane inscriptions, we can find both the limits of public discourse and the outlaw voices that threaten to be heard.

NOTES

1. We have noted elsewhere how the Nazis used graffiti as both a weapon in the persecution of the Jews and as a form of propaganda within occupied territories (Back, Keith, & Solomos, 1996).

2. The notion of *détournement* was first developed by the Belgian surrealist Marcel Mariën, and its meaning is connected with spontaneous moments of subversion or diversion in which conventions are played with and thus revealed. Sadie Plant (1992), in her excellent study of the Situationist International, describes the role of graffiti: "Anonymous, cheap and immediate, the use of graffiti in the May events epitomized the avant-garde dream of art realized in the practice of everyday life. A transformation of its environment as a larger *détournement* of the city it inspired and reported" (p. 104).

3. Sennett (1991), echoing situationist *détournement* favors the suggestive wall writing of Parisian graffiti, which juxtapose images and slogans that "intrigue pedestrians who slow down and look" (p. 211).

4. See particularly Ricard (1981).

5. Jill Posner's (1982) insightful study of feminist graffiti shows how the spray can has also been used by women activists to deface offensive public representations of femininity. One example graphically challenged the advertiser to "Get your ads off my body!" Graffiti, she suggests, offer the means to overwrite the dominant gendered imagery presented in advertising and other public texts. Here, the act of defacement is perhaps another example of a momentary attempt to open up patriarchal imagery to public scrutiny.

6. A similar point is made by Benjamin Barber (1995) about the coincidence of globalism and tribalism. He argues we are caught between "Babel and Disneyland, the planet is falling precipitously apart and coming reluctantly together at the very same moment" (p. 4).

7. See Bethnal Green Trades Council (1979).

8. Meaning the "prolific painting or marking with ink" (Cooper & Chalfant, 1980, p. 27).

9. This research was developed from a project conducted with Anoop Nayak that examined racism in the suburbs (see Back & Nayak, in press). We thank and acknowledge Anoop for all the help he has given us with this material.

10. Malcolm Quinn (1994), in his excellent history of the swastika, points out that it is a symbol that cannot be subverted because of the overburdening legacy of Nazi violence and genocide (see also Solomos & Back, 1996).

REFERENCES

Abel, E. L., & Buckley, B. E. (1977). *The handwriting on the wall: Toward a sociology and psychology of graffiti.* London: Greenwood.

Back, L., Keith, M., & Solomos, J. (1996). Technology, race, and neo-fascism in a digital age: The new modalities of racist culture. *Patterns of Prejudice, 30*(2), 3-27.

Back, L., & Nayak, A. (in press). *The new frontiers of racism: Youth, community, and conflict in the suburbs.* Warwick, UK: Center for Research in Ethnic Relations.

Barber, B. (1995). *Jihad vs. McWorld: How globalism and tribalism are reshaping the world.* New York: Ballantine.

Berman, M. (1987, Winter). Take it to the streets: Conflict and community in public space. *Dissent,* pp. 476-485.

Bethnal Green Trades Council. (1979). *Blood on the streets.* London: Stepney.

Borja, J., & Castells, M. (1997). *Local and global.* London: Earthscan.

Bushnell, J. (1990). *Moscow graffiti: Language and subculture.* London: Unwin Hyman.

Castleman, C. (1982). *Gettin' up: Subway graffiti in New York.* Cambridge: MIT Press.

Cesaretti, G. (1975). *Street writers: A guided tour of Chicano graffiti.* New York: Acrobat.

Cockcroft, E. (1977). *Toward a people's art.* New York: E. P. Dutton.

Cooper, M., & Chalfant, H. (1980). *Subway art.* London: Thames & Hudson.

Cooper, M., & Sciorra, J. (1994). *R.I.P.: New York spray can memorials.* London: Thames & Hudson.

Corrigan, P. (1976). Doing nothing. In T. Jefferson & S. Hall (Eds.), *Resistance through rituals: Youth subcultures in postwar Britain* (pp. 103-106). Birmingham, UK: Center for Contemporary Cultural Studies.

Cresswell, T. (1996). *In place/Out of place: Geography, ideology, and transgression.* Minneapolis: University of Minnesota Press.

Dundes, A. (1966). Here I sit. *Kroeber Anthropological Society, 34,* 91-105.

Ferrell, J. (1993). *Crime of style: Urban graffiti and the politics of criminality.* New York: Garland.

Gilroy, P. (1987). *There ain't no black in the union jack: The cultural politics of race and nation.* London: Unwin Hyman.

Glazer, N. (1974). On subway graffiti in New York. *Public Interest, 54,* 3-11.

Goldstein, R. (1993). Visual punk: Basquiat and graffiti. In R. Marshall (Ed.), *Jean Michel Basquiat.* New York: Witney.

Hagopian, P. (1988). Reading the indecipherable: Graffiti and hegemony. *Polygraph, 1,* 105-109.

Hebdidge, D. (1993). Welcome to the Terrordome: Jean Michel Basquiat and the dark side of hybridity. In R. Marshall (Ed.), *Jean Michel Basquiat.* New York: Whitney.

Henderson, S. (1981). *Billboard art.* London: Angus & Robertson.

Hesse, B. (1993). Racism and spacism in Britain. In P. Francis & R. Matthews (Eds.), *Tackling racial attacks.* Leicester, UK: University of Leicester, Center for the Study of Public Order.

Hesse, B., Dhanwant, K. R., Bennett, C., & Lone, M. (1990). *Beneath the surface: An enquiry into racial harassment in the London borough of Waltham Forest.* Aldershot, UK: Avebury.

Jay, M. (1992). Scopic regimes of modernity. In S. Lasch & J. Friedman (Eds.), *Modernity and identity.* Cambridge, MA: Blackwell.

Lefebvre, H. (1991). *The production of space.* Cambridge, MA: Polity.

Ley, D., & Cybriwsky, R. (1974). Urban graffiti as territorial markers. *Annals of the Association of American Geographers, 64,* 491-505.

Lindsay, J. (1960). *The writing on the wall: An account of Pompeii in its last days.* London: Frederick Muller.

Lomas, H. D. (1973). Graffiti: Some observations and speculations. *Psychoanalytic Review, 68,* 70-75.

Lomas, H. D., & Weltman, G. (1966). *What the walls say today.* Paper presented at a meeting of the American Psychiatric Association, New Jersey.

Moore, J. W. (1978). *Homeboys: Gangs, drugs, and prison in the barrios of Los Angeles.* Philadelphia: Temple University Press.

Mosse, G. (1985). *Toward the final solution: A history of European racism.* Madison: University of Wisconsin Press.

Oliver, A. M., & Steinberg, P. (1993). Information and revolutionary ritual in Intifada graffiti. In A. A. Cohen & G. Wolfsfeld (Eds.), *Framing the Intifada: People and media.* Norwood, NJ: Ablex.

Perry, R. (1976). *The writing on the wall: The graffiti of London.* London: Elm Tree.

Plant, S. (1992). *The most radical gesture: The situationist international in a postmodern age.* London: Routledge.

Posner, J. (1982). *Spray it loud.* Cambridge, MA: Polity.

Quinn, M. (1994). *The swastika: Constructing the symbol.* London: Routledge.

Rees, N. (1979). *Graffiti lives, OK.* London: Unwin Paperbacks.

Reisner, R. (1974). *Graffiti: Two thousand years of wall writing.* London: Frederick Muller.

Rex, J., & Moore, R. (1967). *Race, community, and conflict.* London: Institute of Race Relations.

Rex, J., & Tomlinson, S. (1979). *Colonial immigrants in a British city: A class analysis.* Boston: Routledge Kegan Paul.

Reynolds, R. (1975). *Magic symbols: A photographic study of graffiti.* Portland, OR: Graphic Arts Center.

Ricard, R. (1981, December). The radiant child. *Artforum, 20,* 35-43.

Sennett, R. (1973). *The uses of disorder: Personal identity and city life.* Harmondsworth, UK: Penguin.

Sennett, R. (1976). *The fall of public man.* New York: Knopf.

Sennett, R. (1991). *The conscience of the eye.* New York: Norton.

Sennett, R. (1994). *Flesh and stone: The body and the city in Western civilization.* London: Faber & Faber.

Sennett, R., & Cobb, J. (1972). *The hidden injuries of class.* Cambridge, UK: Cambridge University Press.

Solomos, J., & Back, L. (1996). *Racism and society.* Basingstoke, UK: Macmillan Education.

Sussman, E. (1997). Songs of innocence at the nuclear pyre. In E. Sussman (Ed.), *Keith Haring*. New York: Whitney Museum of Modern Art.

Wilson, J. Q., & Kelling, G. (1982, March). Broken windows: The police and neighborhood safety. *Atlantic Monthly,* pp. 29-38.

Wimsatt, W. (1994). *Bomb the suburbs*. Chicago: The Subway and Elevated Press.

CHAPTER 5

The Art of Subversive Image Making

Carol Becker
The School of the Art Institute of Chicago

Some images conspire to perpetuate illusions, distance people from reality, and create further mystification. When they fill the public space and obliterate real discourse and debate, their effects are lethal to the health of society. Other images, however, are designed to pierce reality, to heighten the understanding of societal contradictions. Such images attempt to create a visual language, a discourse through which to discuss the convergence of the individual with the society. The ability to read such visual language, to *see* such images, has been lost to many because of the elimination of art from public school education (hence the growth of visual illiteracy), because of the hostile response to art and artists (the result of numerous censorship battles), and because artists themselves at times have become too hermetic in their discourse, hiding their meaning from a larger audience. But serious artists *are* working to understand the culture within which they live and to rearticulate that culture to itself, offering insights into the issues of race, class, gender, and general emotional dis-ease, which continue to haunt America. This subversive image making, the work of particular art and artists, the relationship of this work to that of specific writers and intellectuals, and their joint role in the analysis of the collective historical psyche is what I wish to discuss. To do so, I begin with the master of such analyses: Freud himself.

POLITICS AND PATHOLOGY

Freud had been ill and had not written for several years when he began *Civilization and Its Discontents* (1930/1961), a small book designed to challenge the most basic assumptions on which Western civilization is constructed. It was 1929 and therefore not surprising that he would have been motivated to explore such large societal issues. At that time, the struggle (in Freud's terms) between Eros and Thanatos was already underway in Germany and Austria. Hitler was in his ascendancy, and there was foreboding of the unimaginable nightmare to come. The original ending of Freud's sustained argument in this book offered a sense that although humans did have the capacity to exterminate each other "to the last man," he assured his readers that the force of life would most assuredly triumph over the force of death. By 1931, however, Freud clearly understood that the fate of the world could easily go either way. The outcome was definitely less certain. And so, for the second edition, which also ended with the statement that "eternal Eros will make an effort to assert itself against its dreaded adversary," he added one line: "But who can foresee with what success and with what result?" It was a frightening revision.

Many critics have accused Freud and his followers of pathologizing society without addressing concrete social and political issues. And yet, in these philosophical writings, his particular methodology of psychoanalytic and social scrutiny did allow him to take the pulse of his own civilization and find it alarmingly diseased.

What interests me for this discussion is how few models exist for measuring the temper of a society or the motivation of the collective psyche at any particular historical moment, and yet at times such analyses are desperately needed, when madness, or at least neurosis, does rule politics. Freud himself ran into an immediate problem in attempting such an analysis. He asked: How do you diagnose the pathology of cultural communities when everyone in the society is somehow implicated in the troubled behavior? And, I would add, how can you achieve an accurate measure of the collective psyche when part of the pathology is that only certain voices are allowed to be heard?

In my thinking, this is the juncture at which artists, poets, and intellectuals can make their presence felt. Through various creative means, such people create discourses that articulate the multiple collective psyches that actually do exist in the society and attempt to represent their underlying fears about the state of that society. Artists might envision notions of freedom and psychic health that may or may not as yet exist while also presenting the manifestations of psychic unhealth—malaise, racism, hypocrisy, despair—for all to see. But this type of anthropological/analytic work—the theoretical questionings of intellectuals—is not terribly valued within American society at the moment. If we use the cutbacks in governmental allocations to the National Endowment for the Arts and Humanities as any indication, we might deduce, in fact, that the United States has declared war on artists and intellectuals with a progressive agenda and therefore also on the process of critically and poetically analyzing its own behavior. From where would we take our measure of health if those in whom we entrust the life of our dreams were actually ever to become silent?

Perhaps we can say that the well-being of a democracy is, in part, manifested by how openly this representation of its own complexity is embraced by a society. There is no doubt that what Terry Eagleton (1995) says about culture can also be said about the perception of contemporary art in America: It has now become "part of the problem, rather than the solution; the very medium in which the battle is engaged, rather than some Olympian terrain on which our differences can be recomposed" (p. 17). Whereas artists seek to face the present reality, art's fall from such idealization to become itself a zone of contention makes it problematic and a too-easy target for politicians who can turn a general audience against contemporary artists because the experience of art viewing, at this time, often does not satisfy more traditional expectations and desires for immediate gratification.

PRIVATE TESTIMONY AND PUBLIC RECEPTION

Serious intellectual challenges to how things are done, if they come from the Left and not the Right, are often seen as un-American, and complex thought is criticized as elitist. And because the language of postmodernism both in writing and in art making often has been unfortunately obscure, it is not surprising that, after several decades of work by artists and intellectuals on issues of race, identity politics, gender, and youth culture, the popular understanding of these issues as reflected back to us has not changed profoundly. All this collective work accomplished in the academy and in the art world has not sufficiently permeated the popular/projected image of who is an American. Thus, the media continue to present America as a fundamentally homogeneous society with homogeneous values—values with which critically positioned art must inevitably collide.

Much of the work that infuriated politicians and that the National Endowment for the Arts then tried to write off as "mistakes" was art, often performance art, that provided personal testimony, work that said: This is my experience of daily life. Here is how I am seen or not seen in America and in the world as a woman, a gay man, a person of color, a politically and socially conscious being. This is the form within which I engage critically with my environment.

Such art, which was doing the work of bringing subjective experiences into the collective, was too often met without understanding and with scorn. The Nan Goldin retrospective at the Whitney Museum was an interesting example of such an endeavor. In this autobiographical photographic exhibition entitled "I'll Be Your Mirror" (in which the artist's presence over 25 years of photographing is so direct and palpable that the show feels like a protracted performance), it becomes clear that Nan Goldin has loved both men and women, has lost many friends to AIDS, and has come undone herself from drug and alcohol abuse. It is also apparent that she continues to use her skills as an artist, and particularly as a photographer, to unify her fragmented world and ours. This work might terrify those who do not see art as a vehicle for chronicling the intersection of personal and societal realities. Her experience as documented could be evaluated as deviant from the norm or as a representation of the uniqueness of each life and the deep desire we all have at times to permeate the membrane between us and those we love and to hold on to those we have lost. The society outside the art world could claim her as a fellow human being—vulnerable—or it could try to portray her as a Martian. Such work that is capable of generating an understanding of difference and of offering reconciliation, amazingly, can actually also further isolate artists from mainstream society. It completely depends on the political climate into which the work is placed, how well it can control its own contextualization, and whether the public funding is anywhere involved to further skew the issues. What can we say of a society that has become demonstrably afraid of its own most creative people precisely because they try to represent truth and complexity as they experience it?

BREAKING THE SILENCE

Focusing on a different type of testimony, raw testimony without the organizing principles of art, yet searching for what South African writer

Nadine Gordimer calls "restoration," I have been fascinated by the events in South Africa and have been watching that country closely to learn something about how a society may listen to voices that have been silenced and how these voices may revise the collective understanding of what a society is and has been. Since April 1996, South Africa has been involved in a collective catharsis that has already gone through many stages under the guidance of the Truth and Reconciliation Commission. This process is scheduled to continue for 18 months to 2 years from its point of origin. It is designed to drain the collective abscess by allowing the crimes perpetuated under apartheid to be spoken within a government-sanctioned public forum. It is a project completely dependent on personal testimony and, when completed, will actually rewrite the former apartheid historical narrative for the postapartheid era. People are testifying every day in South Africa or are being forced to come forward through the use of subpoenas. Victims who have suffered profound indignities at the hands of torturers and murderers are telling their stories. Those who have committed horrific crimes are being challenged to justify those crimes politically if they wish amnesty. The accusations have already implicated the top strata of the National Party. The daily workings of the commission are broadcast on radio and television, moved around to various sites around the country. Whatever the final outcome—and many questions have been raised about its ultimate efficacy—this government-initiated endeavor reflects a profound desire for collective psychic health and forgiveness. It is performative, theatrical, and takes place in front of an audience potentially as large as the entire population of South Africa.

I was there to attend the Fault Line Conference in Cape Town (July 1996), where writers, artists, and intellectuals from around the world were invited to participate in readings and discussions about "remembering, recollecting, restructuring." In his keynote address, Mark Behr, a young writer whose first novel, *Smell of Apples,* received acclaim for deconstructing the racist sentiments of a prominent Afrikaner military family, told the conference that, from the end of 1986 to 1990, he worked as a police agent infiltrating student antiapartheid groups on the Stellenbosh University campus (a premier Afrikaner institution). Recruited by a high-ranking family member in the South African police force, he used the money he received from serving as an agent to pay his college expenses. Once exposed to the antiapartheid movement, he began to change his feelings about apartheid and turned double-agent, supplying intelligence information to the police, as well as to the ANC in exile. His individual testimony, unmediated by the formal structures of a novel or play, so much less horrific than that being told every day in the hearings, nonetheless had a shocking effect. It demonstrated to many the degree to which apartheid permeated and corrupted all aspects of human relationships and the amount of individual pain still to be reconciled at all levels of society.

ENTERTAINMENT, REPRESSION, AND PROTRACTED ADOLESCENCE

For those of us raised in the United States, this degree of forthrightness, this truth telling and collective catharsis, is unknown to our experience. When has this country actually sought after the truth and encouraged to speak those who have wronged and those who have been wronged and then silenced? When has it deliberately fostered an atmosphere of reconciliation?

America has instead evolved a media apparatus of such proportion that it has come to obfuscate the truth and to mediate every experience we have in the public sphere, and often in the private as well, transforming politics, painful personal testimony, tragedy, and world events into entertainment. Surrounded by a veritable wall of video projection—an extravagant and impenetrable veil of maya that blocks perception and the accurate evaluation of reality—it is difficult for artists and intellectuals to see the impact of their work. The sheer scale of America is prohibitive to the notion of collectivity. And inevitably the commodity nature of late capitalism transforms everything, even audience, into a market.

Writers and artists are free to make the work they choose as long as they can afford to do so without public funding. But there is the distinct possibility that only a small group will actually experience the work, and often no written critical response is forthcoming to amplify and preserve its meaning and effect. If the work becomes controversial and reaches national recognition, then its message likely will be distorted and an aura of fear and repression will be generated around it. This is a very difficult society in which to position strategically one's art or one's intellectual work.

So in keeping with my original inquiry, suppose we were now to attempt to characterize the condition of the dominant image of the collective psyche (the protagonist at the center of the master narrative, the collective persona projected by those who hold power in this country at this time) and then use this profile to measure America's psychic health. We might say that we have a nation controlled by an ego so narcissistic and fragile that it cannot tolerate direct criticism, a psyche so repressed and rigid that each tremor reverberating from the collective knot of cathected energy threatens to explode its cohesion. We might see it as so terrified of its own originality that it would rather be overstimulated by media every waking hour, plugged into a myriad of electronic devices, or drugged into a narcoleptic but nonetheless antidepressed stupor than face its own difficult, rich, complex, and diverse identity. Perhaps we might say that the projected profile of America is of a country that does not want to mature, a *puer* in Jungian terms, arrested in its desire to project and protract its adolescence and therefore admired and emulated by adolescents the world over.

Nineteenth-century American writers like Poe, Melville, and Hawthorne had to explore the underside of their society, that which was hidden from the public view. No one else dared give shape to the collective unconscious. They often presented their findings in the form of adventure stories, appealing to the wildness/wilderness experience of an adolescent nation. They exposed the darkness and complexity at the core, even alluding to the racism on which this country was constructed. This role as archeologist of truth became the adopted position of many artists in America who were then often punished for doing their jobs too well.

IMAGES OF THE ARTIST

In Latin America and Africa, artists have been aligned with the romance of liberation struggles. Their articulation of conflicts within the society has made them significant to groups of people seeking social change. Hence, the popularity of a poet like Pablo Neruda, who became "of the people" because he expressed the imaginings of Chileans to free themselves from fascism. Or South African artists and writers whose voices have been heard and whose place in the process of political change is secured, their work directly associated with the public good.

In the United States, the popular images of artists are also aligned with romance. But it is still either the nineteenth-century romance of the starving artist alone in his garret (always a he) or an image of the most vastly successful artists like Andy Warhol, who are associated with money, Hollywood, and illusion. Warhol himself made it big in America on American terms. He was smart and talented enough to know how to project the media back to themselves in their own riotous narcissism—to embrace their images, replicate them to eternity, and transform them into art. The media loved him for this. But deep, passionate. psychologically serious work, even Warhol's own darker images, have difficulty penetrating the collective psyche as Picasso's *Guernica* (1937) was able to do in and for Europe. Audiences in this country often become angry with any merger of art and politics. They want a pure aesthetic experience, and they want beauty—still caught in the idea that art with a social agenda is not free because it serves a utilitarian function. Such art is still associated with socialist realism, a prejudice reaffirmed even in the art world's own conflicted responses to the 1993 Whitney Biennial.

Poet and artist William Blake believed that it was most assuredly the function of poetry—as both language and visual imagery—to express the faults of humans, as well as to re-form them. Blake believed in the transformation of individual consciousness that would lead to the evolution of societal consciousness, convinced that the world we desire is more real than the world we passively accept. For Blake, art was the bridge linking these realities. But to carry forth this mission, art had to be "corrosive" to the illusions that had encrusted and therefore obscured the ability of the individual and of the body politic to envision the potential of the species.

Some U.S. artists have thought they could achieve such ends through work that was regressive in nature. But childlike rebellion is easily absorbed into a society that already seeks to remain infantile. It might annoy some who associate high art with adult behavior to see such work, but it cannot revolutionize perception. Art that succeeds in Blake's terms is art that attempts to acknowledge the fall from innocence. It does not romanticize that innocence, nor does it confuse rebellion with revolution. It tries to show that it is not innocence we should seek to re-find, but rather greater consciousness, and that the only way to do that is to move through the mass and mess of contradictions that stand in our way. This is why, though many doubts have been raised, I still have faith in the laborious process in which South Africans are engaged. They are insisting on facing up to their political and spiritual history until it becomes transparent, no longer mystified, no longer able to hold them hostage. But for Western society, it is as if the myth of the fall rests in the idea that knowledge and understanding are a curse; movement to greater consciousness therefore is met with resistance. Art certainly attempts such movement. But at least one Gnostic sect believed that even the snake in the garden was God because it brought "consciousness" that does not *keep us* from really seeing the world within which we live and imagining a better one, but is in fact our only way to get there.

The false innocence that America continually perpetuates can be very appealing to the rest of the world as it manifests itself in popular culture. Others often seem drawn to a society that appears to have shed the weight of the past and tradition and that also denies the reality of growing up and older and then unselfconsciously wraps itself in the image of righteousness and the good. But this denial of "what is" has also marginalized the serious art making in America that attempts to move beyond the struggle with form and content to tackle its relationship to society. Perhaps this desire to return art to a childlike, unfallen, prepubescent, nonconflictual, depoliticized state accounts for this most recent movement in public arts debate away from the National Endowment for the Arts to discussions about creating more art classes for children. Who wants to refute such a push for spending? But surely we need to ask: What ever happened to art for adults? And how did we manage to get through an entire presidential campaign without a mention of arts and humanities funding?

THE THERAPEUTICS OF CRITICAL DISCOURSE

At this moment, when the path for art, artists, and all cultural workers in America is uncertain, when the "aesthetic project," as Eagleton (1995) calls it, must not be abandoned, we need to support artists who make truly thoughtful work—work full of thoughts—radical precisely because it refuses to simplify its meaning or to reduce its multiplicity. Radical because it takes a strong stand about where we are as a society and strives to communicate its meaning to many while insisting on creating a moment of private space, an indication of subjectivity within the public sphere. And radical because it shows that neither the mind nor, in the case of performance, the body can be colonized. Such work is an emancipatory practice that relies on intervention and surprise.

Those of us who can, need to continue to defend the intention and importance of such engaged work by creating critical discourses that provide a proper reception for it so that its importance to society is understood, its meaning is not distorted, and it is not lost to us. Such artists as Betye Saar, Suzanne Lacy, Ron Athey, Goat Island, Cindy Sherman, Ana Mendieta, Leon Golub, Guillermo Gómez-Peña, Nancy Spero, Fred Wilson, Susanna Coffey, and Rachel Rosenthal instigate a necessary collision between what is and what wants to be—a vital component of any collective psychosocial analysis. And they do it and have done it in public.

We can say of their work what Heiner Müller (1990) said about Pina Bauch's: Their images are like a "thorn in the eye" (p. 108). I take this metaphor to mean that such images are so piercing of the veil, so penetrating, so unassimilable, even blood-letting and ultimately disruptive to the homeostasis of the body politic as well as to the collective psyche that, unless they are confronted, there can be no cure.

REFERENCES

Eagleton, T. (1995). The crisis of contemporary culture. In P. Buchler (Ed.), *Random access* (Vol. 1). London: Rivers Oram.

Freud, S. (1961). *Civilization and its discontents* (J. Strachey, Trans. & Ed.). New York: Norton. (Original work published 1930)

Muller, H. (1990). *Germania* (B. Schutze & C. Schutze, Trans.). New York: Semiotext(e).

CHAPTER 6

Resisting Whiteness

Revolutionary Multiculturalism as Counterhegemonic Praxis

Peter L. McLaren
University of California at Los Angeles

> *Whitey has screwed everything up. Only whitey would shoot 500 buffalo from a train, just to see them die. Only whitey would hand out disease-ridden blankets and wipe out whole tribes of indigenous people. I'm playing for my son, because I am not going to bring him up in this horseshit. I'd like to slap the faces of the politicians and drag them from office and put some grass-roots people in there.*
>
> Dick Dale, King of the Surf Guitar, *San Louis Obispo New Times* (p. 24)

Rarely assailed as a racialized practice of power and privilege precisely because of its ubiquitous and invisible presence, whiteness has become universalized as an identity that both supersedes and transcends ethnicity. Public discussions of race seldom provide opportunities to recognize the epistemological, phenomenological, metaphysical, political, or ethical implications of racialized social practices in our everyday experiences as racialized subjects. These dilemmas are symptomatic of an image of identity

AUTHOR'S NOTE: An extended version of this chapter appears in McLaren, P. (1997). *Revolutionary multiculturalism: Pedagogies of dissent for the new millennium.* Boulder, CO: Westview Press.

that forecloses consideration of its broader political dimensions. They are also symptomatic of a media culture that has transcoded racial differences as cultural differences, thereby resulting in cultural attributes that join phenotype and skin color as permanently fixed "natural" attributes of different ethnic groups. Within increasingly globalized commodity cultures, such "cultural" differences become transformed into consumer "lifestyle" choices. Rarely are ethnic discourses and practices interrogated for the interests they serve and the social arrangements they privilege. Seldom is the practice of racism explored beyond its expression as a question of individual or group "attitude." Policies of multiculturalism and invocations of diversity are, for the most part, grounded in an integrationist universalism that links truth with the transcendence of racial categories and status. Within such a perspective, white people are encouraged to become "colorblind" and not to recognize the specificity of their own white ethnicity because to do so would reveal whiteness as an invisible marker for conceptualizing normative arrangements of citizenship practices. In fact, the dominant discourse of national identity in the United States motivates certain pernicious forms of social amnesia surrounding the way whiteness is articulated into the practices of the self, as well as taken up as racialized sets of social practices and privileges linked to the social division of labor.

When dealing with issues of racism, inequality, and capitalist exploitation, the ideological state apparatuses, such as the mass media, the schools, and governmental social agencies, serve more to reduce the opportunity for substantive dialogue than to exercise it. As a national policy initiative, multiculturalism functions as a means of understanding the culture of foreign investors so as to increase profits. At the precise historical juncture when we possess the discursive and ideological means of facilitating such a dialogue, less real communication about the processes through which racialized identity constitutes itself is occurring. The sign or image value of racialized identifications in the public media has overwhelmed dialogic attempts at understanding how racialized identities are grounded in everyday social relations. At a time when the racialized practice of fetishizing the classification of difference has resulted in the universalizing of a changing sameness, we need to recognize that most attempts at practicing a form of multiculturalism actually reconfirm existing relations of power and privilege. This is because social practices of whiteness are rarely, if ever, named, let alone interrogated in the clarion call for increasing cultural diversity. Multiculturalists and antiracist activists have transformed difference into a type of fetishized value in itself. *Difference,* on the one hand, becomes the form of particularism that soils the purity of universalism. *Diversity,* on the other hand, becomes a form of "uniqueness" that does not disturb the changing sameness of white hegemony. Diversity is a way of "adding on" cultures to an already whitened cultural center. Within the call for diversity exists little acknowledgment of, let alone complex engagement with, the processes by which racialized difference is grounded in certain moral economies, representational taxonomies, dominant social relations of production and consumption, and the existing social division of labor.

AMERICA AS EUPHEMISM

In the United States, we are living at a time of undeclared war. Each day, we negotiate our way through mine-sown terrains of confrontation and uncertainty surrounding the meaning and purpose of identity. American democracy faces Janus-like in two simultaneous directions: into a horizon of hope and coexistence and into the burning eyes of klansmen in sheets soiled with blood. On the one hand, this current historical juncture is witnessing an unprecedented growth of white supremacist organizations living on the fringes of social life; on the other hand, establishment conservatives are stridently asserting nativistic and populist sentiments that barely distinguish them ideologically from their counterparts in racialist far-right groups and citizen militias: The Ku Klux Klan, Posse Comitatus, The Order, White Aryan Resistance, Christian Identity, National Alliance, Aryan Nations, American Front, Gun Owners of America, United Citizens of Justice, and militia groups have organizations in most, if not all, 50 states.

Young white males and females who may find these racist groups unappealing can still find solace in politicians such as Pete Wilson and Bob Dole, whose anti-immigrant and Latinophobic policies and practices deflect their racializing sentiments through flag waving, jingoism, and triumphalist acts of self-aggrandizement—such as the disguising of Proposition 209 as a civil rights initiative—designed to appeal to frightened white voters who believe that growing numbers of Spanish-speaking immigrants will soon outnumber them. Politicians have become white warriors in blue suits and red ties, dedicated to taking back the country from the infidel. Recently, amid headlines of black churches in the South being razed by arson, a Los Angeles newspaper ran a photograph of Bob Dole at a Southland political rally. The magnetic allure of Dole's head, its skin a translucent blue, tensile; its shiny yellow tongue as if dipped in kerosene, seemingly wagging, appeared in metonymic relationship to his message: Anglos feel under siege from the most alien of alien nations—Mexico—

and it is time that civilized white folks wrestle back the land from the barbarians.

Guillermo Gómez-Peña (1996) writes:

> This identity crisis translates into an immense nostalgia for an (imaginary) era in which people of color didn't exist, or at least when we were invisible and silent. The political expression of this nostalgia is chilling: "Let's take our country back." The far right, like Pete Wilson, Newt Gingrich, Jesse Helms, and Pat Buchanan, along with many Democrats, are in agreement on the following: This country must be saved from chaos and collapse into Third-Worldization; "illegal" immigrants must be deported; the poor should be put in jail (three strikes, you're out); welfare, affirmative action, and bilingual education programs must be dismantled; and the cultural funding infrastructure that has been infiltrated by "liberals with leftist tendencies" (the National Endowment for the Arts and the Humanities and the Corporation for Public Broadcasting) must be decimated. In the euphemistic Contract with America, ethnic "minorities," independent artists and intellectuals, the homeless, the elderly, children, and especially immigrants from the South, are all under close watch. (p. 173)

On the day of General Colin L. Powell's address to the 1996 Republican National Convention in San Diego, former U.S. Education Secretary and current Director of Empower America, William J. Bennett (1996), published a commentary in the *Los Angeles Times* titled "Civil Rights Is the GOP's Mission." Evoking the figure of Dr. Martin Luther King, Jr., Bennett called for the end of racial discrimination through the abolition of affirmative action. Bewailing the civil rights leaders of the past 30 years (with the exception of Dr. King, of course, whose symbolic power he seeks to conscript into his own agenda), who he argued are a group of malcontents who have wielded a "racial branding iron," have "diminished the moral authority of the civil rights movement," have "fanned the flames of racial resentment," and have "helped Balkanize America," Bennett calls for the government to eliminate "race-based preferences" for people of color. He putatively wants African Americans, Latino/as, and other ethnic minority groups to be judged by the "content of their character." He cites African Americans such as Ward Connerly, chairman of the Civil Rights Initiative, and General Powell as continuing "the great civil rights tradition of Dr. King."

Bennett's vision is perniciously shortsighted and maleficent, however, and effectively domesticates King's place in the civil rights struggle. And his logic is disturbingly flawed. It is similar to the conservative school board that abolishes school breakfast programs for hungry children because such programs are "antifamily." Because the children eat at school and not with their parents and siblings at home, they are apparently offending the values that made this country great. Supposedly, it is better to go hungry with your family than to be fed at school. Bennett's arguments are similarly confused. First, he appears to work under the mistaken assumption that U.S. society has reached a point of relative economic justice and that affirmative action is no longer necessary. Second, he appears to be either unable or unwilling to fathom the nearly intractable reality of white privilege and uncontested hegemony in the arena of the economy. Third, he fails to realize that racist white people are going to be suspicious of African Americans and Latino/as whether they are assisted by affirmative action initiatives or not. And fourth, his vision is propelled by a nostalgic view of a United States as a middle-class suburban neighborhood in which people of color don't have so much "attitude" and where whites are the uncontested caretakers of this prelapsarian nation of consensus and harmony. To be color-blind in Bennett's restricted use of the term is to be naive at best and ignorant at worst, because not to see color, in Bennett's view, really amounts in ideological terms to being blind to the disproportionate advantage enjoyed by white people in nearly all sectors of society. Winant (1994) has argued: "In many ways no African American, however affluent, can feel as secure as even the average White: for example, in an encounter with the police. . . . Yet the malevolent attentions of floor walkers in Bloomingdales cannot be compared with those of the Los Angeles Police Department" (p. 283).

Bennett's view is akin to conservative politicians who bemoan critics of tax breaks for the rich (welfare for the rich) for engaging in "class warfare." You don't have to be an economist to realize that, since the Reagan administration, money has been transferred from the ranks of the poor into the coffers of the rich in record proportions. Yet conservative politicians resent people who label these practices "unjust." After all, if rich (mainly white) people can work the system to their advantage, then all the more power to them. Bennett has turned the logic of Martin Luther King, Jr. upside down. He has replaced social analysis with homilies about "character." That a former U.S. secretary of education would take a position like this is especially telling, given the state of critical self-reflection among politicians in this country.

Politicians of Bennett's ilk want to increase the role of charitable institutions in the United States. If economically disenfranchised people of color are to be helped, then it should be done by private individuals or organizations and not the government—or so the conservatives maintain. But wealthy private organizations have benefited from the hegemony of white privilege in the government and the marketplace for centuries.

Unbridled capitalism in our current post-Fordist service economy is ruthlessly uncharitable to the poverty-stricken. Nevertheless, transferring the challenge of economic justice from the government into the hands of philanthropists who feel "pity" for the poor is not the solution.

Bennett misses the crucial point: that not to have affirmative action for people of color in the current social structure amounts to a hidden affirmative action for white people. Bennett's position tacitly seeks the incorporation of racialized groups into the corporate ethics of consumption where white privilege increasingly holds sway. His ethics of racial tolerance can therefore work as a means of social control of populations of color. His motivated amnesia with respect to the history of capitalism causes him to ignore the macrostructures of inequality and injustice and the class-bound hierarchies and institutionalized racism of U.S. society and to act as if U.S. society already obtains on the issue of economic equality across diverse ethnic populations. A false assumption at work in Bennett's logic views culture as essentially self-equilibrating, as providing similar sets of shared experiences to all social groups. The culture of diversity heralded by Bennett is a decidedly homogenized one, cut off from the contingencies of state power and economic practices. He fails to recognize the ideology of colonialism as a founding discourse of U.S. democracy and refuses to acknowledge that the skull-and-crossbones logic of imperial piracy that helped the United States steal the land from its indigenous inhabitants is still largely with us in both domestic and foreign policy.

If Bennett is so intent on character building and fears that African Americans are now being viewed by white people as bearing the "stigma of questionable competence" because of affirmative action, why doesn't he, rather than dismantle affirmative action, place greater emphasis on improving the social practices of white people by encouraging them not to stigmatize, demonize, and peripheralize people of color and women not only in boardrooms but in all walks of life?

Bennett's stubborn unwillingness to recognize the asymmetrical allocation of resources and power overwhelmingly favors white people as much now as during King's era, effectively truncates Bennett's vision, and fashions it into a form of sound bite histrionics.

THE DISCOURSE OF COLOR BLINDNESS

In her article "Whiteness as Property," Cheryl Harris (1993) makes the compelling case that, within the legal system and within popular reasoning, an assumption exists that whiteness is a property interest entitled to legal protection. Whiteness as property is essentially the reification in law of expectations of white privilege. Not only has this assumption been supported by systematic white supremacy through the law of slavery and "Jim Crow" but also by recent decisions and rationales of the U.S. Supreme Court concerning affirmative action. Harris is correct in arguing that whiteness serves as the basis of racialized privilege in which white racial identity provides the basis for allocating societal benefits in both public and private spheres. Whiteness as a property of status continues to assist in the reproduction of the existing system of racial classification and stratification that protects the socially entrenched white power elite. According to Harris, rejecting race-conscious remedial measures as unconstitutional under the equal protection clause of the Fourteenth Amendment "is based on the Court's chronic refusal to dismantle the institutional protection of benefits for whites that have been based on white supremacy and maintained at the expense of Blacks" (p. 1767).

Current legal definitions of race embrace the norm of color blindness and thus disconnect race from social identity and race consciousness. Within the discourse of color blindness, blackness and whiteness are seen as neutral and apolitical descriptions reflecting skin color and unrelated to social conditions of domination and subordination and to social attributes such as class, culture, language, and education. In other words, *color blindness* is a concept that *symmetrizes* relations of power and privilege and flattens them out so that they appear symmetrical or equivalent. But blackness and whiteness are not symmetrical; rather, they exist in society within a dependent hierarchy, with whiteness constraining the social power of blackness: by colonizing the definition of what is normal, by institutionalizing a greater allocation of resources for white constituencies, and by maintaining laws that favor whites. According to Harris (1993):

> To define race reductively as simply color, and therefore meaningless . . . is as subordinating as defining race to be scientifically determinative of inherent deficiency. The old definition creates a false linkage between race and inferiority, the new definition denies the real linkage between race and oppression under systematic white supremacy. Distorting and denying reality, both definitions support race subordination. As Neil Gotanda has argued, color blindness is a form of race subordination in that it denies the historical context of white domination and Black subordination. (p. 1768)

Affirmative action needs to be understood, not through privatizing social inequality through claims of bipolar corrective justice between black and white competitors, but rather as an issue of distributive social justice and rights that focuses, not on guilt or innocence, but on entitlement and fairness.

Bennett's faltering rhetoric and specious logic speak directly to the current crisis of democracy that has deported the hopes and dreams of growing numbers of minority populations across the United States into an abyss of emptiness and despair. The crisis has exposed the infrastructure of U.S. democracy to be made of Styrofoam, trembling spray-painted pillars of a Greek temple in an off-Broadway play. Democracy has been cut at the joints by events currently transpiring both locally and worldwide.

AGAINST WHITENESS

The specific struggle that I wish to address is that of choosing against whiteness. Yet is it possible for us to choose against whiteness, given that historically the practice of whiteness has brought about such a devastating denial, disassembly, and destruction of other races? One would think such a choice against whiteness would be morally self-evident. Precisely because whiteness is so pervasive, however, it remains difficult to identify, to challenge, and to separate from our daily lives. My central argument is that we must create a new public sphere where the practice of whiteness is not only identified and analyzed but also contested and destroyed. Choosing against whiteness is the hope and promise of the future. One task ahead for those who wish to reclaim the dignity offered by true justice is to revivify democratic citizenship in an era of diminishing returns. It is to create critical citizens who are no longer content occupying furtive spaces of private affirmation but who possess the will and the knowledge to turn these spaces into public spheres through the creation of new social movements, anticapitalist struggle, and revolutionary socialist praxis.

The struggle in these new times is a daunting one. Record numbers of disaffected white youths are joining citizen militias and white supremacist organizations at a time when black churches are burning in the South and cross burnings are occurring at an alarming rate across the nation in Louisiana, Georgia, Pennsylvania, Oregon, Maine, southern California, and elsewhere. As white youths search for identity in their lives, many are able to find meaning only in relation to their capacity to hate nonwhites. Although some postmodernists adventitiously assert that identities can be fluidly recomposed, rearranged, and reinvented toward a more progressive politics in these new "pluralistic" times, I maintain that this is a short-sighted and dangerous argument. It would take more than an army of Jacques Lacans to help us rearrange and suture the fusillade of interpolations and subject positions at play in our daily lives. My assertion that the contents of particular cultural differences and discourses are not as important as how such differences are embedded in, and related to, the larger social totality of economic, social, and political differences may strike some readers as extreme. Yet I think it is fundamentally necessary to stress this point.

We are not autonomous citizens who can fashionably choose whatever ethnic combinations we desire in order to reassemble our identities. Although the borders of ethnicity overlap and shade into one another, it is dishonest to assert that pluralized, hybridized identities are options available to all citizens in the same way (Hicks, 1991). Class, race, and gender stratification and objective constraints and historical determinations restrict the choices of some groups over others. The division of labor linked with political organization and the politics of the marketplace regulate choices and often overdetermine their outcome (San Juan, 1995). Identity is more than the ideological trafficking between nationality and ethnicity; the overlapping and mutual intereffectivity of discourses are configured by the social relations of production. In other words, nationalism, ethnicity, and capitalist circuits of production can be seen moving into a shared orbit.

Rather than stress the importance of diversity and inclusion, as do most multiculturalists, I think significantly more emphasis should be placed on the social and political construction of white supremacy and the dispensation of white hegemony. The reality-distortion field know as "whiteness" needs to be identified as a cultural disposition and ideology linked with specific political, social, and historical arrangements.

BORDER WARS

A related theme I would like to emphasize is the need to incorporate, yet move beyond, the politics of diversity and inclusion when discussing multicultural education. The discourse of diversity and inclusion is often predicated on hidden assumptions of assimilation and consensus that serve as supports for neoliberal democratic models of identity.

Neoliberal democracy, performing under the banner of diversity yet actually in the hidden service of capital accumulation, often reconfirms the racist stereotypes already prescribed by Euro-American nationalist myths of supremacy—stereotypes that one would think democracy is ostensibly committed to challenge. In the pluralizing move to become a society of diverse voices, neoliberal democracy has often succumbed to a recolonization of multiculturalism by failing to challenge ideological assumptions surrounding difference that are installed in its current anti-affirmative action and welfare "reform" initiatives. In this sense, people of color are still placed under the threshold of candidacy for inclusion into the universal right to self-determination and are interpolated as exiles from U.S. citizenship. After all, as a shrinking minority, whites are running scared, conscious of their own vulnerability, and are erecting fortresses of social regulation while they still have the power to do so. Todd Gitlin (1995) declares:

> The Republican tilt of white men is the most potent form of identity politics in our time: a huddling of men who resent (and exaggerate) their relative decline not only in parts of the labor movement but at home, in the bedroom and the kitchen, and in the culture. Their fear and loathing is, in part, a panic against the relative gains of women and minorities in an economy that people experience as a zero-sum game, in which the benefits accruing to one group seem to amount to subtractions from another. Talk about identity politics! These white men, claiming they deserve color-blind treatment, identify with their brethren more than their wives or sisters, or minorities. (p. 233)

One of the most hated groups among the poor in the Southland where I live is the Mexican migrant workers. Stereotyped as *crimmegrantes,* they have become the object of xenophobia par excellence. Ron Prince, one architect of Proposition 187, has remarked: "Illegal aliens are a category of criminal, not a category of ethnic group" (Gómez-Peña, 1996, p. 67). Gómez-Peña comments on the imbrication of borders as a perceived crisis-effect by white Americans:

> For many Americans, the border has failed to stop chaos and crisis from creeping in (the origin of crisis and chaos is somehow always located outside). Their worst nightmare is finally coming true: The United States is no longer a fictional extension of Europe, or the wholesome suburb imagined by the screenwriter of *Lassie.* It is rapidly becoming a huge border zone, a hybrid society, a mestizo race, and worst of all, this process seems to be irreversible. America shrinks day by day, as the pungent smell of enchiladas fills the air and the volume of quebradita music rises. (p. 67)

The process of "Mexicanization" has struck fear into the hearts of the Euro-American *cabrone* who views this inevitability as an obdurate political reality. And this fear is only exacerbated by the media and anti-immigration activists. As Gómez-Peña (1996) notes:

> Now, it is the "illegal aliens" who are to take the blame for everything that American citizens and their incompetent politicians have been unable (or unwilling) to solve. Undocumented immigrants are being stripped of their humanity and individuality, becoming blank screens for the projection of Americans' fear, anxiety, and rage. . . . Both the anti-immigration activists and the conservative media have utilized extremely charged metaphors to describe this process of "Mexicanization." It is described as a Christian nightmare ("hell at our doorsteps"); a natural disaster ("the brown wave"); a fatal disease or an incurable virus; a form of demographic rape; a cultural invasion; or the scary beginning of a process of secession or "Quebequization" of the entire Southwest. (pp. 66, 67-68)

I remember the bestial hate mongering among whites after the anti-187 march in East Los Angeles in 1994. The size of the crowd—approximately 100,000 protesters by some estimates—instilled such a fear of a brown planet that many white Angelenos fervently took to the streets in anti-immigration demonstrations. Too much "difference-effect" resulting from the borderization phenomenon has created among previously stable white constituencies a type of fibrillation of subjectivity—a discursive quivering that eventually leads to a state of identity collapse. Wreaking havoc on the social landscape by creating a spectacular demonology around African American and Latino/a gang members, welfare queens, undocumented workers, and gays and lesbians, members of the professional-managerial class made up primarily of cosmopolitan whites have tried to convince white America that its identity is threatened and that white people now constitute the "new" oppressed. Can anyone take this claim seriously, coming as it is from the most privileged group in history?

I believe that an emphasis on the construction of whiteness will help put a different and important focus on the problems surrounding identity formation at this juncture in history. When North Americans talk about race, they inevitably refer to African Americans, Asians, Latinos/as, and Native Americans to the consistent exclusion of Euro-Americans. I want to challenge the prevailing assumption that to defeat racism we need to put our initiatives solely behind the inclusions of minoritarian populations—in other words, of people of color. I want to argue instead that, in addition to making an argument for diversity, we need to put more emphasis on the analysis of white ethnicity and the destabilization of white identity, specifically white supremacist ideology and practice. As David Roediger (1994) notes: "Whiteness describes, from Little Big Horn to Simi Valley, not a culture but precisely the absence of culture. It is the empty and therefore terrifying attempt to build an identity based on what one isn't and on whom one can hold back" (p. 137).

I immigrated to the United States from a country that supplies the United States with a substantial group of undocumented workers—Canada. But you don't see the U.S. government militarizing its northern border. I don't have to be too concerned about harassment from *la migra* if California's Propositions 187 or 209 someday take effect. Consider the vehemently racist comments directed against Mexican and other immigrants of color by Patrick Buchanan, a recent Republican candidate for the U.S. presidency:

> If British subjects, fleeing a depression, were pouring into this country through Canada, there would be few alarms. The central objection to the present flood of illegals is they are not English-speaking white people from Western Europe; they are Spanish-speaking brown and black people from Mexico, Latin America, and the Caribbean. (Bradlee, 1996, p. 1)

Consider Buchanan's remarks in the light of U.S. history. I offer comments made by Abraham Lincoln during a speech in southern Illinois in 1858:

> "I am not," he told his audience, "nor ever have been, in favor of bringing about in any way the social or political equality of the white and black races. . . . I will say in addition that there is a physical difference between the white and black races which, I suppose, will forever forbid the two races living together upon terms of social and political equality; and in as much as they cannot so live, that while they do remain together there must be a position of the superiors and the inferiors; and that I, as much as any other man, am in favor of the superior being assigned to the white man." (Zinn, 1970, p. 148)

Another U.S. hero, Benjamin Franklin, wrote:

> Why increase the Sons of *Africa,* by planting them in *America,* where we have so fair an Opportunity, by excluding all Blacks and Tawneys, of increasing the lovely White and Red? (cited in Perea, 1995, p. 973)

Or consider the views of Thomas Jefferson, who was concerned about the presence of Africans in America, whom he referred to as an impure "blot" on the purity of the land:

> . . . [I]t is impossible not to look forward to distant times, when our rapid multiplication will expand itself . . . & cover the whole northern, if not the southern continent, with a people speaking the same language, governed in similar forms, & by similar laws; *nor can we contemplate with satisfaction either blot or mixture on that surface.* (cited in Perea, 1995, p. 974)

Not only was Thomas Jefferson a mean-spirited racist and slave owner, but he also can arguably be considered the central ideological founder of American apartheid. He advocated an approach to democracy inspired by a mystical reading of the French Revolution that justified mass slaughter in the name of liberty and justice for whites only. It is perhaps no coincidence that when Timothy McVeigh was arrested driving away from Oklahoma City on the day the Murrah Federal Building was bombed, he was wearing a T-shirt that bore the celebrated words of Jefferson: "The tree of liberty must be refreshed from time to time by the blood of patriots and tyrants." Although Jefferson was surely against the practice of slavery, he unhesitatingly called for the banishment of free blacks from the United States because he believed that "nature, habit, opinion has drawn indelible lines of distinction" between white people and black people such that they "cannot live in the same government" (O'Brien, 1996, p. 57).

Jefferson preached against racism, yet he had one of his many slaves, James Hubbard, severely flogged for escaping. In addition, he proposed an amendment to the Virginia legal code that would have banned free blacks from coming to Virginia of their own accord or from taking up residence for more than 1 year. His amendment was rejected by his contemporaries as being too severe. Jefferson even proposed that white women who had children by black fathers were to be ordered out of Virginia within 1 year of the child's birth and that failure to leave the state would place these women "out of the protection of the law," which meant, of course, that they could be lynched. Jefferson also suggested that the government purchase newborn slaves from their owners and pay for their maintenance until the children could work off their debt up to their date of deportation to Santo Domingo (O'Brien, 1996). Fortunately, these other suggestions were also rejected by his contemporaries.

Not to be outdone in the racist department, we have Senator John Calhoun, speaking on the U.S. Senate floor in 1848, where he opposed annexation by the United States of land belonging to Mexico on the grounds of preserving a homogeneous white nation:

> I know further, sir, that we have never dreamt of incorporating into our Union any but the Caucasian race—the free white race. To incorporate Mexico, would be the very first instance of the kind of incorporating an Indian race; . . . I protest against such a union as that! *Ours, sir, is the Government of a white race.* (cited in Perea, 1995, p. 976)

Compare the ideological logic behind California's Proposition 187 with the statements provided by Calhoun, Jefferson, Franklin, and Buchanan. Compare, too, the logic of Proposition 187 to its precursor—California's 1855 "Greaser Act." The Greaser Act was an antiloitering law that applied to "all persons who are commonly known as 'Greasers,' or the issue of Spanish and Indian blood. . . and who go armed and are not peaceable and quiet persons" (cited in López, 1996, p. 145).

This is the same racist logic that fueled David Duke's 1992 comment ". . . that immigrants 'mongrelize' our culture and dilute our values" (cited in López, 1996, p. 143). Comments made by Duke during an appearance in California in 1996 were in support of Proposition 209, an anti-affirmative action effort at creating a "color-blind" society. This effort has been orchestrated by Ward Connerly, an African American, who is a University of California regent and chairman of the Proposition 209 initiative. In addition to accusing minority men of raping white women "by the thousands" and claiming that black New Orleans police officers rape and kill local citizens, Duke remarked:

> I don't want California to look like Mexico. . . . I don't want to have their pollution. I don't want the corruption. I don't want their disease. I don't want their superstition. I don't want us to look like that country. If we continue this alien invasion, we will be like Mexico. (Bernstein, 1996, p. A14)

Duke reflects a perspective that hasn't changed since the days of the Zoot Suit Massacre, Operation Wetback, and when public Los Angeles swimming pools were frequently drained by whites after they were used by Mexican Americans. It is a perspective also shared by the British extreme right, who sexualize racism in order to "generate fear among women and masculine protectiveness among men" in relation to the presence of black men in British inner cities (Rattansi, 1994, p. 63). Such perspectives connote earlier ideas of the empire as a dangerous place where white women need protection (Rattansi, 1994, p. 63). One example is a story that appeared in the National Front youth newspaper, *Bulldog*, titled "Black Pimps Force White Girls Into Prostitution," and that exhorted, "White Man! You Have a Duty to Protect Your Race, Homeland and Family" (p. 63). Of course, this fear of the rape of the white woman is not projected solely onto the African American male. Underwriting Duke's comments on Mexico, for instance, is the image of the Mexican as rapist and beast. In his discussion of the relationship between San Diegans and Tijuanenses, Ramón Gutiérrez (1996) describes how Tijuana—"as a place of unruly and transgressive bodies" (p. 256)—has become fixed in the American psyche. He reports, "Tijuana first developed as an escape valve for the sexually repressed and regulated American Protestant social body of San Diego" (p. 255). And he writes that

> the international boundary between Mexico and the United States has long been imagined as a border that separates a pure from an impure body, a virtuous body from a sinful one, a monogamous conjugal body regulated by the law of marriage from a criminal body given to fornication, adultery, prostitution, bestiality, and sodomy. (pp. 255-256)

HISTORICAL FICTIONS AND THE LOGICS OF EMPIRE

Whereas the United States is constructed as a country governed by nature and the law, such codes of civility that regulate kinship and the body are thought not to exist in Mexico, where only unregulated desire and criminality exist to menace all who come into contact with Mexicans. The image of the undocumented worker as an illegal alien, as a "migrant" living in squalor, spreading disease, raping white women, extorting lunch money from white school children, creating squatter communities, hanging out in shopping centers, and forcing Anglo schools to adopt bilingual education programs to accommodate the offspring of criminals and to appease the foreigner living on U.S. soil has served to identify Mexicans with dirt, filth, and unnatural acts while symbolically constructing Euro-American citizens as pure, law-abiding, and living in harmony with God's natural law (Gutiérrez, 1996).

One of the nation's relatively unblemished heroes of history is Woodrow Wilson. Many U.S. citizens have little, if any, knowledge about Wilson's Palmer Raids against left-wing unions, his segregation of the federal government, and his military interventions in Mexico (11 times beginning in 1914), Haiti in 1915, the Dominican Republic in 1916, Cuba in 1917, and Panama in 1918. Wilson also maintained forces in Nicaragua. He was an unrepentant white supremacist who believed that black people were inferior to white people. In fact, Wilson ordered that black and white workers in federal government jobs be segregated. He vetoed a clause on racial equality in the Covenant of the League of Nations. Wilson's wife told "darky" stories in cabinet meetings while his administration drafted a legislative program designed to curtail the civil rights of African Americans. Congress refused to pass it (Loewen, 1995). Wilson did manage to appoint southern whites to offices traditionally given to blacks. President Warren G. Harding was inducted into the Ku Klux Klan in a ceremony at the White House (Loewen, 1995). How many students can boast knowledge of this event? How can U.S. history books cover up these events and hundreds of others, including the 1921 race riot in Tulsa, Oklahoma, in which whites dropped dynamite from an airplane onto a black community, destroying 1,100 homes and killing 75 people (Loewen, 1995)?

How can we forget the evils of slavery, including the 10,000 native Americans shipped from Charleston, South Carolina, to the West Indies (in 1 year) in exchange for black slaves? Must we forget that the United States is a country conceived in slavery and baptized in racism?

The Protocols of the Learned Elders of Zion was a work that influenced another American hero—Henry Ford. His newspaper ran a series of anti-Semitic articles in the 1920s that were made available to the public in book form under the title *The International Jew.* In this particular sense, the United States is not "post-Fordist" at all. At least in the case of right-wing Christian movements, many of whom fervently believe that whites are the true Israelites, that blacks are subhuman, and that Jews are the issue of Satan. The organization known as Christian Identity is linked to British Israelism, which began as a white supremacist protestant organization in Victorian England. White Europeans were believed to be the 12 lost tribes of Israel. Like many postmillennial religions, Identity proclaims that God gave the Constitution of the United States to the white Christian Founding Fathers and that only white Christian men can be true sovereign citizens of the republic. Identity followers are set to destroy the "Beast"—the government of the United States—in order to hasten Armageddon (Southern Poverty Law Center, 1996). Members of Pat Robertson's Christian Coalition are aligned with the patriot movement. This movement wants to establish God's law on Earth, which in the view of some members of the movement calls for the execution of homosexuals, adulterers, juvenile delinquents, and blasphemers (Southern Poverty Law Center, 1996). After Florida hosted a major gay and lesbian event in 1998, Pat Robertson warned that God might send an asteroid to punish the earth. He remains a powerful political force in the United States.

Buchanan, Duke, Pete Wilson, and countless other conservative politicians currently enjoying considerable popularity among growing sectors of the U.S. population owe a great deal to the racist perspectives they inherited from historical figures such as Jefferson, Franklin, and Lincoln, who have been sanctified and haigiographied in the larger political culture. It appears that it is as patriotic now for white people to proclaim racist sentiments as it was 150 years ago. Today, however, one has to camouflage one's racism in deceptive and sophisticated ways by hiding it in a call for family values, a common culture of decency, and a "color-blind" society, but the racist formations underwriting such a call are clearly in evidence to the discerning cultural critic.

The concept of *whiteness* became lodged in the discursive crucible of colonial identity by the early 1860s. Whiteness at that time had become a marker for measuring inferior and superior races. Interestingly, Genghis Khan, Attila the Hun, and Confucius were at this time considered "white." Blackness was evaluated positively in European iconography from the 12th to the 15th centuries, but after the 17th century and the rise of European colonialism, blackness became conveniently linked with inferiority (Cashmore, 1996). For instance, during the 16th and 17th centuries, blood purity (*limpieza de sangre*) became raised to a metaphysical—perhaps even sacerdotal—status as it became a principle used to peripheralize Indians, Moors, and Jews.

Blackness was not immediately associated with slavery. In the United States, the humanistic image of Africans created by the abolitionist movement was soon countered by new types of racial signification in which white skin was identified with racial superiority. Poor Europeans, however, were sometimes indentured and, in some sense, de facto slaves. They occupied the same economic categories as African slaves and were held in equal contempt by the lords of the plantations and legislatures (Cashmore, 1996). Poor Europeans, however, were invited to align themselves with the plantocracy as "white" to avoid the most severe forms of bondage. This strategy helped plantation owners form a stronger social control apparatus as hegemony was achieved by offering "race privileges" to poor whites as acknowledgment of their loyalty to the colonial land (Cashmore, 1996).

By the early 20th century, European maritime empires controlled over half of the land (72 million km^2) and a third of the world's population (560 million people). Seventy-five million Africans died during the centuries-long transatlantic slave trade (West, 1993). The logics of empire are still with us, bound to the cultural fabric of our daily being-in-the-world; woven into our posture toward others; connected to the lenses of our eyes; folded into the sinewy depths of our musculature; dipped in the chemical reactions that excite and calm us; and structured into the language of our perceptions. We cannot will our racist logics away. We need to work hard to eradicate them. We need to struggle with a formidable resolve to overcome that which we are afraid to confirm exists, let alone confront, in the battleground of our souls. We must destroy the logics of racism and the social division of labor which they serve to naturalize.

RACE AND CAPITAL

According to Alex Callinicos (1993), racial differences are invented. Racism occurs when the characteristics that justify discrimination are held to be inherent in the oppressed group. This form of oppression is peculiar to capitalist societies; it arises in the circumstances surrounding industrial capitalism and the attempt to acquire a large labor force. Callinicos points out three main conditions for the existence of racism as outlined by Marx: (a) economic competition between workers, (b) the appeal of racist ideology to white workers, and (c) efforts of the capitalist class to establish and maintain racial divisions among workers. Capital's constantly changing demands for different kinds of labor can only be met through immigration. Callinicos remarks that "racism offers for workers of the oppressing 'race' the imaginary compensation for the exploitation they suffer of belonging to the '*ruling* nation' " (p. 39).

Callinicos (1993) notes the way Marx grasped how racial divisions between "native" and immigrant workers could weaken the working class. U.S. politicians take advantage of this division, which the capitalist class understands and manipulates only too well. George Bush, Jesse Helms, Pat Buchanan, Phil Gramm, David Duke, and Pete Wilson have effectively used racism to divide the working class. At this point, you might be asking yourselves: Doesn't racism predate capitalism? Here I agree with Callinicos that the heterophobia associated with precapitalist societies was not the same as modern racism. Precapitalist slave and feudal societies of classical Greece and Rome did not rely on racism to justify the use of slaves. The Greeks and the Romans had no theories of white superiority. If they did, that must have been unsettling news to Septimus Severus, Roman Emperor from A.D. 193 to 211, who was, many historians claim, a black man. Racism developed at a key turning point in capitalism during the 17th and 18th centuries on colonial plantations in the New World where slave labor stolen from Africa was used to produce tobacco, sugar, and cotton for the global consumer market (Callinicos, 1993). Callinicos cites Eric Williams, who remarks: "Slavery was not born of racism; rather, racism was the consequence of slavery" (p. 24). Racism emerged as the ideology of the plantocracy. It began with the class of sugar planters and slave merchants that dominated England's Caribbean colonies. Racism developed out of the "systemic slavery" of the New World. The "natural inferiority" of Africans was a way that whites justified enslaving them. According to Callinicos:

> Racism offers white workers the comfort of believing themselves part of the dominant group; it also provides, in times of crisis, a ready made scapegoat, in the shape of the oppressed group. Racism thus gives white workers a particular identity, and one moreover which unites them with white capitalists. We have here, then, a case of the kind of "imagined community" discussed by Benedict Anderson in his influential analysis of nationalism. (p. 38)

To abolish racism, we need to abolish global capitalism. Callinicos is very clear on that point.

While obviously we cannot wait for the working class as a class "in itself" to realize its revolutionary potential and work "for itself" (by unloosing such potential in the form of revolutionary class struggle) before we begin to engage in anti-racist work, nevertheless we need to remind ourselves that anti-racist practices congealed around identity politics can obscure the connection between racial oppression and capitalist exploitation.

THE CULTURAL LOGIC OF WHITENESS

The educational left has failed to address sufficiently the issue of whiteness and the insecurities that young whites harbor regarding their future during times of diminishing economic expectations. With their "racially coded and divisive rhetoric," neoconservatives may be able to enjoy tremendous success in helping insecure young white populations develop white identity along racist lines. Consider the comments by David Stowe (1996):

The only people nowadays who profess any kind of loyalty to whiteness *qua* whiteness (as opposed to whiteness as an incidental feature of some more specific identity) are Christian Identity types and Aryan Nations diehards. Anecdotal surveys reveal that few white Americans mention whiteness as a quality that they think much about or particularly value. In their day-to-day cultural preferences—food, music, clothing, sports, hairstyles—the great majority of American whites display no particular attachment to white things. There does seem to be a kind of emptiness at the core of whiteness. (p. 74)

Cornel West (1993) has identified three white supremacist logics: (a) Judeo-Christian racist logic, (b) scientific racist logic, and (c) psychosexual racist logic. *Judeo-Christian racist logic* is reflected in the Biblical story of Ham, Son of Noah, who, in failing to cover Noah's nakedness, had his progeny blackened by God. In this logic, unruly behavior and chaotic rebellion are linked with racist practices. *Scientific racist logic* is linked to the evaluation of physical bodies in the light of Greco-Roman standards. Within this logic, racist practices are identified with physical ugliness, cultural deficiency, and intellectual inferiority. *Psychosexual racist logic* identifies black people with Western sexual discourses associated with sexual prowess, lust, dirt, and subordination. A serious question is raised by West's typology in relation to the construction of whiteness: What are the historically concrete and sociologically specific ways that white supremacist discourses are guided by Western philosophies of identity and universality and capitalist relations of production and consumption? West has located racist practices in the commentaries by the Church Fathers on the Song of Solomon and the Ywain narratives in medieval Brittany, to name just a few historical sources. West has also observed that human bodies were classified according to skin color as early as 1684 (before the rise of modern capitalism) by French physician François Bernier. The famous 18th-century naturalist Carolus Linnaeus produced the first major written account of racial division in *Natural System* (1735).

People do not discriminate against groups because they are different, but rather the act of discrimination constructs categories of difference that hierarchically locate people as "superior" or "inferior" and then universalizes and naturalizes such differences. When I refer to whiteness or to the cultural logics of whiteness, I need to qualify what I mean. Here I adopt Ruth Frankenberg's injunction that cultural practices considered to be white must be seen as contingent, historically produced, and transformable. White culture is not monolithic, and its borders must be understood as malleable and porous. It is the historically specific confluence of economic, geopolitical, and ethnocultural processes. According to Alastair Bonnett (1996), whiteness is neither a discrete entity nor a fixed, asocial category. Rather, it is an "immutable social construction" (p. 98). White identity is an ensemble of discourses, contrapuntal and contradictory. Whiteness— and the meanings attributed to it—are always in a state of flux and fibrillation. Bonnett notes:

> [E]ven if one ignores the transgressive youth or ethnic borderlands of Western identities, and focuses on the "center" or "heartlands" of "whiteness," one will discover racialized subjectivities that, far from being settled and confidant, exhibit a constantly reformulated panic over the meaning of "whiteness" and the defining presence of "non-whiteness" within it. (p. 106)

According to Frankenberg, white culture is a material and discursive space that "is inflected by nationhood, such that whiteness and Americanness, though by no means coterminous, are profoundly shaped by one another. . . . Similarly, whiteness, masculinity, and femininity are coproducers of one another, in ways that are, in their turn, crosscut by class and by the histories of racism and colonialism" (p. 233).

Whiteness needs to be seen as *cultural,* as *processual,* and not ontologically different from processes that are nonwhite. It works, as Frankenberg (1993) notes, as "an unmarked marker of others' differentness—whiteness not so much void or formlessness as norm" (p. 198). Whiteness functions through social practices of assimilation and cultural homogenization; whiteness is linked with the expansion of capitalism in the sense that "whiteness signifies the production and consumption of commodities under capitalism" (p. 203). Yet capitalism in the United States needs to be understood as contingently white because white people participate in maintaining the hegemony of institutions and practices of racial dominance in different ways and to greater or lesser degrees. Frankenberg identifies the key discursive repertoires of whiteness as follows:

> . . . modes of naming culture and difference associated with west European colonial expansion; second, elements of "essentialist" racism . . . linked to European colonialism but also critical as rationale for Anglo settler colonialism and segregationism in what is now the USA; third, "assimilationist" or later "color- and power-evasive" strategies for thinking through race first articulated in the early decades of this century; and, fourth, . . . "race-cognizant" repertoires that emerged in the latter half of the twentieth century and were linked

both to U.S. liberation movements and to broader global struggles for decolonization. (p. 239)

Whiteness is a sociohistorical form of consciousness, given birth at the nexus of capitalism, colonial rule, and emergent relationships among dominant and subordinate groups. Whiteness operates by means of its constitution as a universalizing authority by which the hegemonic white bourgeois subject appropriates the right to speak on behalf of everyone who is nonwhite while denying voice and agency to these others in the name of civilized humankind. Whiteness constitutes and demarcates ideas, feelings, knowledges, social practices, cultural formations, and systems of intelligibility that are identified with, or attributed to, white people and that are invested in by white people as "white." Whiteness is also a refusal to acknowledge how white people are implicated in certain social relations of privilege and relations of domination and subordination. Whiteness, then, can be considered a form of social amnesia associated with certain modes of subjectivity within particular social sites considered normative. As a lived domain of meaning, whiteness represents particular social and historical formations that are reproduced through specific discursive and material processes and circuits of desire and power. Whiteness can be considered a conflictual sociocultural, sociopolitical, and geopolitical process that animates commonsensical practical action in relationship to dominant social practices and normative ideological productions. Whiteness constitutes the selective tradition of dominant discourses about race, class, gender, and sexuality hegemonically reproduced. Whiteness has become the substance and limit of our common sense articulated as cultural consensus. As an ideological formation transformed into a principle of life, into an ensemble of social relations and practices, whiteness needs to be understood as conjunctural, as a composite social hieroglyph that shifts in denotative and connotative emphasis, depending on how its elements are combined and on the contexts in which it operates. Whiteness is an accretion of and a tributary to a regime of truth predicated upon social amnesia and an impoverished social imagination in which social power is sanctioned by a willingness and an ability to forget.

Whiteness is not a pre-given, unified ideological formation, but rather a multifaceted collective phenomenon resulting from the relationship between the self and the ideological discourses that are constructed out of the surrounding local and global cultural terrain. Whiteness is fundamentally Euro- or Western-centric in its episteme, as it is articulated in complicity with the pervasively imperializing logic of empire.

Whiteness in the United States can be understood largely through the social consequences it provides for those who are considered nonwhite. Such consequences can be seen in the criminal justice system, in prisons, in schools, and in the boardrooms of corporations such as Texaco. It can be defined in relation to immigration practices and social policies and practices of sexism, racism, and nationalism. It can be seen historically in widespread acts of imperialism and genocide and linked with an erotic economy of "excess." Eric Lott (1993) writes:

> In rationalized Western societies, becoming "white" and male seems to depend upon the remanding of enjoyment, the body, an aptitude for pleasure. It is the other who is always putatively "excessive" in this respect, whether through exotic food, strange and noisy music, outlandish bodily exhibitions, or unremitting sexual appetite. Whites in fact organize their own enjoyment through the other, Slavoj Zizek has written, and access pleasure precisely by fantasizing about the other's "special" pleasure. Hatred of the other arises from the necessary hatred of one's own excess; ascribing this excess to the "degraded" other and indulging it—by imagining, incorporating, or impersonating the other—one conveniently and surreptitiously takes and disavows pleasure at one and the same time. This is the mixed erotic economy, what Homi Bhabha terms the "ambivalence" of American whiteness. (p. 482)

Whiteness is a type of articulatory practice that can be located in the convergence of colonialism, capitalism, and subject formation. It both fixes and sustains discursive regimes that represent self and Other; that is, whiteness represents a regime of differences that produces and racializes an abject Other. In other words, whiteness is a discursive regime that enables real effects to take place. Whiteness displaces blackness and brownness—specific forms of nonwhiteness—into signifiers of deviance and criminality within social, cultural, cognitive, and political contexts. White subjects discursively construct identity through producing, naming, "bounding," and marginalizing a range of others (Frankenberg, 1993, p. 193).

Whiteness constitutes unmarked patriarchal, heterosexist, and Euro-American practices that have negative effects on, and consequences for, those who do not participate in them. Inflected by nationhood, whiteness can be considered an ensemble of discursive practices constantly in the process of being constructed, negotiated, and changed. Yet it functions to instantiate a structured exclusion of certain groups from social arenas of normativity. Coco Fusco (1995) remarks, "To raise the specter of racism in the here and now, to suggest that despite their political beliefs and sexual preferences, white people operate within, and benefit from, white supremacist social structures is still tantamount to a declaration of war" (p. 76).

Whiteness not only is mythopoetical in the sense that it constructs a totality of illusions formed around the ontological superiority of the Euro-American subject but also is metastructural in that it operates across specific differences; it solders fugitive, breakaway discourses and re-hegemonizes them. Consumer utopias and global capital flows rearticulate whiteness by means of relational differences.

Whiteness is dialectically reinitiated across epistemological fissures, contradictions, and oppositions through new regimes of desire that connect the consumption of goods with the everyday logic of Western democracy. The cultural encoding of the typography of whiteness is achieved by remapping Western European identity onto economic transactions, by recementing desire to capitalist flows, by concretizing personal history into collective memory linked with place, with a myth of origin. Whiteness offers a safe "home" for those imperiled by the flux of change.

Whiteness can be considered a conscription of the process of positive self-identification into the service of domination through inscribing identity into an onto-epistemological framework of "us" against "them." For those who are nonwhite, the seduction of whiteness can produce a self-definition that disconnects the subject from his or her history of oppression and struggle, exiling identity into the unmoored, chaotic realm of abject otherness (and tacitly accepting the positioned superiority of the Western subject). Whiteness provides the subject with a known boundary that places nothing "off limits," yet provides a fantasy of belongingness. It's not that whiteness signifies preferentially one pole of the white-nonwhite binarism. Rather, whiteness seduces the subject to accept the idea of polarity itself as the limit-text of identity, as the constitutive foundation of subjectivity.

There exists no intrinsic link between whitenes and European capitalist expansion and imperialism. The link is, of course, contextual and historically specific. I am not arguing that whiteness as a form of ideological hegemony is homogeneous, seamless, or all of one piece. There exists within the various cultures of whiteness contradictions and antagonisms, including class struggle. Capitalism can shape the subjectivities of social agents of different ethnicities and those who inhabit different continents. Insofar as capitalist practices have inflected white patriarchal ideology, whiteness can be considered motorized by capitalist social relations of exploitation. To resist whiteness means developing a politics of difference linked to anti-capitalist revolutionary struggle. Because we lack the full semantic availability to understand whiteness and to resist it, we need to rethink difference and identity outside sets of binary oppositions. We need to view identity as coalitional, as collective, as processual, as grounded in the ideological and material struggle for social justice grounded in socialist praxis.

DISMANTLING WHITENESS

Although an entire range of discursive repertoires may come into play, jostling against, superseding, and working in conjunction with each other, white identity is constructed in relation to an individual's personal history, geopolitical situatedness, contextually specific practices, and his or her location in the materiality of the racial order. In other words, many factors determine which discursive configurations are at work and the operational modalities present.

In his important volume *Psychoanalytic-Marxism,* Eugene Victor Wolfenstein (1993) describes the whiteness of domination as the "one fixed point" of America's many racisms. He argues that whiteness is a social designation and a "history disguised as biology" (p. 331). Whiteness is also an attribute of language. Wolfenstein claims:

Languages have skin colors. There are white nouns and verbs, white grammar and white syntax. In the absence of challenges to linguistic hegemony, indeed, language *is* white. If you don't speak white you will not be heard, just as when you don't look white you will not be seen. (p. 331)

Describing white racists as "virtuosos of denigration," Wolfenstein (1993, p. 337) maintains that the language of white racism illustrates "a state of war" (p. 333). Yet the battles are fought through lies and deceit. One such lie is the idea of "color blindness."

Wolfenstein (1993) notes that color blindness constitutes more than a matter of conscious deceit:

White racism is rather a mental disorder, an ocular disease, an opacity of the soul that is articulated with unintended irony in the idea of "color blindness." To be color-blind is the highest form of racial false consciousness, a denial of both difference and domination. But one doesn't have to be color-blind to be blinded by white racism. . . . Black people see themselves in white mirrors, white people see black people as their own photographic negatives. (p. 334)

Wolfenstein (1993) suggests that two epistemological tasks be undertaken: (a) Black people need to look away from the white mirror, and (b) white people need to attempt to see black people as they see themselves and to see themselves as they are seen by other black people. Wolfenstein links white racism with what he terms "epidermal fetishism." Epidermal fetishism reduces people to their skin color and renders them invisible. It is a type of social character formed within a process of exchange and circulation. As such, whiteness represents the super-ego (the standard of social value, self-worth, and morality). Because the ego is affirmatively reflected in the super-ego, it also must be white. What is therefore repressed is blackness, which "becomes identified with the unwanted or bad parts of the self" (p. 336). Wolfenstein writes:

At the level of social character, white racism is self-limiting for white people, self-destructive for black people. White people alienate their sensuous potentialities from themselves. They are devitalized and sterilized. Blackness, officially devalued, comes to embody their estranged life and desire. They are able, however, to see themselves reflected in the mirrors of selfhood. But if black people have their selfhood structured by the whitened-out form of social character, they become fundamentally self-negating. Their blackness, hated and despised, must be hidden away. Hair straighteners and skin lighteners testify to the desire to go further and eradicate blackness altogether. (pp. 336-337)

The incorporeal luminescence of whiteness is achieved, according to Wolfenstein (1993), by the subsumption of blackness within whiteness. What cannot be subsumed and digested is excreted. White people both despise and lust after blackness. Arguing that "you can count on sex or love to defeat the disuniting of America," Arthur Schlesinger Jr. claimed recently that the antidote to multiculturalism is intermarriage (i.e., Jews and non-Jews, blacks and whites, Japanese and Caucasians) because it is effective in promoting assimilation (Newfield, 1998). Schlesinger fails to acknowledge the structured modalities within the social field that shape such unions, or the dominant ideology of whiteness that exerts pressure on them.

It is important to recognize that white racism is neither purely systemic nor purely individual. Rather, it is a complex interplay of collective interests and desires. White racism in this instance "becomes a rational means to collective ends" (Wolfenstein, 1993, p. 341) when viewed from the standpoint of ruling-class interests. Yet for the white working class, it is irrational and a form of false consciousness. White racism also circumscribes rational action for black people in that they are encouraged to act in terms of their racial rather than class interests.

Alastair Bonnett (1996) notes that a reified notion of whiteness "enables 'white' people to occupy a privileged location in antiracist debate; they are allowed the luxury of being passive observers, of being altruistically motivated, of knowing that their 'racial' identity might be reviled and lambasted but never actually made slippery, torn open, or, indeed, abolished" (p. 98). Bonnett further notes: "To dismantle 'blackness' but leave the force it was founded to oppose unchallenged is to display both a political and theoretical naivety. To subvert 'blackness' without subverting 'whiteness' reproduces and reinforces the 'racial' myths, and the 'racial' dominance, associated with the latter" (p. 99).

Ian F. Haney López's book *White by Law* (1996) offers a view of white transparency and invisibility at odds with the thesis that whites are growing more conscious of their whiteness. López cites an incident at a legal feminist conference in which participants were asked to pick two or three words to describe themselves. All the women of color selected at least one racial term, but not one white woman selected a term referring to her race. This uncoils a disturbing observation that only white people in this society have the luxury of having no color. An informal study conducted at Harvard Law School underscores this point. A student interviewer asked 10 African Americans and 10 European Americans how they identified themselves. Unlike the African Americans, most of the European Americans did not consciously factor in their "whiteness" as a crucial or even tangential part of their identity.

López (1996) argues that one is not born white but becomes white "by virtue of the social context in which one finds oneself, to be sure, but also by virtue of the choices one makes" (p. 190). But how can one born into the culture of whiteness, one who is defined as white, undo that whiteness? López addresses this question in his formulation of whiteness. He locates whiteness in the overlapping of *chance* (e.g., features and ancestry over which we have no control, morphology); *context* (context-specific meanings attached to race, the social setting in which races are recognized, constructed, and contested); and *choice* (conscious choices with regard to the morphology and ancestries of social actors) to "alter the readability of their identity" (p. 191).

In other words, López (1996) maintains that chance and context are not racially determinative. He notes:

> Racial choices must always be made from within specific contexts, where the context materially and ideologically circumscribes the range of available choices and also delimits the significance of the act. Nevertheless, these are racial choices, if sometimes only in their overtone or subtext, because they resonate in the complex of meanings associated with race. Given the thorough suffusion of race throughout society, in the daily dance of life we constantly make racially meaningful decisions. (p. 193)

López's perspective offers new promise, it would seem, for abolishing racism because it refuses to locate whiteness only as antiracism's "other." I agree with Bonnett (1996) when he remarks that "to continue to cast 'whites' as antiracism's 'other,' as the eternally guilty and/or altruistic observers of 'race' equality work, is to maintain 'white' privilege and undermine the movement's intellectual and practical reach and utility" (p. 107). In other words, whites need to ask themselves to what extent their identity is a function of their whiteness in the process of their ongoing daily lives and what choices they might make to escape whiteness. López (1996) outlines—productively, in my view—three steps in dismantling whiteness. They are worth quoting in full:

> First, Whites must overcome the omnipresent effects of transparency and of the naturalization of race in order to recognize the many racial aspects of their identity, paying particular attention to the daily acts that draw upon and in turn confirm their whiteness. Second, they must recognize and accept the personal and social consequences of breaking out of a White identity. Third, they must embark on a daily process of choosing against Whiteness. (p. 193)

Of course, the difficulty of taking such steps is partly attributable to the fact that, as López (1996) notes, the unconscious acceptance of a racialized identity is predicated on a circular definition of the self. It is difficult to step outside whiteness if you are white because of all the social, cultural, and economic privileges that accompany whiteness. Yet whiteness must be dismantled if the United States is to overcome racism. Lipsitz (1995) remarks: "Those of us who are 'white' can only become part of the solution if we recognize the degree to which we are already part of the problem—not because of our race, but because of our possessive investment in it" (p. 384).

An editorial in the book *Race Traitor* (Ignatiev & Garvey, 1996) puts it thus:

> The key to solving the social problems of our age is to abolish the white race. Until that task is accomplished, even partial reform will prove elusive, because white influence permeates every issue in U.S. society, whether domestic or foreign. . . . Race itself is a product of social discrimination; so long as the white race exists, all movements against racism are doomed to fail. (p. 10)

I am acutely aware that people of color might find troubling the idea that white populations can simply reinvent themselves by making the simple choice of not being white. Of course, this is not what López and others appear to be saying. The choices one makes and the reinvention one aspires to as a race traitor are not "simple," nor are they easy choices for groups of whites to make. Yet from the perspective of some people of color, offering the choice to white people of opting out of their whiteness could seem to set up an easy path for those who do not want to assume responsibility for their privilege as white people. Indeed, there is certainly cause for concern. David Roediger (1994) captures some of this when he remarks that "whites cannot fully renounce whiteness even if they want to" (p. 16). Whites are, after all, still accorded the privileges of being white even as they ideologically renounce their whiteness, often with the best of intentions. Yet the possibility that whites might seriously consider nonwhiteness and antiwhite struggle is too important to ignore, to dismiss as wishful thinking, or to associate with a fashionable form of code switching. Choosing not to be white is not an easy option for white people, as simple as deciding to make a change in one's wardrobe. To understand the processes involved in the racialization of identity and to choose nonwhiteness consistently is a difficult act of apostasy because it implies a heightened sense of social criticism and an unwavering commitment to social justice (Roediger, 1994). Of course, the question needs to be asked: If we can choose to be nonwhite, then can we choose to be black or brown? Insofar as blackness is a social construction (often "parasitic" on whiteness), I would answer yes. Theologian James H. Cone, author of *A Black Theology of Liberation* (1986), urges white folks to free themselves from the shackles of their whiteness:

> [I]f whites expect to be able to say anything relevant to the self-determination of the black community, it will be necessary for them to destroy their whiteness by becoming members of an oppressed community. Whites will be free only when they become new persons—when their white being has passed away and

they are created anew in black being. When this happens, they are no longer white but free. (p. 97)

But again I would stress that becoming black is not a "mere" choice but a self-consciously political choice, a spiritual choice, and a critical choice. To choose blackness or brownness merely as a way to escape the stigma of whiteness and to avoid responsibility for owning whiteness is still very much an act of whiteness. To choose blackness or brownness as a way of politically disidentifying with white privilege and instead identifying with, and participating in, the social struggles of nonwhite peoples is, in contrast, an act of transgression, a traitorous act that reveals a fidelity to the struggle for justice. And it frequently requires courage and irrefragable insight.

Because ethnic identity is constructed diacritically, whiteness requires the denigration of blackness and brownness (López, 1996). Therefore, I do not argue for the construction of a positive white identity no matter how well intentioned. Rather, I argue against celebrating whiteness in any form. As López (1996) notes, whiteness retains its positive meanings only by denying itself. I call for the denial, disassembly, and destruction of whiteness as we know it and advocate instead a form of critical agency dedicated to social struggle in the interests of the oppressed.

AUTHENTICITY AND POSTCOLONIAL HYBRIDITY

The work of critical multiculturalists attempts to unsettle both conservative assaults on multiculturalism and liberal paradigms of multiculturalism, the latter of which in my view simply repackage conservative and neoliberal ideologies under a discursive mantle of diversity. In undertaking such a project, I have tried in a modest way to advance a critical pedagogy that will service a form of postcolonial hybridity.

It is true that the concept of *hybridity* has been used in a powerful way to counter essentialized attempts at creating monolithic and "authentic" forms of identity (Hicks, 1991; McLaren, 1995). Fusco (1995), however, rightly reminds us:

Too often . . . the postcolonial celebration of hybridity has been interpreted as the sign that no further concern about the politics of representation and cultural exchange is needed. With ease, we lapse back into the integrationist rhetoric of the 1960s, and conflate hybridity with parity. (p. 76)

Because not all hybridities are equal, we must attach to the term an ideological tacit nominal qualifier (Radhakrishnan, 1996). In making this assertion, Ragagopalan Radhakrishnan provides us with an important qualification. He maintains that we should distinguish between a metropolitan version of hybridity and postcolonial hybridity. Whereas the former is a ludic form of capricious self-styling, the latter is a critical identitarian mode. *Metropolitan hybridity,* notes Radhakrishnan, is "characterized by an intransitive and immanent sense of jouissance," whereas *postcolonial hybridity* is marked by a "frustrating search for constituency and a legitimate political identity" (p. 159). Metropolitan hybridity is not "subjectless" or neutral but is a structure of identitarian thinking informed by the cultural logic of the dominant West. Postcolonial hybridity, in contrast, seeks authenticity in "a third space that is complicitous neither with the deracinating imperatives of Westernization nor with theories of a static, natural, and single-minded autochthony" (p. 162). Within such a perspective educators are called to create *una pedagogía fronteriza.*

Critical multiculturalism as a point of intersection with critical pedagogy supports the struggle for a postcolonial hybridity. Gómez-Peña (1996) captures the concept of *postcolonial hybridity* when he conceptually maps what he calls the "New World Border,"

> a great trans- and intercontinental border zone, a place in which no centers remain. It's all margins, meaning there are no "others," or better said, the only true "others" are those who resist fusion, *mestizaje,* and cross-cultural dialogue. In this utopian cartography, hybridity is the dominant culture; Spanish, Franglé, and Gringoñol are *linguas francas;* and monoculture is a culture of resistance practiced by a stubborn or scared minority. (p. 7)

Whites need to do more than remember the history of colonialism as it affected the oppressed; they need to remember such history critically. As Homi Bhabha (1986) reminds us: "Remembering is never a quiet act of introspection or retrospection. It is a painful re-membering, a putting together of the dismembered past to make sense of the trauma of the present" (p. xxiii). This means piercing the vapors of mystification surrounding the objectification of human relations within bourgeois consciousness to construct new forms of subjectivity and agency that operate within a socialist political imaginary and praxis.

What I am advocating is a revolutionary multiculturalism that moves beyond the ludic, metrocentric focus on identities as hybrid and hyphenated assemblages of subjectivity that exist alongside or outside the larger social totality. Revolutionary multiculturalism, as I am articulating the term, takes as its condition of possibility the capitalist world system; it moves beyond a monoculturalist multiculturalism that fails to address identity formation in a global context and focuses instead on the idea that identities are shifting, changing, overlapping, and historically diverse (Shohat, 1995). Revolutionary multiculturalism is a politics of difference that is globally interdependent and raises questions about intercommunal alliances and coalitions. According to Ella Shohat (1995), intercommunal coalitions are based on historically shaped affinities, and the multicultural theory that underwrites such a coalitionary politics needs "to avoid either falling into essentialist traps or being politically paralyzed by deconstructionist formulations" (p. 177). Shohat articulates the challenge as follows:

> Rather than ask who can speak, then, we should ask how we can speak together, and more important, how we can move the dialog forward. How can diverse communities speak in concert? How might we interweave our voices, whether in chorus, in antiphony, in call and response, or in polyphony? What are the modes of collective speech? In this sense, it might be worthwhile to focus less on identity as something one "has," than on identification as something one "does." (p. 177)

Revolutionary multiculturalism recognizes that the objective structures in which we live, the material relations tied to production in which we are situated, and the determinate conditions that produce us are all reflected in our everyday lived experiences. In other words, lived experiences constitute more than subjective values, beliefs, and understandings; they are always mediated through ideological configurations of discourses, political economies of power and privilege, and the social division of labor. Revolutionary multiculturalism is a socialist-feminist multiculturalism that challenges the historically sedimented processes through which race, class, and gender identities are produced within capitalist society. Therefore, revolutionary multiculturalism is not limited to transforming attitudinal discrimination but is dedicated to reconstituting the deep structures of political economy, culture, and power in contemporary social arrangements. It is not about reforming capitalist democracy, but rather about transforming it by cutting it at its joints and then rebuilding the social order from the vantage point of the oppressed and within the context of socialist revolutionary struggle.

Revolutionary multiculturalism must not only accommodate the idea of capitalism but also advocate a critique of capitalism and a struggle against it. The struggle for liberation on the basis of race and gender must not remain detached from anticapitalist struggle. Often, the call for diversity and pluralism by the apostles of postmodernism is a surrender to the ideological mystifications of capitalism. The fashionable apostasy of preaching difference from the citadels of postmodernist thought has dissolved resistance into the totalizing power of capitalist exploitation. In this regard, Ellen Meiksins Wood (1995) rightly warns:

> We should not confuse respect for the plurality of human experience and social struggles with a complete dissolution of historical causality, where there is nothing but diversity, difference and contingency, no unifying structures, no logic of process, no capitalism and therefore no negation of it, no universal project of human emancipation. (p. 263)

The challenge is to create at the level of everyday life a commitment to solidarity with the oppressed and an identification with past and present struggles against imperialism, against racism, against sexism, against homophobia, against all those practices of unfreedom associated with living in a white supremacist capitalist society.

Subaltern ethnicities can become a focal point for a critique of Enlightenment rationality and its stress on universalizing Western notions of sameness and difference. They can also become a pivot position from which to challenge the structuring of intersubjective relations by global white supremacist patriarchal capitalism. In this case, the illusion of symmetrical intersubjectivity is countered from the standpoint epistemology of the oppressed. As Linda Martin Alcoff (1996) notes, identity in this case does not constitute an opposition to sameness, but rather an opposition of substance to absence—of having an identity to not having an identity. Identity can give a person substantive visibility in a world that tries to make her invisible. Yet another way of situating agency is not compatible with ethnic identification but becomes important in developing a coalitional politics of anticapitalist struggle. I believe that this concept of *agency*— agency as singularity—is also important in developing forms of critical agency as a counterpraxis of resistance to the globalization of capital and consumer ethics.

OTHERNESS AS POSITIVE DISCOURSE

Although identity politics can provide points around which a counterhegemonic politics can coalesce, there exists the frequent problem of essentialized identities and the difficulty of developing necessary coalitions among new social movements that do not rely on the modernist logic of difference and a humanist conception of the subject. Because identity politics largely relies on a modernist logic of difference, we strongly need to consider a rethinking of agency that does not rely on identity politics to mount a challenge to the dominate social order (Yudice, 1995). This suggests approaching the concept of *subjectivity* as a position from which one experiences the world and thus as a "contextually produced epistemological value" (Grossberg, 1996, p. 98) that is "always inscribed or distributed within cultural codes of differences that organize subjects by defining social identities" (p. 99). Such an understanding of subjectivity can lead to a theory of otherness based on positivity and effectivity, rather than on negatively defined difference. In this sense, agency has more to do with identifications or affiliations than with ethnicity. Whereas subjectivity operates in terms of the types of experiences available, agency has to do with "a distribution of acts" (p. 102). The questions surrounding agency that need to be asked by critical educators include, What forms of agency can schools make available to individuals and groups? and How can subject positions and identities be articulated into specific fields of activity and along particular socialist and revolutionary vectors?

I agree with Larry Grossberg (1996) that agency may be more a matter of "singular belonging" than structures of ethnic or political membership, and more the case of an "elective community" that exists within the "structured mobilities" of everyday life. In my view, agency cannot easily be conflated with questions of cultural identity in the sense that it marks, not a modernist subject-agent of liberal humanism, but a place where one acts practically and tactfully and with revolutionary purpose. Agency has to do with the spatial relations of places and how people are distributed within them. It has to do with the global division of labor.

Grossberg (1996) notes that often a politics of ethnic identity is grounded in a modernist logic of difference in which the "other" is defined by its negativity and gives rise to a politics of resentment. It is necessary, therefore, to develop a theory of agency in which culture is not grounded in the idea of difference and the logic of individuality, but rather is viewed as productive. Second, this calls for educators to move beyond the modernist concept of the subject-agent underwritten by a liberal humanism. The alternative, according to Grossberg, "is to begin to construct a theory of otherness which is not essentialist, a theory of positivity based on notions of effectivity, belonging and, as Paul Gilroy describes it, 'the changing same' " (p. 97). Grossberg argues that agency is not so much a question of cultural identity built around a modernist logics of difference and individuality as it is a matter of spatial relations built on a logic of temporality and overlapping mobilities. Grossberg notes:

> The question of agency is, then, how access and investment or participation (as a structure of belonging) are distributed within particular structured terrains. At the very least, this suggests that agency as a political problem cannot be conflated with issues of cultural identity or of epistemological possibilities. In other words, agency is not so much the "mark of a subject, but the constituting mark of an abode." (p. 100)

My position is not to decry identity politics. Identity politics is undeniably important in assisting ethnic groups to resist oppressive relations within a white supremacist capitalist patriarchy. My fundamental concern is organizing revolutionary praxis and social transformation productively around the revolutionary pivot points of anticapitalist struggle in which agency is not limited to—but neither does it exclude—agential spaces of ethnic struggle. In my view, collective agency needs to be produced within spaces of mobility and belonging articulated within the spacial and temporal axes of resistive and transformative power. Here it is important to emphasize that social agency must be rethought within a criticalist project of revolutionary transformation in such a way that does not discursively privilege an economic determinism that universalizes the historical inevitability of labor and the economy or that relegates individual identity to a bourgeois swindle of fulfillment. Further, social agency (race, class, gender, sexuality, nationality) needs to be understood, not as a form of economic overdetermination, but as the product of social relations that are constitutive of the agency of class. That is, social agency needs to be analyzed within the contextual specificity of its historical effects. Social agency is always played out within larger webs of social relations within global arenas of capitalist exploitation. I am maintaining that cultural, political, and economic processes are mutually constitutive of social agency, as agency can be more productively read as an historically specific confluence of material, and social relations based on class antagonism.

Critical agency formulated both as a singularity linked to place and as a form of critical ethnicity is necessary for the development of a counterpraxis capable of challenging both local and globalized forms of white patriarchal capitalism.

The movementism valorized by post-Marxists is not enough to enable African-Americans, Latinolas, gays, and lesbians to overthrow white supremacist capitalist social relations. As long as their efforts take place within the existing capitalist hierarchy, such a struggle is limited. The revolutionary multiculturalism that I advocate must be articulated within a working class alliance and toward a revolutionary politics of socialist struggle. We must advance toward an unconditional assent to struggle, to victory, to life.

REFERENCES

Alcoff, L. M. (1996, January/February). Philosophy and racial identity. *Radical Philosophy, 75,* 5-14.

Bennett, W. J. (1996, August 13). Civil rights is the GOP mission. *Los Angeles Times,* p. B5.

Bernstein, S. (1996, September 11). Storm rises over ex-Klansman in debate. *Los Angeles Times,* pp. A3, A14.

Bhabha, H. (1986). Remembering Fanon. In F. Fanon, *Black skin, white masks.* London: Pluto.

Bonnett, A. (1996). Antiracism and the critique of white identities. *New Community, 22*(1), 97-110.

Bradlee, B., Jr. (1996, March 3). The Buchanan role: GOP protagonist. *Boston Sunday Globe,* pp. 1, 12.

Callinicos, A. (1993). *Race and class.* London: Bookmarks.

Cashmore, E. (1996). *Dictionary of race and ethnic relations* (4th ed.). London: Routledge.

Cone, J. H. (1986). *A black theology of liberation.* New York: Orbis.

Frankenberg, R. (1993). *The social construction of whiteness: White women, race matters.* Minneapolis: University of Minnesota Press.

Fusco, C. (1995). *English is broken here: Notes on cultural fusion in the Americas.* New York: New Press.

Gitlin, T. (1995). *The twilight of common dreams: Why America is wracked by culture wars.* New York: Metropolitan Books.

Gómez-Peña, G. (1996). *The new world border.* San Francisco: City Lights Bookstore.

Grossberg, L. (1996). Identity and cultural studies: Is that all there is? In S. Hall & P. duGay (Eds.), *Questions of cultural identity* (pp. 87-107). Thousand Oaks, CA: Sage.

Gutiérrez, R. (1996). The erotic zone: Sexual transgression on the U.S.-Mexican border. In A. Gordon & C. Newfield (Eds.), *Mapping multiculturalism* (pp. 253-262). Minneapolis: University of Minnesota Press.

Harris, C. I. (1993). Whiteness as property. *Harvard Law Review, 106*(8), 1709-1791.

Hicks, E. (1991). *Border writing.* Minneapolis: University of Minnesota Press.

Ignatiev, N., & Garvey, J. (1996). *Race traitor.* London: Routledge.

Lipsitz, G. (1995). The possessive investment in whiteness. *American Quarterly, 47*(3), 369-387.

Loewen, J. W. (1995). *Lies my teacher told me: Everything your American History textbook got wrong.* New York: Touchstone.

López, I. F. H. (1996). *White by law.* New York: New York University Press.

Lott, E. (1993). White like me: Racial cross-dressing and the construction of American whiteness. In A. Kaplan & D. E. Pease (Eds.), *Cultures of United States imperialism* (pp. 474-498). Durham, NC: Duke University Press.

McLaren, P. (1995). *Critical pedagogy and predatory culture.* London: Routledge.

McLaren, P. (1997). *Revolutionary multiculturalism: Pedagogies of dissent for the new millennium.* Boulder, CO: Westview Press.

Newfield, J. (1998, July-August). Schlesinger speaks. *Tikkun,* pp. 56-58.

O'Brien, C. C. (1996, October). Thomas Jefferson: Radical and racist. *Atlantic Monthly, 278*(4), 53-74.

Perea, J. F. (1995). Los olvidados: On the making of invisible people. *New York University Law Review, 70*(4), 965-991.

Radhakrishnan, R. (1996). *Diasporic mediations.* Minneapolis: University of Minnesota Press.

Rattansi, A. (1994). "Western" racisms, ethnicities, and identities in a "modern" frame. In A. Rattansi & S. Westwood (Eds.), *Racism, modernity, and identity on the Western front* (pp. 143-86). Cambridge, MA: Polity.

Roediger, D. (1994). *Toward the abolition of whiteness.* London: Verso.

San Juan, E., Jr. (1995). *Hegemony and strategies of transgression.* Albany: State University of New York Press.

Shohat, E. (1995). The struggle over representation: Casting, coalitions, and the politics of identification. In R. de la Campa, E. A. Kaplan, & M. Sprinker (Eds.), *Late imperial culture* (pp. 166-178). London: Verso.

Southern Poverty Law Center. (1996). *False patriots: The threat of antigovernment extremists.* Montgomery, AL: Author.

Starkey, G. (1998, August 6). Loud and outspoken: Surf-guitar legend Dick Dale still wails. *San Louis Obispo New Times, 12*(50), 24-25.

Stowe, D. W. (1996). Uncolored people: The rise of whiteness studies. *Lingua Franca, 6*(6), 68-77.

West, C. (1993). *Keeping faith: Philosophy and race in America.* New York: Routledge.

Winant, H. (1994). *Racial conditions: Politics, theory, comparisons.* Minneapolis: University of Minnesota Press.

Wolfenstein, E. V. (1993). *Psychoanalytic-Marxism: Groundwork.* New York: Guilford.

Wood, E. M. (1995). *Democracy against capitalism: Renewing historical materialism.* Cambridge, UK: Cambridge University Press.

Yudice, G. (1995). Neither impugning nor disavowing whiteness does a viable politics make: The limits of identity politics. In C. Newfield & R. Strickland (Eds.), *After political correctness: The humanities and society in the 1990s* (pp. 255-285). Boulder, CO: Westview.

Zinn, H. (1970). *The politics of history.* Boston: Beacon.

PART III

BORDERS AND BOUNDARIES: THE ACADEMY AT THE EDGE OF DISCOURSE

A variety of inappropriate comparisons may be appropriate here. Compare the academy to television talk shows, with the testifying, the posturing, the personal declarations and accusations based on autobiography and institutional authority—but with no discernible host. Perhaps the host is virtual or a projection, with each participant referring to an imagined moderator who is an ideal from different scholarly origins and biases. Or additionally, think of a seminar, a post-, postgraduate, postmodern seminar, because in the three chapters included in this section, the emphasis is on the lack of exchange and the type of exchange taking place within academic discourse. It is as if all the really bright students in this seminar have had too much coffee and too little sleep and are trying to impress the professor and will not allow the other students to talk. Interrupting. Speaking over others and out of turn. Denying the credibility and theoretical stance (style) of the others present: school rivalries. The environment is performative, uncivil, and self-serving. What's worse, it is combative, done to impress, to establish, and to confirm a privileged and often anomic identity. And what's even worse, the imagined professor directing this imagined post-, postdoctoral seminar is not there, and will not be there. Because in the extended classroom of postmodern discourse, the authority and confirmation that will confer victory, that will brand as current or right, is not there. The center will not hold in this widening gyre. That this sort of conclusive authority was ever there is an illusion and one we no longer need to indulge.

In Chapter 7, Peter Kellett and H. L. Goodall examine the public and private responses to the scholarly essay "Sextext," which appeared in the January 1997 issue of *Text and Performance Quarterly*. In doing so, they note the production and consumption of a problematic and disheartening "superior" attitude that calls into question the "legitimacy of the existence of the voice itself" of the other side. And this practice is seen as perilous because it threatens any community's ability to carry on a democratic dialogue, particularly with the proliferation of electronic media interfaces and screen-oriented behaviors that reinforce oppositional, self-serving exchange.

In Chapter 8, Henry Giroux points out the absence of an engaged, interdisciplinary, and public discourse, noting that, until the 1990s, very few critical educators had incorporated some insights of cultural studies into the field of critical pedagogy. Yet, the two areas overlap, with the work of one group of theorists informing the other:

> [B]oth . . . engage in forms of cultural work that locate politics in the relations that articulate among symbolic representations, everyday life, and the machineries of power; both engage cultural politics as an experience of sociality and [engage] learning as the outcome of diverse struggles rather than a passive reception of information; both critical traditions [cultural studies and critical pedagogy] have emphasized what theorists such as Lawrence Grossberg and Paul Gilroy call the act of doing, being in transit . . ., and the importance of understanding theory as the grounded basis for "intervening into contexts and power."

So even though academics in cultural studies and critical pedagogy have common concerns both pedagogically and politically, they address vastly different audiences and themselves "rarely are in dialogue with each other, in part, because of the disciplinary boundaries and institutional borders that atomize, insulate, and prevent diverse cultural workers from collaborating across such boundaries."

Giroux proposes a project, the justification for which is the common ground shared by cultural studies and critical pedagogy. His idea is that the pedagogical as a performative practice not only can provide an opportunity to create an exchange across disciplinary boundaries but is also connected with a wider project "to further racial, economic, and political democracy." The result will be a revitalization of public life.

In Chapter 9, Charles Davis asks us to rethink harmful words and discourse in the schoolhouse, pointing out that although significant differences exist between the college campus and the public schoolhouse and these difference have yielded differing legal projections, "discourse in the classroom rightly serves as a barometer of the general condition of discourse in a society theoretically supportive of learned discussion and of empirical progress." Yet, central questions arise from noting this existing set of conditions, and these questions that face academia are both constitutional and philosophical in nature. Davis asks: "How does the university protect the free speech so important to its educational mission while identifying and punishing only 'harmful speech'? Should 'hate speech' be punished at all, or should the university take a content-neutral approach to all academic expression?" The notion of unfettered discourse must be restored to a position of primacy in the university.

And this gets us to the fundament: What is exchange for? To say *ideally* that it is an airing of views—but not to reach a conclusion by way of one side assenting to the other—is irrelevant. The point is that this practice is not ideal; this inconclusiveness, this continuum, is the reality of exchange. Why? Because as each author in this section shows, exchange is not domination, not victory, and not agreement. It is exchange. And if the academy is not the place where we can agree to disagree, then what place might there be? Where is it? Or what is it?

CHAPTER 7

The Death of Discourse in Our Own (Chat) Room

"Sextext," Skillful Discussion, and Virtual Communities

Peter M. Kellett
H. L. Goodall, Jr.
University of North Carolina at Greensboro

His face is turned towards the past. Where we perceive a chain of events, he sees one single catastrophe which keeps piling wreckage upon wreckage and hurls it in front of his feet. The angel would like to stay, awaken the dead, and make whole what has been smashed. But a storm is blowing from Paradise; it has got caught in his wings with such violence that the angel can no longer close them. This storm irresistibly propels him into the future to which his back is turned, while the pile of debris before him grows skyward. This storm is what we call progress.

—Walter Benjamin (1973)

The power of specific elite groups may be a direct function of the measure of access to, and control over, the means of symbolic reproduction in society, that is, over public discourse.

—Teun A. van Dijk (1995)

She arrived almost innocently. There she was in our mailboxes, at first glance just another academic journal, sheathed in a smooth two-color cover, her initial textual allure, her slick, serene surfaces, her too-blueness half-concealed by the usual memos, letters, and reminders that long-forgotten library books are now overdue. With the telltale blue cover, this is TPQ, a feminine, sometime feminist, disciplinary Other, a performative text that struggles to achieve professional voice and stature among an archetypal array of more traditional offerings, those historically testoster-one-heavy SCA-sponsored quarterlies that always contain modernist for-mulaic writing that is the old dominant white boys'—and unreconstructed dominant white girls'—collective definition of what Michael McGee calls "good ol' 'merican, scholarship" (March 5, 1997) in communication should look like, read like, and therefore be. For this reason, we coauthors have always rather liked TPQ, admired her in-your-face boldness, her resistance to scholarly genre-domination, her dedication to celebrate stylistic diver-sity, to promote minority and other typically marginalized (within our discipline) views, to stand up for what so often gets left completely out of our literature, which is to say, in sum, her bravery and passion. You've got to admit, it's hard to look like that, to act like that, to stand out when you are the only obvious girrrrl member of this particular discursive crowd.

So, we didn't immediately open her up, examine her contents. Not in our mailroom. TPQ is better entertained alone, at home. In the privacy of our own, shall we say, quarters?

Later that evening, dry martini in hand, we open the blue cover and cruise the title page, noting with pleasure the presence of some familiar authors—Rodden, Pelias, Welker—and the theme of this "special issue": Alternatives in Writing About Performance. A quick scan of the contents reveals a particularly spicy issue, with literary interviews, a confession, a divination, an Osun festival, gender role playing, and a photographic essay in addition to "a fictional account of text and body as fields of pleasure" that calls itself "Sextext" (Corey & Nakayama, 1997).

SEXtext? In an SCA journal?

SexTEXT, more probably. In our field, it is perfectly all right to theorize about sex via an examination of texts or to use sexual metaphors as sources of language critique. Both of us, in fact, had been guilty of such pleasures recently. In a chapter called "Sexing His Text for Plurals," Goodall (1995) read Gerald R. Miller's call for applied communication research through a sexual lens; Kellett (1995) had deconstructed the testimony of convicted rapists for ways that narratives about sexual power dramatize capitalized cultural archetypes. Sex *in* the text was one thing. Sex *as* the text?

Thus bidden, we approached "Sextext" with some genuine anticipation. It begins:

> I cruise theories. A look, a glance, a turn of the head. I walk away, pause, wait for the theory to follow. I let theories pursue me, and when I am ready, I turn to say hello, to ask, "Are you ready?" (Corey & Nakayama, 1997, p. 58)

A slow smile appears on our lips. Well . . . What have we here? The martini swirls suggestively, dangerously, metaphorically, along the edge of the glass. This is definitely not what we expected. The promise offered in the first four sentences is coy, a little saucy, a kind of seductive challenge, really: "Are [we] ready?" Ready for what? Certainly, the prose ante has been seriously upped. In truth, we are enticed by the attitude, decentered by it in an impurely sexual, ironic way, but we are also a little worried. Are [we] ready? Some girrrrls do take advantage of their circumstances, grab our attention with rhetorical heat that changes the context entirely, and then, usually, let us down with a quick grin and a turn of the head. Only kidding. Just seeing if you were looking at us. Paying attention. You didn't think we were . . . did you?

Ultimately, our reactions to such teasing are far more telling than the teasing itself. And that is always the point. Always.

AND NOW WE PAUSE FOR A MESSAGE FROM OUR DISCIPLINARY SPONSORS . . .

Our aim in this essay is to examine public and private responses made to a scholarly essay called "Sextext" that appears in the January 1997 issue of *Text and Performance Quarterly* (TPQ). The public responses that we have chosen for this study occurred from February through April 1997 on a computer-mediated list called CRTNET, which is sponsored by the then Speech Communication Association (now National Communication Association), the same organization that sponsors TPQ.[1] The private responses include e-mails written to us about the exchanges on CRTNET from scholars in the field, as well as some off-line comments gathered from conversations with colleagues over the controversy generated by the piece.

The purpose of our examination is threefold. First, we aim to apply to ourselves—in this case, to our discipline's electronic public forum on "Sextext"—the same set of recognized standards for conducting rational, democratic, and purposeful public discussions that we teach students in our classes. Second, we use the palette of Senge, Kleiner, Roberts, Ross, and Smith (1994) for developing communal dialogue to analyze the texts that comment on "Sextext" in order to locate the discursive strategies that construct both the terms of this controversy and the strategies through which this electronic public debate is manifested. Third, we want to see whether within this particular set of exchanges we might glean a new understanding of electronic public discourse as a vehicle for cultural production and consumption of messages and ideas. Although it may at first appear that this chapter only serves to reveal a familiar rhetorical analogue (e.g., those [girrrrls] who test the boundaries of rhetorical fashion [writing strategies, structures of production and consumption of scholarship, and styles of academic discourse] simultaneously unite and divide audiences to it [Burke, 1989]); in fact something more perilous is going on. However divisive the responses are, the ability to produce rational and democratic conversation appears to be less important than producing and consuming a "superior" attitude by condemning the other side and by calling into question the legitimacy of the existence of the voice itself. As you will read, mostly what gets produced in this disciplinary narrative is a bricolage of surface moments that only look like or feel like discourse and that ultimately serve to affirm the self by denying the discursive plurality of others. Our concluding section addresses how electronic media induce in us screen-oriented behaviors that seriously threaten any community's ability to engage in democratic dialogue.

OUR PUBLIC PERSONAE: THE MODERN NATURE OF WHAT WE TEACH ABOUT PUBLIC DISCUSSION AND CIVIL DEBATE

Let us begin this comparison of our standards for civil debate with the CRTNET discussion of "Sextext" with a brief examination of what criteria our discipline purports to warrant when it comes to public discussion and debate over ideas. To do this, we rely on commonly accepted standards for the conduct of public argument as found in a convenience sampling[2] of basic speech communication, argumentation and debate, and public speaking textbooks. On the basis of our review, the major themes of public argument are as follows:

1. That, all things being equal, the truth will prevail.
2. That to make "all things equal" is to issue a general invitation for knowledgeable disputants to give public voice to their claims about the world and to

provide good reasons why others—presumably audience members—should also hold those views.

3. That a structured process capable of allowing for the free exchange of those views for public consideration should be used (a well-organized and well-argued speech; a facilitated discussion that moves from definition of a problem toward an implementable solution; a formal debate that, after producing at least two sides to a given case, asks the audience for a judgment).

4. That fallacious forms of argument, including personal attacks, should be avoided; the substance of the discussion or debate should focus on the ideas and how they are supported by the weight of credible evidence.

In the end, the audience will determine the victor or the finer idea or both.

These standards are drawn from, and therefore represent, a decidedly modernist version of communication. By "modernist," we mean to reference the idea that public debate is best conducted when rational, well-informed, and ethical communicators advance their claims by using inductive and/or deductive modes of reasoning, support their claims with appropriate evidence and warrants, and make every effort to present audiences with both sides of the issue at hand. As argued elsewhere (see Goodall, 1996, pp. 245-251; Rushing, 1993), this modernist view of communication supports a view of power that is derived from a perceived unity of social and political manifestations in modern philosophy, commodity capitalism, and scientifically driven technologies. Such a view of power privileges a "sovereign rational subject" who is conceived of as an autonomous, disembodied, individualistic Self, and whose goal for public debate is to win over the audience and any opponents, via critical and judicious applications of Western logic, to some predetermined truth that will or at least can stand as an ahistorical certainty.

Admittedly, this is an ideal for public debate that is—or has been, historically—seldom achieved; we are, after all, only human. Nevertheless, it does largely supply a powerful *mythos* for the conduct of public argument within our discipline, at least as that discipline is widely represented in its basic texts.[3] Furthermore, modernist standards for public speaking, argumentation, discussion, and debate also promote elite forms of discourse; only the most well-educated, argumentatively trained, and eloquent members of a community (who can afford to spend the time and effort engaging in moderated public exchanges) are entitled to practice it (see van Dijk, 1995). One clear characteristic of elite discourse is the overall attitude of privilege that entitles the elite speakers to their views, as well as to their claims of the natural superiority of the beliefs and values that inform them.[4] Electronic media formats, such as chatrooms, challenge this idealistic and elite view of public discussion and debate. Both in format for the discussion (e.g., electronic chatrooms are not analogous to actual face-to-face encounters before public audiences) and in time bracketed for the communication process (e.g., a 1-hour public debate vs. being able to "enter" a chatroom at one's own convenience, day and/or night), these changes in communication processes tend to bring with them alterations in communicative form. Even if we allow for the differences that could be explained by random access to a chatroom, however, such as the ability to reproduce, reread, and critically analyze the entire text, verbatim, of an opponent's argument before crafting a response, a response that itself can be carefully written, scrupulously edited, even tried out on friends and colleagues and otherwise "polished" prior to actual "delivery," we might expect a more refined form of argument, a more civil form of public discussion and debate. After all, the heated passions of the moment that do occur in public face-to-face debates, or simply the ability to look up facts prior to posting a message, should improve the rationality of the arguments, wouldn't you agree?

But apparently, this is indeed not the case. As we demonstrate in the following section, the discursive strategies used in the actual postings concerning "Sextext" rarely measure up to either the textbook standards we supposedly teach or to the improvements and refinements to civil public discussions we can imagine as a result of the textual and time advantages afforded by an electronic medium. Before we examine the discourse strategies that are used to conduct these public forums in the case of "Sextext," however, we want to ask why the use of this new information technology may have something to do with the kinds of exchanges that go on there.

Marshall McLuhan (1964) taught us that "the medium is the message." In part, this phrase was used to signal the advent of television as a new form of information-processing technology, but it was also used to explain how visual technologies speed up the ability of humans to process information and how reliance on visual images would increasingly be used to compress—and thereby reduce—meanings associated with written or spoken language. As cultural critic Lewis Lapham (1997) puts it: "[T]elevision bears more of a resemblance to symbolist poetry than it does even to newspaper prose. The camera looks but doesn't see, and the necessary compression forces both the words and the images to become less literal and more figurative" (p. 10). For Lapham:

Instead of narrative we have montage, and our perceptions being tuned to the surfaces of film rather than to the structures of print, we tell one another stories not by lining up rows of words but by making connections (sometimes synchronous, sometimes in juxtaposition) between the film loops stored in our heads. Words define themselves not as signs of a specific meaning but as symbols bearing lesser or greater weights of cinematic association. (p. 10)

Lapham's concern, in part, is for how this imagistic, screen-based process influences perceptions of history. Relatedly, our concern is with how screen-based technologies influence the perceptions and practices of civil discourse. For Lapham, screen logic breaks down narrative into iconic images that reference other iconic images; for us, screen logic takes rational, linear, structured, modernist argument and morphs it into post-modern, nonlinear fragments. By some sort of evolutionary—if unnatural—selection, chatrooms inherit features of both screen-based worlds: Perceptions of visual displays of words are narratively fragmented, and their meanings are both more compressed and more figurative. The result is a brave new medium that is more powerful than McLuhan's oft-quoted dictum; the medium is no longer equivalent to the message, it is greater than the message because it frames the available perceptions of decreased screen meanings while increasing the associated iconic referents. Perhaps, in sum, the activity we engage in is aptly named: Screen logic dictates that we cannot really "argue," we can only "chat."

Without warrantable argument as a discursive foundation for civil discourse, we move from being "citizens" in a modern sense to "consumers" in a postmodern one. We replace "the marketplace of ideas" with a market in which ideas traffic as signs of "identity politics," or political membership in various commodity-based systems of meaning. We "surf" messages, not so much for the substance of arguments aimed at a generalized public truth, but for rushes of feelings we have been driven to need. Our idiom moves from claims supported by evidence and warrantable assent to a variety of powerful and power-seeking emotive metaphors—blasting, slamming, and so on—that support immediate gratification for screen-based screams, divisions along political lines, and a general call to discursive combat.

So much for our framing. In the following section, we move from this general concern for the loss of the rational process of civil discourse to a more specific concern for how this loss of discourse threatens democratic community.

TEXTUAL RESPONSES TO GAY MALE PORNOGRAPHY

Blasting Toward a Scholarly Community

> Submissions to this list are evidence of how communication functions to create
> and sustain community in a social system. As you can see, sometimes commu-
> nity is achieved through messages that separate the members by what they
> say/do. . . . We can see how communication is working by observing who gets
> blasted, and for what. We can see how the participants in this community are
> all trying to come toward some satisfying agreement on identity. . . . In other
> words what is happening right in front of you is a great example of how
> communication constructs community. (Carlos Aleman, February 23, 1997)

This quote captures one of the main paradoxical tensions we are working
with in this essay, and one central to our analysis of the textual responses
to "Sextext." Some CRTNET participants have the perception that the
chatroom is building or constructing community that, by contrast, appears
to be constituted out of a communicative norm of "Blasting" people with
opinions and methodological stances different from our own. This unor-
thodox notion of community suggests the following main question: What
kind of scholarly community is being created through emotive, combative
discourse based on images, short stylized arguments that are often fictionalized?

Related to this question is the perception in the above quote that the
purpose of the discourse is to come to agreement on a common definition
or at least common ground on our "disciplinary identity." Yet, at the same
time, much of the communicative work in this chatroom appears to be
driven by a desire to separate members from the discipline—from the
community—by affirming oneself as "right" and others as "wrong." This
paradox generates the question, How does talk that, in many cases, fore-
grounds difference and division contribute to the creation of a scholarly
community that balances unity and diversity? Additional questions derived
from these general ones include, How close is this discursive style of the
chatroom to the rational, reasoned debate or participative discussion models that we teach our students? Why does the discourse evolve as it does
into "blasting" and other divisive practices? In this part of the chapter, to
address these issues we need to identify the discursive strategies that
characterize this particular form of organized communication. To accomplish this, we compare our discourse practices to Peter Senge's model of

the learning community. We use the learning community model because academic disciplines seem by definition to be learning communities and because the basis of a learning community is public talk in the form of skillful discussion.

If a scholarly community—whether this chatroom or our discipline more generally—aspires to be an enduring and productive learning community, its participants should be concerned with balancing inquiry (community) and advocacy (scholarship) through "skillful discussion."[5] Skillful discussion involves being genuinely curious, making one's reasoning explicit, and asking others about their assumptions without being critical or accusing. When skillful discussion is the norm, scholarship is likely to be produced and consumed within a context that balances both constructive criticism and collegiality. If the discourse is not skillful discussion, Senge et al. (1994) show us that forms of dysfunctional talk will be produced and reproduced. For example, "Dictating" ("Here's what I say and never mind why") has its equivalent in the chatroom as "Blasting." Also, "Withdrawing" (mentally checking out of the room and not paying attention) has its equivalent in the chatroom as "Lurking." Other common strategies are "Interrogating," "Withdrawing," and "Politicking." We use this "palette" evaluatively to explicate the discourse style of the CRTNET chatroom.[6] We do this by asking simply, Is the chatroom talk about "Sextext" skillful discussion? If not, what is it? How and why does it take the form that it does? and What are the implications for our scholarly communities?

> Although the dialogue here has included many heavyweights in our field, it is completely accessible to all of us. I would encourage all lurkers to dive in and participate, that's what it's all about. (Ted & Stephanie Coopman, Tuesday, February 25, 1997)

When we entered this discourse, we were initially struck, as Ted and Stephanie Coopman appear to be, first by the vibrancy of exchange, a quality rarely seen in the more typical face-to-face conference-based exchanges of the National Communication Association. People taking the time to "dive in and participate" and to be deep, playful, creative, honest, and smart in ways that often our more traditional journals do not, seemed like a wonderful discursive opportunity.[7] Second is the immediacy of intellectual exchange not seen much in our discipline. Third, as the above quote suggests, is what appears at first to be a wonderfully inclusive conversation emerging, one in which young scholars and teachers are conversing with "big names" in a medium that, because of its lack of paralinguistic and nonverbal framing of power/status differences, levels people to seemingly equal voices in an evolving collaborative discussion. The medium appears to offer some corrective opportunities to our increasingly fragmented field, a way of stimulating a broad and accessible forum, something the NCA convention largely fails to do, which is, to create and consume ideas and insights about communication as a living and evolving learning community.[8] The chatroom offers seductive glimpses of these possibilities in action. Some participants do use skillful discussion. Much of the talk, however, though more immediate and accessible than most other forms of academic exchange, is (with a few exceptions) neither productively vibrant nor, in practice, particularly inclusive. While studying this discourse, we have spent a lot of time watching people struggle to be cleverly pointed. We have also wondered, at times, whether this medium is being used merely to re-create a clubby group where clever members blast and zap each other as if locked in the violent excitement of a do-or-die computer game. We move on from these initial impressions to a closer interpretive reading of the discourse style of this CRTNET chatroom.

Some key discursive strategies are used to attempt to establish authority for particular positions—specifically, on the scholarly value of "Sextext"—throughout this discussion. As you will see from the following examples, at stake are what people consider or do not consider to be "scholarship" in our field, defined operationally as what and who deserves to get published. This discussion is therefore always also about the powered interests of who gets to be productive and how scholarship should be consumed, as much as it is about what counts as appropriate scholarship in the community. Hence, the ongoing struggle between "authority" (those mostly against "Sextext") and "radical" (those mostly for "Sextext") voices throughout the chatroom discourse.

It Looks Like Fashion, Not Scholarship

My guess is that the only test this article was required to pass was the test of TPQ's ideology du jour. (Ted Wendt, Friday, February 14, 1997)

Derogation of alternative forms of inquiry—namely, autoethnography—as mere passing fancy is one main way of avoiding the possibility that "Sextext" might offer valuable contributions to our field, both in a substantial sense and in the sense of opening up talk about who we are and what we produce.[9] One argument is that autoethnography is only evocative and therefore insubstantial in any scholarly sense. As the following narrative indicates, this is a deeply held belief for some:

> I agree—autoethnography is evocative. But sadly that's about all it is. And that's why it's not scholarship. It may be a lot of other things, but it ain't scholarship. And the fact that there is now a critical mass of self-reinforcing devotees to this drivel who can be called upon to defend it doesn't make it scholarship either. Scholarship must involve something more than the mere ability to evoke a feeling or response. Stepping on a piece of broken glass will do that. (Malcolm Parks, Friday, January 31, 1997)

In this cutting dismissal, autoethnography is relegated to drivel that exists to express and reinforce the feelings of a particular trendy subculture. The implication is that, as it is not scholarship, then it must be mere fashion, the alternative, transitory, and somewhat annoying identity statement of a marginal few. (Ironically, the signature after Parks's message begins, "Honor Cultural Diversity . . . [!]") Unlike the enduring truth that exists beyond paradigm forces that Parks might have us believe we have been producing in our field, autoethnography is mere surface fashion.[10] This move to define scholarship as necessarily excluding autoethnography, for some, involves the strategy of linking autoethnography with other, more readily demonizable fashion icons in the field, such as "postmodernism." The argument is broadened to a more familiar modern versus postmodern dialectic. For example, in a (presumably) fictional conversation between a goldfish and David Sutton, the seemingly wiser goldfish explains:

> . . . This is the Postmodern age, my friend. You've got to get with the times. The idea of going back to a QJS *(Quarterly Journal of Speech)* of the 1970's in which essays were brief and clear is over, mi amigo. It is all cultural trends. Intellectual fads and fashions. You are out of date, David. You're still wearing the intellectual version of an electric blue polyester leisure suit. (David Sutton, Thursday, February 6, 1997)

What the not-so-smart goldfish does not seem to realize in this conversation is that even though the 1970s style seems to make more sense—information in brief and clear forms—like the leisure suit, it too was guided by fashion, although academic. And 1970s scholarship, like the leisure suit, is clear and sharp as an icon only in retrospect. What was clear and apparently good at one point in our disciplinary history also obeys a similar paradigmatic fashion sense as the apparently less clear and identifiable style of the late 1990s, embodied as autoethnography. Perhaps, as in popular culture these days, academic trends turn over and are replaced faster that ever (it is difficult to think of a single style dominating a whole decade any more), and perhaps this is what is making the contribution of autoethnography "unclear" for those like Sutton, who seems to believe in the absolute integrity of an academic body outside cultural forces of production and consumption.

It Doesn't Look or Act Like Scholarship

> Sextext is much ado about nothing. (Ted Wendt, Monday, February 10, 1997)

The argument against autoethnography as scholarship builds through another authority strategy. That is, not only is this mere emotive fashion in its subcultural consumption, but it also does not even follow established practices of the field in its production and does not address established questions or problems of the field as its product or outcome. Therefore, it must be insignificant. Consider the following part of a post by Don Ellis:

> These issues about certain types of writing and analytical efforts (e.g. autoeth-nography) are intellectual ones that demand justification, statements of as-sumption, and some form of validation. . . . I will however argue when I think these things are not accomplishing what they say they are, or when they are simply the result of individual idiosyncrasies rather than established methods, procedures or what have you. Moreover, there is also the question about disciplinarity and what problems are communication problems, and what constitutes communication approaches. When a thousand flowers bloom, you have diversity but plenty of weeds. (Don Ellis, Tuesday, February 4, 1997)

The assumption here is that fully established and generally believed traditional criteria for judging scholarship cut across the boundaries of methodological genres and styles. These criteria establish that traditional social science approaches really just are the way that scholarship should get done. Anything else is mere solipsistic self-gratification—idiosyn-crasy—that misses the mark because it does not even try to deal with traditional "communication problems."[11] Communication problems that are deemed appropriate for our scholarship do not, according to David Sutton, involve references to sexual activity, particularly homosexual ac-tivity. As his alter-ego, Goldfish, amusingly states,

"Suck my dick" is scholarship? Not in my aquarium. (David Sutton, Thursday, February 6, 1997)

The discourse strategy here is to represent selectively the scholarship being discussed in terms of its least desirable part. Selective and extreme evidence is taken out of its context and given as representative of the whole. The result is that we are led to believe that the article—and, by implication, autoethnography more generally—is about the promotion of "sucking dicks" and probably not much more.[12] These forms of argument also illustrate two deeper strategic tendencies throughout these posts. First is the reliance on organizing arguments around icons that are easily identifiable as "good" or "bad." This reflects the tendency toward short, fast, seductive, image-based claims that are more representative of mass mediated "persuasion" such as television advertising. Second is that the goldfish narratives and other similarly fictionalized presentations of arguments reflect the tendency to draw on argumentation styles reminiscent of soap opera or situation comedy styles of representation. These deeper strategic themes imply that our own academic discussion is necessarily tied to postmodern themes of image-based representation and logic.

Polarizing Language

Naming, whether name calling, playing with names, or renaming, is a powerful discourse strategy that can be used to unite, show respect, change selves and relationships, divide, derogate, or express cynicism. The following statement illustrates the power of naming in both displaying cynicism and creating division and, thus, undermining the possibility for reasonable discourse to happen:

An eight page article devoted to stagefright; oops, sorry: "Performance apprehension." No "scholarship," you understand—just "personal narrative" or "autoethnography." AKA: Talking to yourself. (Ted Wendt, Friday, February 7, 1997)

This strategy positions autoethnography as the contemporary (read fashionable) rearticulation or renaming of "Talking to yourself" in the same way that "performance apprehension" is just a trendy renaming of "stagefright." In renaming as "talking to yourself," the autoethnographic style of research scholarship is again marginalized to egocentric idiosyncrasy.

Beyond division, naming can also set up mutually exclusive categories that imply a hierarchy of relative value. For example, the argument that "Sextext" is pornography *and* therefore has nothing to do with scholarship is an exclusionary distinction promoted by some throughout this discourse. For example,

> Does their (TPQ) editorial board have the right to publish gay pornography? Yes, but SCA members should ask themselves what they're paying for. Scholarship? I don't think so. (Ted Wendt, Friday, February 7, 1997)

The exclusive distinction sets up a deductive argument consisting of the following progressive propositions:

1. Scholarship is valuable;
2. As (gay) pornography is not scholarship, and "Sextext" is a case of gay pornography,
3. Therefore, "Sextext" is not valuable. That is, as scholarship it is worthless.

Throughout the postings, these oppositions serve to create bipolar either/ or options in viewing, and therefore judging, "Sextext" as scholarship or not. Another opposition is constructed between "scholarship" and "drivel." When names such as "Gay Porn," "Idiosyncrasy," and "drivel," are taken together, they form both a dismissal of autoethnography and a reification of self as producers of widely read and valuable scholarship, as well as policers of these scholarly standards.

Another polarizing strategy is to use the language of intense conflict, such as war, to structure and make sense of the flow of discourse back and forth between "positions" or "camps." For example:

> As editor of the new Sage, Inc. series on Rhetoric and Society, I'd welcome a well argued, well researched rhetorical analysis of org comm scholarship, of the sort Palmieri has in mind. Even better, I'd welcome a jointly authored "attack" and "defense." Any takers? (Herb Simons, Thursday, February 13, 1997)

Using combative imagery to illustrate points can escalate conflicted relationships into deeper oppositions. This is particularly "effective" when communication itself takes on warlike imagery as in the following:

McGee did some ad hominem in both missiles . . . (Herb Simon, Tuesday, March 11, 1997)

When messages are viewed as missiles, communication metaphorically becomes the battle to outblast the other, rather than being the process of reasonable discussion by which scholarly issues can be discussed and minds broadened.

Constructing the Motives and Experiences of Others for Them

When a participant in a conflicted discourse begins to decide, guess at, and embellish what he or she thinks the motives of the other participants are and what they should be and then decides what their experiences are for them, usually a deeply divisive and marginalizing construction of Others emerges. This happens frequently in this chatroom. For example, Ted Wendt asks:

Prominent scholars have published in TPQ. I agree. And what must they be thinking now? That, by the way, is not a "rhetorical" question. I'd really like to know. Are they happy being associated with "Sextext"? (Ted Wendt, Monday, February 10, 1997)

His implied answer, of course, is that they would agree with him and say that, yes, the quality of TPQ submissions (and therefore our scholarly publications) has changed for the worse. This strategy appropriates others into the "side" of the argument by constructing their motives and experiences in line with the current position in the argument being asserted.

Another strategy used to marginalize autoethnography is to construct the expressions as coming from meaningless and absurd lives; therefore, by implication, the value of their research is meaningless and absurd. It is a simple argumentative step from this analogy, then, to assert that the meaningless and absurd research really belongs in an alternative place where it might make more sense. For example, John Hollwitz constructs an argument by which the "Sextext" research and TPQ research more generally belongs in a locker room:

TPQ exists for a small isolated group of people who exemplify what some-one . . . metaphorically as the ultimate academic absurdity: A few dozen PhD's locked in a room for five decades, furiously scribbling notes to each other full of self-applauding but increasingly meaningless jargon.

People can spend their careers any way they want. But it seems to me inappropriate to the point of self-delusion to concretize Gardner's metaphor and then to get misty eyed about how progressive they are because they can print stuff appropriate mainly for the locker room, with less scholarly value. (John Hollwitz, Friday, February 14, 1997)

Wendt mirrors Hollwitz's attack and personalizes the issue further through strategically accusing others of what he does himself—that is, of being judgmental:

Aside from Dwight Conquergood and a handful of others, performance studies doesn't have much going for it. I think it's very telling that people of Mumby's professional stature (he's tall too) hold back on passing judgment—something he probably does on a daily basis with his grad students. (Ted Wendt, Monday, February 24, 1997)

Wendt's strategy of assigning aspects of motive or identity not revealed in the messages evokes the same strategic response. The conflict escalates. For example, then McGee playfully imagines Wendt in a scene he is not likely, on the basis of the persona he projects through his messages, to be involved in:

I judge the Dean (Wendt) will not likely do field research to observe what may be a connection between sexual performance and what gets counted as knowledge. Nor can I imagine Dean Wendt curling up with books by Lacan, Kristeva, Foucault, Freud, Jung, Plato and others—in an open frame of mind. (Michael McGee, Wednesday, March 5, 1997)

Another way that autoethnography is marginalized is to construct physical images of those who represent their identity as faddish rebellious teens passing through a phase well before scholarly maturity. For example:

The one thing I always admire about postmodernists, deconstructionists, poststructuralists, queer theorists, autoethnographers, and the like is that they get to maintain that revolutionary stance. They get to stand there with leather and orange hair and piss off the adults. (Don Ellis, Wednesday, March 5, 1997)

Assigning negative perceptions and values that undermine the credibility and perceived character of the other—putting words in their mouths—is another discrediting strategy used in the chatroom. For example:

> See, he knows you're this red neck, 'cause you live in Kentucky, and you work at this hick school. (Ted Wendt, Thursday, March 6, 1997)

Nothing has been stated in previous postings about Ted Wendt being a redneck, and neither has an evaluative statement been made about where Wendt teaches. This strategy assigns motives, reasons, and qualities of character and identity to others and provides reasons both for why they argue certain things and for why others are wrong.

Blaming the Other for the Lack of Quality Talk

A common tactic in escalating conflicts is to blame others for the lack of collaborative communication—that is, for the conflict—and for engaging the tactics that they themselves are using—hence, the old adage that we tend to accuse others of the things we are most guilty of ourselves. Amid the conflicted discourse, Ted Wendt finds an opportunity to blame the conflict on the so-called postmodern ideologues. The posting thinly hides the very ad hominem attack on postmodernists that he claims they typically use on him. Hence, the voice of authority is equated with the voice of reason and the victim of the others' unreasonable behavior. The posting states:

> Anyone presuming to have an opinion about "Sextext" (this author included) needs to be prepared for a deluge of ad hominem attacks. Has anyone noticed how post-modern ideologues wrap themselves in a protective cocoon of politically-correct defenses, designed to pre-empt criticism? Thus, "Sextext" is a self styled fiction. It is convoluted, irrational, poorly-written, derivative, and disorganized because it is post-modern theory. Its personae are Gay, Gay, Gay. (Ted Wendt, Friday, February 7, 1997)

Here, so-called postmodern styles of writing and inquiry are reduced to excuses for poor scholarship. Postmodern ideologues are also blamed for dampening the spirit of "genuine" critical inquiry that Ted and his pals are bringing to the chatroom discourse. Defensive and politically guided mystification is blamed for the apparent lack of critically constructive discourse. How such charges are supposed to generate constructive discourse and not more defensiveness is also, to us, a mystery.

When participants blame others for the conflicted quality of talk, the language of blaming is pointed and evaluative, thus escalating an already pointed style of conflict. For example, misreading/interpreting the talk of the other as motivated by derogation is one tactic for escalating the talk. Ted Wendt is particularly skilled at this debate tactic, justifying his ad hominem attacks by accusing the other of the same, hence justifying his attack. This quality of talk has the quality of gaming, jousting, and bating the other:

> . . . Just finished reading the hardcopy of Michael Calvin McGee's trashing of my concerns about Sextext . . . In academic circles we refer to this as an ad hominem attack. Seems out-of-character coming as it does from someone who signs off with the quote, "Violence is the last resort of the incompetent." (Ted Wendt, Thursday, March 6, 1997)

Here again, the other is portrayed as unreasonable, provocative, and divisive, and Wendt uses this to justify attacking McGee by using the very tactics he accuses McGee of using.

Taking the Moral High Ground

Another way to undermine the possibility of productive discussion is to assign lower moral status to others when moral issues are not even necessarily part of the discussion. That is, the argument—and therefore the truth—become part of a broader system of moral and ethical judgment in which the expression of ideas different from ones own becomes immoral, impure, and even dishonorable. Once such a moral high ground is taken, the argument is easily personalized into a bipolar opposition:

Moral ——————————————————————— Immoral
(agree with me)   (do not agree with me)

For example, in the following post, Stacy Vatne weaves in the evaluative descriptors of degradation, dishonor, and impurity to morally denounce such open expression:

> In commenting on an article in *Text and Performance Quarterly,* his persona Goldfish uses highly graphic sexual imagery. As a Christian and a lover of

metaphor, I was saddened to see our incredible gift—language—degraded. Surely, Goldfish could have just as creatively presented his argument using a vehicle other than the sexual. Even if Goldfish uses sexual imagery because he thinks that that is the best way to criticize the Text and Performance Quarterly article, it is still an unacceptable method. Sometimes employing the most rhetorically effective technique is not the most honorable and pure way to respond in life. (Stacy Vatne, Friday, February 7, 1997)

It is a short argumentative leap to reach the judgment that it is "unacceptable" and that, as Donna Reinstrata dismissively suggests,

Perhaps this type of writing could have its own scholarly journal? (Donna Reinstrata, Wednesday, March 5, 1997)

The implication here is that a community of scholarship is unattainable and even undesirable, so why not accept the fundamental fragmentation of the field? Such a position effectively makes open, skillful discussion obsolete as a way of engaging in scholarship.

Recognizing Male Discourse Styles

Quite often, the style and content of the discussion takes on a distinctly masculine character.[13] Although we do not know for certain, we strongly suspect that this might affect the willingness of some women to participate who might otherwise "dive in" if the style and imagery of the talk were less aggressive. The talk has a masculine style in two main senses. First, masculine imagery and humor permeate many of the chatroom messages, particularly the conflicted exchanges. For example, masculine imagery is used to create a coherent defense against posts that question the following distinctly masculine "Goldfish narrative":

. . . You haven't stroked your ideas long enough. You haven't massaged your arguments until they can stand erect on their own. Your introduction must caress the reader with soft touches, gently previewing your argument. Then, as you lead into the body of your essay, you slowly and gently penetrate the quivering, moist folds of your readers' consciousness. Throughout the body of your essay you use repetition and restatement, working your arguments in and out again and again, until both of your minds are joined in passionate undulations. With your conclusion you explode in one massive stream of enlightenment. Afterwards you and your reader will bask in the afterglow of a shared understanding. (David Sutton, Thursday, February 6, 1997)

Objections to the sexual imagery of the post are met with highly masculine-style responses in the same vein. For example, Scott Johnson's response defends the image through additional male sexual imagery:

The Goldfish's "graphic sexual imagery" fits the crime! A lesser response would have been LIMP! (Scott Johnson, Friday, February 7, 1997)

The person objecting to the sexual imagery is immediately also marginalized (ironically, by another woman) as a petty prude who ought to be more worldly wise in her responses to such imagery:

I was shocked to see Stacy Vatne's prim little slap on the wrist because of the sexual nature of Sutton's analogy. (Jane Banks, Friday, February 7, 1997)

Other masculine sexual imagery is used to add humor to the discussion. Cute wordplays are used to continue the sexual themes of "Sextext" into discussion about the text. For example:

What is the intent? . . . Is it persuasion? I'm not persuaded. The (assumed) gay reader needs no persuasion. So the intent must be to do something else. The authors call it friction. Oops, sorry, fiction. (Ted Wendt, Friday, February 14, 1997)

Second, talk that describes the chatroom itself as a (virtual) place often draws on particularly male images in that identity construction. For example, the chatroom is seen by some as a place to "fight out" an issue. Talk then becomes a form of fighting. Consider the following image for its male perspective on communication:

. . . I've been enjoying my role as the drunk who threw the first punch then slipped behind the bar to watch the ensuing brawl. Suddenly out of nowhere a hard, direct question—pow! (Bob Craig, Tuesday, February 4, 1997)

Male images of debate such as this lead to the marginalization of women as the chatroom takes on a masculine persona as a place of hard punches and straight talk that might be too tough for women. The warlike image is continued through the following post and is used to construct a gendered opposition in that men are involved in fighting about the issues, whereas women stay on the sidelines to facilitate:

> She (Judith Trent) added that she did not wish to enter the debate arena with the rest of the CRTNET gladiators but would prefer to ask a few genteel questions from the sidelines. (David Sutton, Sunday, February 23, 1997)

This construction of chatroom as a masculine context in which ideas get advocated in particular ways that reduce the relevance of inquiry functions, such as considering the other, serves to structure and limit the style and content—and the skill level—of talk that emerges from that context.

Fortunately, there are moments when the maleness of the discourse is recognized and where that gendered experience of the talk can then be deconstructed. What is it about how we do academic discussion that is characteristically male? How are women and women's styles of entering the discussion responded to? These are useful questions that Carlos Aleman shows sensitivity to in the following post:

> WHAT I HEARD NEXT WAS A TRANSFORMATION OF (STACY) VATNE'S IDENTITY TO A CHRISTIAN, FEMALE, OUTSIDER; AN IL-LOGICAL AND CONTRADICTING PLAINTIFF AGAINST OUR LOCAL BOYS, SUTTON AND GOLDFISH (I PRESUME GOLDFISH IS ONE OF "US" SINCE WE ALL HAVE SALUTED HIS ENTRIES DESPITE THAT HE HAS NOT POSTED HIS ACADEMIC CREDENTIALS). (Carlos Aleman, Sunday, February 9, 1997)

Central to this discussion, and Aleman's post that follows, is the question of how we construct boundaries to organized discussion that maintain inclusive and productive discussion. Are we (unobtrusively) creating a good old boys club as a way of closing off the boundaries of discursive relevance or membership? Is there a way of talking in the chatroom that, in our presumably tolerant discussion of "Sextext" and surrounding issues, effectively excludes particular forms of objecting and particular issues? For example, Aleman, again shouting his point for emphasis, questions the norms of the chatroom as follows:

> I WOULD LIKE TO EXPRESS MY RESPECTFUL DISAGREEMENT WITH PROFESSOR JAFFE'S ASSESSMENT OF THE STATUS OF "OUR GROUP," AND HOW WE ARE TALKING WITH EACH OTHER AND WITH OTHERS. WE HAVE DENIGRATED VATNE BY TAKING HER ISSUE AND MAKING IT ONE OF MEMBERSHIP AND OF DISCIPLINED, IF

NOT SYMPATHETIC, PARTICIPATION IN "OUR GROUP." THE EX-
CHANGED MESSAGES PROVIDE SOME EVIDENCE FOR THE CLAIM
THAT, LIKE OUR JOURNALS, THE CRNET IS SPACE RESERVED FOR
"OUR MEMBERS ONLY." (Carlos Aleman, Sunday, February 9, 1997)

DISCOURSE DYNAMICS

Questioning the Quality of Our Scholarly Community

As we have shown so far, the style of talk evolves largely into strategies
that reflect dysfunctional relationships between inquiry and advocacy.
These dysfunctional styles include *dictating* (Here's what I say, and never
mind why), *withdrawing* (mentally checking out of the room and not
paying attention), *interrogating* (Why can't you see that your point of view
is wrong?), and *politicking* (giving the impression of balancing advocacy
and inquiry while being close-minded). In this chatroom, particular strategies we have explicated can be categorized into these main communication
styles. For example, strategies that connect with the dictating form of
communication include blasting others, derogating the other to fashion,
and using combative imagery. Some strategies constitute a dictating style
because they are central to taking on a style of asserting the "truth" without
consideration—much less acceptance—of what the other believes or
thinks. Thus, advocacy for particular ideas takes preeminence over inquiry
into why this is so and how people feel about that.

Withdrawing has its equivalent in the chatroom as the strategy of lurking.[14] That is, many people observed the talk without actually participating.
We can guess that perhaps some of those lurkers were dissuaded from
contributing because the style of communication in the chatroom was not
always inviting or collegial. Hence, the lack of inquiry that characterized
much of the chatroom talk leads to a lack of advocacy for any position by
those who withdraw.

Interrogating takes place in the chatroom through strategies such as
arguing that autoethnography does not look or act like scholarship and
taking the moral high ground such that the other looks "wrong." These are
interrogation strategies in that if the other is morally lower and what he or
she produces is not scholarship, then the person ought to realize that he or
she is inherently wrong.

Politicking is evident through such strategies as blaming the other for
the quality of talk, using male discourse styles, using polarizing language,

and constructing the motives of others for them. These are politicking strategies in that they create the sense that we desire a high quality of talk and a discursive style that is inclusive (inquiry), but at the same time the strategies of talk actually used serve to derogate and accuse others, escalate conflict, and marginalize voices that do not fit the dominant male style (of advocating). In practice, these are close-minded strategies through which others are portrayed as close-minded.

Besides allowing us to categorize strategies within broader categories of styles, the palette also enables us to view strategies as ways of creating the context of choice for other participants. Simply, particular forms of talk narrow the range of what appropriately follows that talk. Sequences and cycles of discourse are created through this flow of action and reaction. For example, dictating leads to dictating, and politicking leads to interrogating, and all of these lead to a certain amount of withdrawing. Hence, cycles of escalated talk emerge that undermine both inquiry and advocacy. Advocacy for ideas is undermined as people do not participate or spend time reacting to being attacked. Inquiry into the communicative quality of the community is undermined as the collegial dimension of scholarly talk is quickly challenged by attacks, by pointed and marginalizing talk, and by people mentally (or physically) checking out of the room.[15] Within this system of actions and reactions that constitute the flow of the chatroom talk, we have also found moments of discussion that lead to profound insight and disciplinary reflection. We have also found a playful and creative context in which some people are attempting to balance inquiry (community) and advocacy (scholarship) through insightful but collegially humorous talk and styles of writing that, by their presence in our discussion, open up textual possibilities. Overall, however, given the possibilities of this medium and context, we have been largely disappointed with the quality of skillful communication. The practices of skillful discussion appear sprinkled throughout the chatroom talk. We move on to discuss how skillful discussion generates opportunities to enliven this adversarial discourse and how skillful discussion may be more effectively practiced in virtual organizations like the chatroom.

Creating a Virtual Scholarly Community Through Skillful Discussion

If we want to have a debate about the integrity of performance studies, let's all do that work first. Such work may benefit each of us more than demanding a simple account for Sex Text that is somehow supposed to resolve deep-seated epistemological conflicts. (Bryan Taylor, Friday, February 14, 1997)

While I disagree with his conclusions, it is productive for me to engage Don Ellis's critique of post-structuralism because he has done his homework. (Bryan Taylor, Monday, February 24, 1997)

Perhaps we should avoid the scare terms ("pornography") and focus on the merits of the article (or lack thereof). (Ed Schiappa, Monday, February 24, 1997)

These discourse moves are examples of skillful discussion as they all suggest a spirit and quality of talk that promotes curiosity about the value of "Sextext"; they make explicit the reasoning and judgment made in the statements; and they avoid approaching others in a critical or accusing style. These and other examples of skillful discussion that occurred serve the crucial functions of balancing inquiry and advocacy in the chatroom discourse.

Exploring the Value of Evocation and Evocative Research

And what is the nature of "orgasmic" knowing? (Michael McGee, Wednesday, March 5, 1997)

Although such a question may be beyond the purview of most communication scholarship at this time, it does point to the fact that evocation, and more specifically evocative research, is central to how many in our field believe that communication can be productively explicated (see Goodall, 1989, pp. 91, 96). Skillful discussion leads to the exploration of the issue of the often evocative ways that autoethnography describes experience. For example, Lesa Lockford insightfully suggests that evocation of desire, as it is expressed in communication, suggests the value of autoethnographic inquiry as it is able to descriptively account for such experience:

I believe that Corey and Nakayama are among other things attempting to represent desire. . . . The article is, I believe, not attempting to get to conclusion (as is so often the case with traditional scholarship). I believe it is best viewed as an inquiry into this communicative phenomena. They are trying to get at something that is elusive and, therefore, they are almost certain not to reach a conclusion in the usual sense. . . . I am left wondering if desire is therefore unreportable, unrepresentable. (Lesa Lockford, Tuesday, February 11, 1997)

A particularly insightful way of evoking the meaning of "Sextext" involves carrying the sexual metaphor of "cruising" through to describe the stages of our relationship to particular methodologies and theories. For example, in the polygamy stage of allure, the evocative appeal of theories drives their ability to create interest and a following of other interested scholars. For example:

> There are those scholars who excel at the one night stand. I suggest many grad students (myself included) fit well into this category. We are always searching for the best, hottest, coolest theory that has immense sexual charms. One theory does not quench our sexual cravings so we begin to explore the charms of another—a busy bee going from flower to flower collecting pollen along the way. (Dutch Driver, Monday, March 10, 1997)

The second stage involves a monogamous relationship to one's methodology. In this stage, there may be tendencies to believe that this is morally right and that it ought to be how others live. This association may be significant in accounting for the indignation with which some participants speak out against "Sextext."

The third stage involves people becoming "Dissatisfied with security (and) beginning illicit affairs, while in their infidelity, they leave behind broken homes and promises to find and fulfill their more Epicurean delights."

This is a particularly useful image, as some responses to "Sextext" read somewhat like the aftermath of an affair. The relationship between our discipline and methodological standards has been compromised through this lewd and unforgivable act of betrayal of the established standards of research. That is, relational normality has been ruptured through the publication of "Sextext." Some want to find out how the overconstraining patterns of the relationship would generate this kind of act; others want to condemn because the rules have been broken, irrespective of reason. Still others just want to walk away.

The quality of this image parallels another important aspect of autoethnographic research, and of performance based research more generally— that is, resonation. Although *resonation,* as the quality of research that connects emotionally or even spiritually with an audience, may not obey the rules of scholarship set out by some in this chatroom, it does suggest the value of research that connects with people's lived experience—that is, research that resonates with lived communicative reality. As Dennis Mumby rightfully questions,

If these people (performance studies) are so isolated, how come their work resonates with so many scholars across our discipline? (Dennis Mumby, Friday, February 14, 1997)

Stimulating Reflections on Identity

Studying ourselves and our world is a noble cause we should be proud of. . . . If we cannot effect our society and make changes for the better, then what is our purpose. (Ted & Stephanie Coopman, Tuesday, February 25, 1997)

Compare the above sense of nobility in studying both ourselves and the world with Art Bochner's lament that follows:

What depresses me most is the unwillingness or inability for the mainstream in our field to acknowledge the legitimacy of the profound changes in the ways in which "communication studies" is practiced. What it shows again, I suppose, is what Geertz said about anthropology in AFTER THE FACT, that we're really just a sprawling consortium of dissimilar scholars held together largely by will and convenience. (Art Bochner, Tuesday, February 18, 1997)

This contrast between the ideal and the reality check of one of the leading proponents of autoethnography indicates two main issues. First, many in autoethnographic research are challenging the tenets of more traditional social science approaches to communication studies in their paradigm claim to be a unified, unitary, or unchanging body. Second, chatroom talk has the ability to explicate these issues of identity and to generate valuable talk about who we are, what our boundaries are, and what those boundaries could be. As Bryan Taylor indicates, making connections across disciplinary boundaries is a very valuable way of thinking through and focusing our disciplinary identity:

As the field of work concerned with evaluating relationships between power, culture and discourse—"Pornography" is a legitimate object of communication scholarship. The fields are not exclusive. (Bryan Taylor, Monday, February 24, 1997)

This sort of productive cross-disciplinary discussion can be expedited through organized electronic contexts such as the chatroom.

Lesa Lockford insightfully discusses these issues of identity and specifically the importance of advocacy, as well as inquiry in creating tolerant scholarly communities:

> . . . As I read through the myriad of postings on the list, the buried question of "what is scholarship?" keeps rising through the mire. . . . Surely the point is not to conform to some standard form of scholarly reporting; rather it is to get at communicative phenomena, to unearth meaning, and to engage in scholarly discussion and debate by presenting our understandings to our peers. . . . "Rebel discourses" challenge because the traditional forms have obscured, silenced, or dominated others. And/or because they are inadequate to the task of representing that knowledge. (Lesa Lockford, Tuesday, February 11, 1997)

She points out that so-called rebel discourses (including autoethnography) come out of a need to question the marginalizing forces that traditional forms of inquiry have exerted. That is, they should be seen as an inevitable systemic expression of being marginalized.

SKILLFUL DISCUSSION GENERATES SKILLFUL DISCUSSION

Skillful discussion has two main generative functions in this chatroom. First, skillful discussion often leads to further skillful discussion of substantive issues. As James Roever states,

> . . . This is the first time that I can recall that one article has produced such a level of discussion. (James Roever, Wednesday, February 26, 1997)

If this rupture in the taken-for-granted style of scholarship is skillfully discussed in terms of its deeper systemic meaning, then "Sextext" is treated as an opportunity to open up discussion, and more discussion emerges.[16] Second, the discussion also generates moments of realization where a sense of responsibility and accountability are taken for the talk that the chatroom generates. As Aleman states,

> I believe, like most I'm sure, that our talk about Corey and Nakayama's SEXTEXT has been both segregating and communing for the speech community called CRTNET. But it has been our talk, not Corey and Nakayama or the article SEXTEXT that has done it. (Carlos Aleman, Tuesday, March 4, 1997)

Skillful discussion can create a sense of ownership over what is produced by that talk.[17] In this case, valuable talk about the similarities and differences that are central to our scholarly community are produced. Another way that skillful discussion leads to further skillful discussion is in generating an understanding of the context in which particular forms of scholarly expression are generated. For example, Rob Drew points to the need to understand the context for the apparent "transgression" of "Sextext." He helps us see "Sextext" as a reaction to the exclusivity that social sciences creates in our field. He puts this succinctly:

> The fact is that a lot of people in qualitative research are feeling drawn to a more personal, evocative style of research and writing. This is a reaction to years of accumulated research written in putatively objective, neutral authorial voices, voices that remained strangely detached and unmoved by the worlds they described; voices that were often not only unengaged but unengaging— boring, frankly. (Rob Drew, Tuesday, February 4, 1997)

"NETIQUETTE": NEGOTIATING NORMS OF COMMUNITY DISCOURSE

At one slow period in the debate, talk turned momentarily to the negotiation of norms of talk (for some, the rules of combative engagement). How people should talk in the chatroom for maximum clarity became important enough to address. One line of discussion focuses on the style of expression. Should chatroom talk be written as scholarship or written as personal communication or even as conversational speech? is an important question in generating cultural norms of communication. For example, as one participant in favor of more formal written personal style states,

> I don't think we should write as though we were presenting a piece of scholarly research. . . . However, I think that we have let our guard down a bit too much when we enter conversations and discussions on listservers. (Alec Hosterman, Wednesday, March 5, 1997)

Additionally, another participant in favor of either informal written style or spoken conversational style states,

> There are many ways to personally choose how to correspond with e-mail. I personally choose most often to correspond as if I were writing a letter; in this

way, I force myself to reread and edit and double check if my ideas are clearly stated. . . . I see no reason to "chide" another's choosing to correspond via e-mail as if it were a spoken conversation that is free-flowing. (Anastacia Serro-Boim, Wednesday, March 5, 1997)

Either formal or informal, at least this level of open discussion generates the co-construction of norms.

How people are treated in chatrooms and how they should be treated is another important line of discussion. One participant laments the lack of invitational style for newcomers to the chatroom:

A couple of newbies wandered into the public square recently. . . . They bravely joined the fray, but behaved in ways that were considered inappropriate. Of course, we snapped and growled and made snide inside jokes to insure that they knew their squeamishness about sexual and verbal hygiene were not "normal" in our community. They haven't been heard from since. (Dale Cyphert, Monday, March 10, 1997)

Skillful discussion can lead to an understanding of accountability in that we are asked to think about how we might have created this loss of participation in the community. Similarly, inquiry is nurtured in that participants can move on to discuss how to communicate such that "newbies" or others can be effectively socialized and not chased away in the future.

On a deeper level, the norms of chatroom discourse do point to ways we should consider how we do academic discourse more generally. Specifically, one discussion point relates to the ways discourse styles chosen in the chatroom actually damage the possibility for discourse. Carole Blair, for example, insightfully points to the damaging implications for discourse when "Sextext" is represented as "pornography." Her argument is characterized as follows:

It reinforces hostility to difference, harms the careers of creative and interesting people, and demands that work be read in a particular way. . . . I'm not sure how that "advances the discipline." (Carole Blair, Monday, February 3, 1997)

Accepting Blair's argument, we are challenged in the following ways: First, we are challenged to create a discourse style in which hostility to difference gives way to more reasoned discussion of differences as starting points for discussion, rather than as end points or boundaries that must be defended at all costs to collegiality. Second, rather than blast anonymous game players in the chatroom, we are challenged to respect the people involved in the discussion as colleagues with lives and desires similar to our own in some fundamental ways. Third, rather than try to impose our hierarchy of values and priorities of scholarly styles onto others, we are challenged to be tolerant of the variety of interpretive possibilities that make up "our" scholarly community, whether virtual or face to face. To develop such a discourse style is one way to ensure that both the opportunities for scholarly discourse that this chatroom represents and the opportunity to maintain the civility of discussion we talk so much about in our classes are not lost.

CONCLUSION

This chapter has presented and analyzed an example of public debate in the electronic era. Our concern has been for how discursive strategies within the context of the debate function to construct and promote combativeness between or among politically divided discourse communities and for how such public conduct fails to live up to our disciplinary standards for civil discussion while at the same time shedding light on the death-producing influences of electronic media in our public discourse.

Our analysis of the screen-based logics displayed in the controversy over "Sextext" induce postmodern forms of expression characterized by (a) shorter, less well-supported claims that are speedier to produce and consume; (b) a preference for more informal, individually stylized utterances that draw from conversational and fictional forms of display; (c) discursive strategies that emphasize conversational put-downs, slams, blasts, and an overall emotional tone and combative style reminiscent of television sitcoms and political talk shows; and (d) an attitude among most speakers of a natural superiority—revealed as personally stylized argumentative rape—of audiences within these electronic chatrooms. Collectively, these four characteristics reveal how disputants in an electronic chatroom generally tend to behave, which is both counter and contrary to what—we can only assume—these same spokespersons have been trained to teach students about public argument and themselves to value.

A second characteristic of these discourses concerns the "tolerance" strategy. Although "tolerance" for disciplinary differences appears to be a common way of denying sexist beliefs and values, such tolerance merely appears to be a discourse strategy designed to dismiss the value of the difference to—much less the struggle to attain voice within—the discipline's culture, thereby reinforcing the dominance of the elite. "Sextext" as an example of scholarship about gay male pornography is "tolerated" by those who would ban it as a form of discourse by arguing that it should appear somewhere else (not in an NCA-sponsored publication) or be classified as something other than scholarly work (e.g., gay male pornography).

A third characteristic of the discourse about "Sextext" is that it seldom engages the piece itself. Aside from Michael McGee's long post in which he treats the arguments within the essay as scholarship that informs our discipline's reading of poststructuralists, and two or three other attempts to talk about the difficulty in representing "desire" in a scholarly form or performance as a valuable form of scholarship, the vast majority of debate over "Sextext" never references the material in the essay. Elite discourse doesn't have to. By and large, a superior attitude about one's own scholarly values supersedes any need to apply those values to some "lesser" form of expression. What is being argued in these exchanges has far more to do with gay males and stylistic choices to represent gay male experiences than it does with quality of the piece as scholarship.

Fourth, we are reminded throughout our reading of these exchanges of the wisdom of Stuart Hall (1996), particularly in his analysis of representation as cultural ideology. Hall teaches us that one consistent use of media by dominant elites is found when the idea of representation means "stands in the place of," rather than its original, modernist sense "to re-present something that already is." Cultural stereotypes in media, for example, convey powerful messages about marginalized groups that, for a large segment of the viewing public, may in fact "stand in the place of" any real experience with members of those groups. Repeated exposure via circulation of cultural stereotypes tends to reify those stereotypical characteristics, therefore reinforcing the cultural power of the representation while ensuring the ideology of the dominant media. Viewed in this way, stereotypical characterizing of gay males, gay male pornography, and its association with performance studies and TPQ becomes a way in which our electronic chatroom contributes to the power of negative representations in circulation, as well as to the dominant nondemocratic ideology of the discipline.

Communication studies, like any other academic discipline, has never been a democratic community. As a discourse community, we are representatives of a dominant cultural elite—academics—whose participation and leadership in intellectual issues both benefits and suffers from our position in society, certainly in the world culture. While we claim to admit anyone to our associations, to admit any style of inquiry into our scholarly community, and to prefer no particular methodology or theory, we in fact do. The controversy over "Sextext" is but one recent example of how much we do, as well as how we do it.

Stuart Hall (1996) explains that it is not enough to replace a negative stereotype with a positive one; in many ways, this form of counterrepresentation itself is complicit with the evil it attempts to combat. Instead, what he suggests—and what we endorse—is far more difficult than merely claiming that our discipline's outlets will be more willing in the future to accept "rebel" work or become more tolerant of discursive differences. What we must do is be willing to expose our own disciplinary practices to critical scrutiny. By "opening up" that which we do when we create and constitute our community, we make possible democratic dialogue. The end is not consensus, nor is it agreement; it is dialogue, or the very important ability to keep the conversation going.

Peter Senge's model for how skillful conversation may lead to dialogue provides us with a way to think publicly about, if not to improve, the conduct of public discourse. Certainly, it provides us with a useful palette on which to open up that discourse to critical inquiry.

OUTRO

"I told you that you would be surprised," she said. "I asked if you were ready." She was naked. Where once there was only a slick two-color surface of blueness, there was now only skin. She seemed to be enjoying this, enjoying the public display of her nakedness, although no doubt the enjoyment of herself was part of the performance she was giving.

That we were studying.

Her statement was hard to respond to. Are we ready?

Are we?

Ready for what?

To touch the naked body of another soul is to become vulnerable to the truths, the needs, the unspoken but well-understood desires that we mistakenly believe are only our own. They are, in fact, more than that.

These desires, these needs, these truths speak not only to us but about us. They connect us to each other in ways that nothing else can.

They teach us about each other, if we let them.

They are how we practice being human, together.
This is what she means when she asks that question. This is the moment of a
kind of truth. Are we ready?
Are we?

NOTES

1. We analyzed 85 posts during this period. An archive of all CRTNET postings is
available from LISTSERV@PSUVM; send the command INDEX.

2. The texts used were found on our shelves or on the shelves of our colleagues in the
department. Although some people may quibble with this method, we believe that it represents
a fair sampling of what currently passes for literature on the subject.

3. Irving J. Rein once published a text that countered these idealistic formations titled
Rudy's Red Wagon: Communication Strategies in Contemporary Society (1969), in which he
demonstrated that, in everyday life, far less rational and well-organized appeals are everywhere
found and disseminated; ironically, Professor Rein's book was widely disregarded or rebuked
for catering to popular culture and thereby debasing the argumentative nobility of our field. In
retrospect, Professor Rein was merely documenting the reality of our culture, and these days
can fairly be said to have been well before his time.

4. Wayne Brockriede (1972), following Plato's *Phaedrus,* suggested that modern argument could also be understood through the attitudes of the rhetor toward the audience, attitudes
that reveal the discursive strategies lovers employ. One of these approaches, in which an arguer
aggressively imposes his or her will on an audience while offering little or no warrantable
support for claims (the "dark horse" in Plato's dialogue) was characterized as "argumentative
rape"; it seems that, in the electronic forum on "Sextext," we have another example of how
Brockriede's characterization of a rhetor's attitude figures into the argumentative mix.

5. We are using learning community here in Stephanie Ryan's (1995) sense of a community of inquirers where the participants value the collective process of discovery and value
living with the additional questions that the process of inquiry continually generates. We are
using the concept of *skillful discussion* in Senge et al.'s (1994) sense of communication that
balances the need to advocate particular ideas (advocacy) with the need in contemporary
organizations to think and work together at collective decision making (inquiry). Hence, in
skillful discussion, people state their ideas, reasoning, and thinking and encourage others to
challenge and respond to those ideas.

6. For a more detailed discussion of dysfunctional communication styles, see Senge et al.
(1994, pp. 253-255).

7. The chatroom offers what Fred Kofman and Peter Senge (1995) call a "transitional
medium" (p. 36). That is, the chatroom offers the opportunity of a place where it is safe to
experiment and reflect. Ideas can be collectively played with outside the more formal and static
journal context. The chatroom medium could be a learning laboratory.

8. That is, as a place where what Kofman and Senge (1995) call "generative conversations
and coordinated actions" can take place (p. 32). Hence, the community evolves constantly
through a high quality of communication.

9. We use the term *autoethnography* in John Fiske's (1990) sense as scholarship that
attempts to account for the relationship between experiences described "from the inside" and

interpreted "from the outside" (p. 89). This intersection necessarily places the self, and specifically the body, at the site of such inquiry. For an excellent collection of essays that make the evocation of experience an explicit goal of communication research, see Ellis and Bochner (1996). See also Behar (1996).

10. This opposition in the field of communication is paralleled in anthropology, where, as Judith Okley (1992) points out, explicitly reflexive or autobiographical work is often characterized as "mere navel gazing" (p. 2).

11. For a skillful discussion of how autoethnography is positioned within context of the failure of social science methodology and the need to view research as communication, see Bochner and Ellis (1996).

12. Part of this derogation may be attributable to "Sextext" being what Norman Denzin (1997) calls a "messy text" (p. 224). That is, "Sextext" is committed to cultural criticism while remaining resistant to theoretical holism. Such ambiguity is difficult for social scientists to tolerate. Coupled with this, autoethnography is always involved on some level with a concern for the intersection of narrative, context, and power (Peterson & Langellier, 1997). These are the very dimensions of research that social science typically most wants to deny about its own production—hence, the overly aggressive attack on research that makes those dimensions into explicit concerns.

13. For a useful discussion of both the traditional oppositions of masculine and feminine styles of communication and the value of exploring how such styles in practice open and close opportunities for discourse and learning, see Anderson (1995).

14. We did not participate in this forum either and so are lurkers ourselves. Neither of us wanted to get involved in yet another disciplinary debate over the scholarly value of work identified with autoethnography.

15. We have focused on disciplinary tensions and oppositions as generating this adversarial discourse. As James Perley (1997) points out, however, the broader context of academia is suffering from a lessening of collegiality as competitiveness for resources increases in an ever more vulnerable profession. The strategies of the chatroom may, in part, be linked with these broader shifts in academic culture.

16. This is what Susan Bethanis (1995) means by language being "generative action."

17. Skillful discussion leads to what Kofman and Senge (1995) call "communities of commitment." This is particularly the case when that skillful discussion evolves into dialogue.

REFERENCES

Anderson, M. (1995). Ahead of the wave: Valuing gender perspectives in learning cultures. In S. Chawla & J. Renesch (Eds.), *Learning organizations: Developing cultures for tomorrow's workplace* (pp. 57-70). Portland, OR: Productivity.

Behar, R. (1996). *The vulnerable observer: Anthropology that breaks your heart.* Boston: Beacon.

Benjamin, W. (1973). *Illuminations.* London: Fontana.

Bethanis, S. J. (1995). Language as action: Linking metaphors with organizational transformation. In S. Chawla & J. Renesch (Eds.), *Learning organizations: Developing cultures for tomorrow's workplace* (pp. 185-196). Portland, OR: Productivity.

Bochner, A. P., & Ellis, C. (1996). Talking over ethnography. In C. Ellis & A. P. Bochner (Eds.), *Composing ethnography* (pp. 13-45). Walnut Creek, CA: AltaMira.

Brockriede, W. (1972). Arguers as lovers. *Philosophy and Rhetoric, 5,* 1-11.

Burke, K. (1989). *Symbols and society.* Chicago: University of Chicago Press.

Corey, F. C., & Nakayama, T. K. (1997). Sextext. *Text and Performance Quarterly, 17,* 58-68.

Denzin, N. K. (1997). *Interpretive ethnography: Ethnographic practices for the 21st century.* Thousand Oaks, CA: Sage.

Ellis, C., & Bochner, A. P. (1996). *Composing ethnography: Alternative forms of qualitative writing.* Walnut Creek, CA: AltaMira.

Fiske, J. (1990). Ethnosemiotics: Some personal and theoretical reflections. *Cultural Studies, 4,* 85-98.

Goodall, H. L. (1995). Sexing his text for plurals. In K. Cissna (Ed.), *Applied communication in the 21st century* (pp. 57-78). Mahwah, NJ: Lawrence Erlbaum.

Goodall, H. L. (1996). *Divine signs: Connecting spirit to community.* Carbondale: Southern Illinois University Press.

Hall, S. (1996). *Race and the floating signifier* [Video]. Northampton, MA: Media Education Foundation.

Kellett, P. M. (1995). Acts of power, control, and resistance: Narrative accounts of convicted rapists. In R. Whillock & D. Slayden (Eds.), *Hate speech* (pp. 142-162). Thousand Oaks, CA: Sage.

Kofman, F., & Senge, P. (1995). Communities of commitment: The heart of learning organizations. In S. Chawla & J. Renesch (Eds.), *Learning organizations: Developing cultures for tomorrow's workplace* (pp. 15-44). Portland, OR: Productivity.

Lapham, L. (1997, April). Notebook: The Spanish armadillo. *Harper's Magazine,* pp. 8-11.

McLuhan, M. (1964). *Understanding media.* New York: McGraw-Hill.

Okley, J. (1992). Anthropology and autobiography: Participatory experience and embodied knowledge. In J. Okley & H. Callaway (Eds.), *Anthropology and autobiography.* London: Routledge.

Perley, J. E. (1997, April 4). Tenure remains vital to academic freedom. *Chronicle of Higher Education, 68*(30), p. A48.

Peterson, E. E., & Langellier, K. M. (1997). The politics of personal narrative methodology. *Text and Performance Quarterly, 17,* 135-152.

Rein, I. J. (1972). *Rudy's red wagon: Communication strategies in contemporary society.* Glenview, IL: Scott, Foresman.

Rushing, J. (1993). Power, other, and spirit in cultural texts. *Western Journal of Communication, 57,* 159-168.

Ryan, S. (1995). Learning communities: An alternative to the "expert model." In S. Chawla & J. Renesch (Eds.), *Learning organizations: Developing cultures for tomorrow's workplace* (pp. 279-292). Portland, OR: Productivity.

Senge, P. M., Kleiner, A., Roberts, C., Ross, R. B., & Smith, B. J. (1994). *The fifth discipline fieldbook: Strategies and tools for building a learning organization.* New York: Currency.

van Dijk, T. A. (1995). Elite discourse and the reproduction of racism. In R. Whillock & D. Slayden (Eds.), *Hate speech* (pp. 1-27). Thousand Oaks, CA: Sage.

CHAPTER 8

Performing Cultural Studies as a Pedagogical Practice

Henry A. Giroux
Penn State University

It is commonly accepted that the field of education was one of the first disciplines in the United States to incorporate the ongoing work of British cultural studies. For instance, Paul Willis's book *Learning to Labor* played a significant role in the educational debates of the late 1970s and early 1980s concerning theories of reproduction and resistance within critical educational thought. In the 1980s and 1990s, a few cultural studies scholars in the United States attempted to address the importance of pedagogy as a continuing and significant dimension of cultural studies, but such attempts were uneven and often ignored.[1] Surprisingly, few critical educators attempted in the 1980s either to keep up with the developing work in cultural studies or to incorporate some of its best insights into the field of critical pedagogy. Fortunately, more and more critical educators are incorporating cultural studies into their work in the 1990s.

Although critical educators and cultural studies scholars have traditionally occupied separate spaces and have addressed vastly different audiences, the pedagogical and political nature of their work appears to converge around a number of points. At the risk of overgeneralizing, both cultural studies theorists and critical educators engage in forms of cultural work that locate politics in the relations that articulate among symbolic representations, everyday life, and the machineries of power; both engage cultural politics as an experience of sociality and learning as the outcome of diverse struggles rather than a passive reception of information; both critical traditions have emphasized what theorists such as Lawrence Grossberg and Paul Gilroy call the act of doing, being in transit (see Gilroy, 1996; hooks, 1996), and the importance of understanding theory as the grounded basis for "intervening into contexts and power . . . in order to enable people to act more strategically in ways that may change their context for the better" (Grossberg, 1996, p. 143). Moreover, theorists working in both fields have argued for the primacy of the political by calling for and struggling to produce critical public spaces, regardless of how fleeting they may be, in which "popular cultural resistance is explored as a form of political resistance" (Bailey & Hall, 1992, p. 19). But although both groups share certain pedagogical and ideological practices, they rarely are in dialogue with each other, in part, because of the disciplinary boundaries and institutional borders that atomize, insulate, and prevent diverse cultural workers from collaborating across such boundaries.

I want to address how the pedagogical as a performative practice might provide cultural studies theorists and educators with an opportunity to engage pedagogical practices that are not only interdisciplinary, transgressive, and oppositional but also connected with a wider project designed to further racial, economic, and political democracy.[2] The meaning and primacy of the notion of the project I am using is drawn from Jean Paul Sartre's *Search for a Method* (1968). For Sartre, the project has a double meaning. It refers to engaging critically that which exists, as well as to a praxis that opens into that which "has not yet been. A flight and a leap ahead, at once a refusal and a realization" (p. 92). Implicit in Sartre's notion of the project is both an expanded notion of the political informed by the discourses of critique and possibility, and a challenge for critical theorists. The challenge I want to address is how critical pedagogy as a political and performative project may provide a theoretical umbrella under which critical studies and critical pedagogy may join together in a radical project and practice informed by a theoretically rigorous discourse that affirms the critical but refuses the cynical, establishes hope as central to a critical pedagogical and political practice but eschews a romantic utopianism. Fundamental to such a project is a notion of the performative that expands the political possibilities of the pedagogical by highlighting how education as a critical practice may be used to engage the tension between existing social practices produced in a wide range of shifting and overlapping sites of learning and the moral imperatives of a radical democratic imaginary. Pedagogy in this context becomes performative because it opens a space for disputing conventional academic borders and raising questions "beyond the institutional boundaries of the disciplinary organization of question and answers" (Grossberg, 1996, p. 145), reclaims the pedagogical as a power relationship that participates in authorizing or constraining what is understood as legitimate knowledge, and links the critical interrogation of the production of symbolic and social practices with alternative forms of democratic education that foreground considerations of power and social agency.

A performative practice in its more orthodox register largely focuses on events as cultural texts that link the politics of meaning with deconstructive strategies of engagement. Such a pedagogy in Judith Butler's terms focuses on representations and "discourses that bring into being that which they name" (Osborne & Segal, 1994, p. 33). Within this form of pedagogical practice is a great deal of emphasis on texts and how they are "presented, 'licensed,' or made 'excessive' " (Frith, 1996, p. 204). The tendency within cultural studies as it becomes more popular, especially in its North American versions, of "privileging cultural texts over practice as the site of the social and political" (Gray, 1996, p. 211) is growing. The exclusive emphasis on texts, however, runs the risk of reproducing processes of reification and isolation as when the performative is framed outside the context of history, power, and politics. In this instance, texts occupy a formalistic space that might disavow a universalistic aesthetic yet views issues such as one's commitments to the other, the ethical duty to decide between what is better and what is worse and, by extension, human rights as meaningless, irrelevant, or leftovers from a bygone age. In its most reductive moment, Lewis Gordon argues, performativity as a pedagogical practice often falls prey to a

> focus on politics as rhetoric . . . [in which] the political dimension of the
> political is rendered invisible by virtue of being regarded as purely performa-
> tive—or, as in more Foucauldian/Nietzchean articulations of this drama, purely
> manifestations of will to power. What one performs is rendered immaterial.
> Whatever "is" is simply a performance. (Gordon cited in James, 1997, p.175)

Progressive cultural studies theorists recognize that the complex terms of cultural engagement are produced performatively, but unlike Gordon, many believe that the issue is still open regarding how the performative can have some purchase in terms of social action or contribute to producing new forms of identity and politics while simultaneously developing a political and ethical vocabulary for creating the conditions of possibility for a politics and pedagogy of economic, racial, and social justice.

I want to address the importance of a politically progressive notion of the performative and its relevance for highlighting the mutually determining role of theory and practice, on the one hand, and the related project of making the political more pedagogical, on the other. This is especially important as pedagogy becomes more central to shaping the political project(s) that inform the work of educators and cultural workers in a variety of sites, especially within a present marked by the rise of right wing politics, a resurgent racism, and ongoing punitive attacks on gays, urban youths, and people of color. The invocation of a wider political context suggests that the intersection at which cultural studies and critical pedagogy meet be analyzed more critically in the light of a cultural politics in which power is addressed primarily through the issues of meaning and ideology, rather than the material organization and contexts of everyday life.

Engaging the pedagogical as a performative practice that both connects and affirms the most important theoretical and strategic aspects of work in cultural studies and critical pedagogy might begin with Raymond Williams's (1989) insight that the "deepest impulse (informing cultural politics) is the desire to make learning part of the process of social change itself" (p. 159). For Williams, a cultural pedagogy signals a form of permanent education that acknowledges "the educational force of our whole social and cultural experience . . . [as an apparatus of institutions and relationships that] actively and profoundly teaches" (Williams, 1967, p. 15). Education as a cultural pedagogical practice takes place across multiple sites and signals how, within diverse contexts, education makes us both subjects of and subject to relations of power.

As a performative practice, the pedagogical opens up a narrative space that affirms the contextual and the specific while simultaneously recognizing the ways such spaces are shot through with issues of power. Central to this referencing of the ethical and political is a pedagogical practice that refuses closure, insists on combining theoretical rigor and social relevance, and embraces commitment as a point of temporary attachment that allows educators and cultural critics to take a position without standing still. The pedagogical as performative also draws on an important legacy of cultural studies work in which related debates on pedagogy can be understood and addressed within the broader context of social responsibility, civic courage, and reconstruction of democratic public life. Cary Nelson's insight that cultural studies exhibits a deep concern with "how objects, discourses, and practices construct possibilities for and constraints on citizenship" (Nelson & Goankar, 1996, p. 7) provides an important starting point for designating and supporting a project capable of bringing together various educators, academics, and cultural workers within and outside the academy.

At stake here is a notion of the performative that provides diverse theoretical tools for educators and cultural workers to move within and across disciplinary, political, and cultural borders in order to raise new questions, provide the context in which to organize the energies of a moral vision, and draw on the intellectual resources needed to understand and transform those institutions and forces that keep "making the lives we live, and the societies we live in, profoundly and deeply antihumane" (Hall, 1992, p. 18). In this instance, such a project offers the promise of challenging the current return to literature and simultaneous retreat from politics so evident in the recent work of theorists Stanley Fish, Frank Lentricchia, William Cain, and others.[3] Professionalist relegitimation in a troubled time seems to be on the march as an increasing number of academics both refuse to recognize the university as a critical public sphere and offer little or no resistance to the ongoing vocationalization of the university, the continuing evisceration of the intellectual labor force, and the current assaults on the poor, the elderly, children, racial minorities, and working people in this country.[4]

Rooted in ongoing cultural exchanges, translations, and border engagements, the pedagogical as a performative practice rejects any rendering of the pedagogical that conveniently edits out the difficulties and struggles posed by institutional constraints, historical processes, competing social identities, and the expansive reach of transnational capitalism. Similarly, the pedagogical as performative practice acknowledges the full range of multiple, shifting, and overlapping sites of learning that, in part, produce, mediate, legitimate, and challenge those forces that are waging an assault on democratic public life in the United States and other parts of the world. In this instance, the political becomes more pedagogical as diverse cultural workers recognize the need to work collectively to create/perform/ construct those spaces in which desire, memory, knowledge, and the body reconfigure discourses of critique and possibility that enable multiple ways of speaking and acting as part of an ongoing engagement around the crucial issues of identity, agency, and democracy. By focusing on the pedagogical and political dimensions of culture, educators and cultural studies advocates can interrogate texts as a form of ethnography, expanding the range of ideology critique and pedagogical encounters to images, symbols, myths, and narratives, as well as diverse systems of belief.

As a form of cultural production, pedagogy takes on the goal of challenging canonicity and interrogating the conditions of exclusion and inclusion in the production, distribution, and circulation of knowledge. Critical pedagogy, in this instance, joins cultural studies in raising questions about the way culture is related to power—why and how it operates in both institutional and textual terms—within and through a politics of representation. But a performative pedagogy does more than textualize everyday life and contest dominant forms of symbolic production; it also calls for resistant readings and the development of oppositional practices. Pedagogical work, in this sense, informs and extends cultural studies' long-standing concern with mobilizing knowledge and desires that may lead to significant changes in minimizing the degree of oppression in people's lives. At stake in making the pedagogical more fundamental to the diverse work done in cultural studies is a political imaginary that extends the possibilities for creating counterpublic spheres; for within such counterpublic spheres, the principles of equality, liberty, and justice become the normative rather than absolute standards for a cultural politics that translates knowledge back into practice, translates theory into the political space of the performative, and invigorates the pedagogical as a practice through which collective struggles can be waged to revive and maintain the fabric of democratic institutions.

The pedagogical as a performative practice also points to the necessity of an integrative language for reconstituting educators and cultural studies scholars as public intellectuals. Seizing on the role that critical theorists and educators may play as part of a wider oppositional strategy of engagement, cultural critics such as Stuart Hall, Lawrence Grossberg, Carol Becker, Stanley Aronowitz, Kobener Mercer, Tony Bennett, and Meghan Morris have attempted to create critical discourses and forms of social criticism through which people can understand and produce culture within democratic and shared structures and spaces of power. Rejecting the well-policed distinctions that pit form against content, professionalism against politics, and subjective experience against objective representations, many critical educators and cultural studies theorists have endeavored in different ways to break down the rigid boundaries and binary oppositions between teaching and politics, ethics and power, high and low culture, margins and center, and so on. Rather than take up the notion of public intellectual as academic fashion plate ready for instant consumption by the *New York Times,* some critical theorists have reconstituted themselves within the ambivalencies and contradictions of their own distinct personal histories while simultaneously recognizing and presenting themselves through their role as social critics and public intellectuals. By connecting the biographical, pedagogical, and performative, cultural workers such as Suzanne Lacy and Guillermo Gómez-Peña rearticulate the relationship between the personal and the political without collapsing one into the other (Gómez-Peña, 1996; Lacy, 1995). As public intellectuals, such cultural workers not only refuse to support the academic institutionalization of social criticism thus contributing to "its effective demise as a socially active force" (Eagleton, 1984, p. 65), they also take seriously their role of critic as teacher and the potentially oppositional space of all pedagogical sites, including but not restricted to the academy.

Of course, few of these cultural workers define themselves self-consciously as public intellectuals. And, yet, what is so remarkable about their work is the way they render the political visible through pedagogical practices that attempt to make a difference in the world, rather than simply reflect it. The pedagogical as performative should provide cultural workers within and outside education with the opportunity to grapple with new questions and, as Peggy Phelan puts it, ways of mis/understanding that address and critically engage the central and most urgent social problems of our time (1993, especially "Afterword: notes on hope"). For instance, the pedagogical as performative does not merely provide a set of representations/texts that imparts knowledge to others; it also becomes a form of cultural production in which one's own identity is constantly being rewritten. In this instance, cultural politics and the authority to which it makes a claim are always rendered suspect and provisional—not to elude the burden of judgment, meaning, or commitment but to enable teachers and students alike to address "the central, urgent, and disturbing questions of a society and a culture in the most rigorous intellectual way . . . available" (Hall, 1992, p. 11).

The interrelationship among critical pedagogy, cultural studies, and the performative is, in part, exemplified through what Jacques Derrida (1994) calls "performative interpretation"—that is, "an interpretation that transforms the very thing it interprets" (p. 51). As a pedagogical practice, performative interpretation suggests that how we understand and come to know ourselves and others cannot be separated from how we represent and imagine ourselves. This is not merely an attempt to reassert the pedagogical/political significance of cultural criticism as a performative practice as much it is to reaffirm such discourses as an integral component of memory-work and the need for people to speak affirmatively and critically out of their own histories, traditions, and personal experiences. Refusing to reduce politics to the discursive or representational, performative interpretation suggests reclaiming the political as a pedagogical intervention that links cultural texts with the institutional contexts in which they are read, the material grounding of power to the historical conditions that give meaning to the places we inhabit and the futures we desire. Within this notion of pedagogical practice, the performative becomes a site of memory-work, a location and critical enactment of the stories we tell to assume our role as public intellectuals willing to make visible and challenge the grotesque inequalities and intolerable oppressions of the present moment.

A cultural politics that makes the performative pedagogical engages cultural texts within specific contexts and practical sites that register how power operates so as to make some representations, images, and symbols under certain political conditions more valued as representations of reality than others. Texts in this instance become pedagogical sites through which educators and others may labor to analyze the mechanisms that inform how a politics of representation operates within dominant regimes of meaning so as to produce and legitimate knowledge about gender, youth, race, sexuality, work, public intellectuals, pedagogy, and cultural studies. At stake here are a politics and pedagogy of representation that interrogate how texts/textuality work to make specific claims on public memory and to shape how we construct our relations to others and what it might mean to use such knowledge as part of a larger struggle to engage and transform the economic, political, and cultural life of a society.

Critical pedagogy as a theory and practice neither legitimates a romanticized notion of the cultural worker who can only function on the margins of society nor refers to a notion of teaching/performance/cultural production in which formalism or the fetish of method erases the historical, semiotic, and social dimensions of pedagogy as the active construction of responsible and risk-taking citizens. At the same time, cultural studies as a performative pedagogical practice presupposes the primacy of educators to take a stand without standing still, to affirm the pedagogical as a political practice if they are to take seriously the challenge of citizenship as a critical educational project and not abandon the radical project and practice of cultural studies. In this scenario, educators and other cultural workers must recognize the performative as that space where theory and practice seize upon power as a pedagogical practice but without having by default to engage in pedagogical or cultural terrorism. Pedagogy and other cultural practices whose aim is to inform and empower are rarely as doctrinaire or impositional as critics claim. Moreover, such criticism fails to make a distinction between what can be called a political education and a politicizing education. *Political education* means teaching students to take risks, challenge those with power, honor critical traditions, and be reflexive about how authority is used in the classroom. *A political education* provides the opportunity for students not merely to express themselves critically but to alter the structure of participation and the horizon of debate through which their identities, values, and desires are constructed. A *political education* constructs pedagogical conditions to enable students to understand how power works on them, through them, and for them in the service of constructing and expanding their roles as critical citizens. In contrast, a *politicizing education* refuses to address its own political agenda and often silences through an appeal to a specious methodology, objectivity, or notion of balance. Politicizing education polices the boundaries of the disciplines, is silent about its own cultural authority, and ignores the broader political, economic, and social forces that legitimate pedagogical practices consistent with existing forms of institutional power.

In politicizing education, the language of objectivity and methodology runs the risk of replacing an ethical discourse concerned with the political responsibility of university professors, including the issue of how they might help students identify, engage, and transform relations of power that generate the material conditions of racism, sexism, poverty, and other oppressive conditions (Graff, 1992). Lacking a political project, the role of the university intellectual is reduced to a technician engaged in formalistic rituals unconcerned with the disturbing and urgent problems that confront the larger society.

In conclusion, I want to argue that pedagogy as a critical and performative practice becomes a defining principle among all those cultural workers—journalists, performance artists, lawyers, academics, media representatives, social workers, teachers, academics, and others—who work in popular culture, composition, literary studies, architecture, and related fields. In part, this suggest the necessity for cultural workers to develop dynamic, vibrant, politically engaged, and socially relevant projects in which traditional binarisms of margin/center, unity/difference, local/national, and public/private can be reconstituted through more complex representations of identification, belonging, and community. As Paul Gilroy (1994) has argued, cultural workers need a discourse of ruptures, shifts, flows, and unsettlement, one that functions less as a politics of transgression than as part of a concerted effort to construct a broader vision of political commitment and democratic struggle. This implies a fundamental redefinition of the meaning of the educators/cultural studies workers as public intellectuals. As public intellectuals, we must begin to define ourselves, not as marginal, avant-garde figures, professionals, or academics acting alone, but as critical citizens whose collective knowledge and actions presuppose specific visions of public life, community, and moral accountability.

Crucial to this democratic project is a conception of the political that is open yet committed, respects specificity without erasing global considerations, and provides new spaces for collaborative work engaged in productive social change. Such a project, I hope, can begin to enable educators and other cultural studies scholars to rethink how pedagogy as a performative practice can be expressed through an "integrative critical language through which values, ethics, and social responsibility" (Lacy, 1995, p. 43) are fundamental to creating shared critical public spaces that engage, translate, and transform those vexing social problems that mark the current historical period. The time has come for educators and other cultural workers to join together to defend and construct those cultural sites and public spheres that are essential for a viable democracy. I hope that such a project can reformulate the relationship between cultural studies and critical pedagogy, not as new academic fashion, but as a broader effort to revitalize democratic public life.

Such a project suggests developing new discourses that are both accessible and offer concrete proposals for affecting social movements and legislation aimed at pressing social problems. This may include calling for a coherent employment policy, funding for public education, a national health insurance policy, and an adequate housing and child care program for the poor and middle class. Progressive educators and other cultural workers need to create a public language and politics—that both link academic work with broader social concerns and provide an opportunity for educators to expand their political and social relations within and outside the university.

NOTES

1. I am thinking specifically of the work of Roger Simon, Linda Brodkey, bell hooks, Lawrence Grossberg, Stanley Aronowitz, Henry A. Giroux, Peter McLaren, and David Trend.

2. My notion of transdisciplinary comes from Zavarzadeh and Morton (1992, p. 10). At issue here is neither ignoring the boundaries of discipline-based knowledge nor simply fusing different disciplines, but creating theoretical paradigms, questions, and knowledge that cannot be taken up within the policed boundaries of the existing disciplines.

3. For example, see Fish (1995), Lentricchia (1996), and Cain (1996). The literature on this debate is too extensive to sight, but a few sources stand out and are worth reading. For a

historical analysis of the battle over the politics of the curriculum and classroom pedagogy, see Levine (1966), Spacks (1996), and Giroux (1992).

4. The term *professionalist legitimation* comes from a personal correspondence with Professor Jeff Williams of East Carolina University.

REFERENCES

Bailey, D., & Hall, S. (1992). The vertigo of displacement. *Ten 8, 2*(3), 19.

Cain, W. (1996, December 13). A literary approach to literature: Why English departments should focus on close reading, not cultural studies. *Chronicle of Higher Education,* p. B4.

Derrida, J. (1994). *Specters of Marx.* New York: Routledge.

Eagleton, T. (1984). *The function of criticism.* New York: Verso.

Fish, S. (1995). *Professional correctness: Literary studies and political change.* New York: Oxford University Press.

Frith, S. (1996). *Performance rites.* Cambridge, MA: Harvard University Press.

Gilroy, P. (1994). *The black Atlantic.* Cambridge, MA: Harvard University Press.

Gilroy, P. (1996). ". . . to be real": The dissident forms of black expressive culture. In C. Ugwu, (Ed.), *Let's get it on* (pp. 12-33). Seattle, WA: Bay Press.

Giroux, H. A. (1992). *Border crossings.* New York: Routledge.

Gómez-Peña, G. (1996). *The new world border.* San Francisco: City Lights Bookstore.

Graff, G. (1992). Teaching the conflicts. In D. J. Gless & B. H. Smith (Eds.), *The politics of liberal education* (pp. 57-73). Durham, NC: Duke University Press.

Gray, H. (1996). Is cultural studies inflated? In C. Nelson & D. P. Goankar (Eds.), *Disciplinarity and dissent in cultural studies.* New York: Routledge.

Grossberg, L. (1996). Toward a genealogy of the state of cultural studies. In C. Nelson & D. P. Goankar (Eds.), *Disciplinarity and dissent in cultural studies.* New York: Routledge.

Hall, S. (1992, Spring). Race, culture, and communications: Looking backward and forward at cultural studies. *Rethinking Marxism, 5*(1), 11-18.

hooks, b. (1996). Performance practice as a site of opposition. In C. Ugwu, (Ed.), *Let's get it on* (pp. 210-221). Seattle, WA: Bay Press.

James, J. (1997). *Transcending the talented tenth: Black leaders and American intellectuals.* New York: Routledge.

Lacy, S. (1995). Introduction: Cultural pilgrimages and metaphoric journeys. In S. Lacy (Ed.), *Mapping the terrain: New genre public art* (pp. 19-47). Seattle, WA: Bay Press.

Lentricchia, F. (1996, September/October). Last will and testament of an ex-literary critic. *Lingua Franca, 6*(6), 59-67.

Levine, L. W. (1966). *The opening of the American mind.* Boston: Beacon.

Nelson, C., & Goankar, D. P. (1996). Cultural studies and the politics of disciplinarity: An introduction. In C. Nelson & D. P. Goankar (Eds.), *Disciplinarity and dissent in cultural studies.* New York: Routledge.

Osborne, P., & Segal, L. (1994). Gender as performance: An interview with Judith Butler. *Radical Philosophy, 67,* 33.

Phelan, P. (1993). *Unmarked: The politics of performance.* New York: Routledge.

Sartre, J. P. (1968). *Search for a method* (H. E. Barnes, Trans.). New York: Vintage.

Spacks, P. M. (Ed.). (1996). *Advocacy in the classroom: Problems and possibilities.* New York: St. Martin's.

Williams, R. (1967). *Communications.* New York: Barnes & Noble.

Williams, R. (1989). Adult education and social change. In *What I came to say.* London: Hutchinson-Radus.

Zavarzadeh, M., & Morton, D. (1992). Theory, pedagogy, politics: The crisis of the "subject" in the humanities. In M. Zavarzadeh & D. Morton (Eds.), *Theory, pedagogy, politics: Texts for change.* Urbana: University of Illinois Press.

CHAPTER 9

Rethinking Harmful Words

The Demise of the Critical Education Model and Discourse in the Schoolhouse

Charles N. Davis
Southern Methodist University

Central to any discussion of discourse in a civil society is an examination of the role of speech in the educational setting and the vitality of expression in an arena traditionally revered for its tolerance of minority viewpoints. Although significant differences between the college campus and the public schoolhouse have yielded differing legal protections, discourse in the classroom rightly serves as a barometer of the general condition of discourse in a society theoretically supportive of learned discussion and empirical progress.

Discourse suffers from the introduction of legal obstacles aimed at punishing speech purely on the basis of its content. As such, courts have attempted to minimize content-based restrictions in recognition of the threat such regulations pose to public discourse (Schauer, 1981). Society, meanwhile, generally has acquiesced to the legal doctrine of free expression, for it is generally tolerant, if not supportive, of minority viewpoints (Richards, 1987).

Societal changes, however, often precede legal changes, and the rapid sociological and technological transformation of the past 50 years has created a new body of legal thought that challenges the very notion of unimpeded discourse. The cornerstone of legal thought on public discourse—that "speech is free under the First Amendment, not so much because free speech is inherently good as because its suppression is inherently bad" (*People v. Huss,* 1966)—is under assault from a disparate collection of scholars, policy analysts, and lawmakers who view the power of discourse, not as the central value of speech, but as one of several equally important societal values (see, e.g., Freedman, 1996).

This shift in societal appreciation for, and toleration of, unpopular public discourse is rooted in the U.S. Supreme Court's historical treatment of speech as a two-dimensional concept; in other words, our struggles with speech begin with the Court's view that speech falls either "inside" or "outside" First Amendment protection.[1] Such an approach encourages those opposed to particular forms of discourse to attempt to place an ever-growing portion of that discourse outside the First Amendment, instead of fostering a societal appreciation for all forms of public discourse regardless of societal acceptance.

As Eric Freedman (1996) points out in a well-reasoned and thoroughly researched treatise, until the Court reconsiders its dichotomy between speech inside and outside the First Amendment, the paramount value of societal discourse will suffer from would-be censors intent on controlling its very core—its content (p. 884). The gradual demise of reasoned discourse will continue unless the Court restores to primacy the value of discourse in a democratic society.

The Court's contribution to the death of discourse can be illustrated by the legal issues surrounding freedom of expression in academia. Predictably enough, the threat to academic speech and student expression has been fueled by acts proscribed by the criminal law but seemingly triggered by speech acts. The upsurge in campus crime motivated by race, religion, or sexual preference is one of the most troubling developments in academia during recent years.[2] Labeled "hate speech," its proliferation on university campuses has sparked debate among academicians, students, and others as the institutions struggle to protect both the free speech "marketplace of ideas" integral to the university and the right of minorities to receive an education free from harassment and intimidation.[3] The central questions facing academia are both constitutional and philosophical in nature: How does the university protect the free speech so important to its educational mission while identifying and punishing only "harmful speech"? Should "hate speech" be punished at all, or should the university take a content-neutral approach to all academic expression?

The answer to both questions is tied to the Court's tortured First Amendment jurisprudence, for so long as the Court attempts to identify and regulate "harmful" speech, college and public school administrators must follow along the tainted path of analyzing speech, not on the basis of potential value of *all* discourse, but on presuppositions as to the value of particular kinds of expression. Value-based analyses of speech fly in the face of the First Amendment, which exists, not to place limits on public discourse, but to protect its uninhibited ebb and flow.

Universities have no choice but to conform to the Court's "inside-outside" view of speech, and so in an attempt to reconcile the irreconcilable values of free discourse and "civil" discourse, many universities have enacted codes prohibiting speech or conduct or both that demean persons on the basis of, for example, race, gender, religion, ancestry, or sexual orientation.[4] The constitutionality of these codes is, at best, suspect, as the courts have found them to be overbroad, content-based restrictions lacking the requisite compelling governmental interest.[5]

Some critical race theorists would move beyond simple administrative punishments to criminalization of harmful speech. Richard Delgado (1991), for example, proposes that courts create a tort for racial insults whenever a plaintiff can prove that

> [l]anguage was addressed to him or her by the defendant that was intended to demean through reference to race; that the plaintiff understood as intended to demean through reference to race; and that a reasonable person would recognize as a racial insult. (p. 137; see also Delgado & Yun, 1994)

Critical race scholars, such as Delgado, Mari Matsuda, and Charles Lawrence, have argued for an evolution in constitutional thought that would recognize the harm visited by such racially hateful speech. Among other things, they argue that such speech does not simply cause offense; it censors its targets. As a consequence, it impedes discourse and the search for truth in the marketplace of ideas (Delgado & Yun, 1994, p. 891; Lawrence, 1990; Matsuda, 1989).

The debate over harmful speech—whether on college campuses, in federally protected workplaces, or on the local basketball court—comes down to a single, inescapable conclusion: Those who would punish harmful speech by placing it beyond the parameters of First Amendment protection deny the efficacy of discourse as a moderator of social conflict. They deny the power of discourse in which society has long placed its faith as at least a partial means of addressing hateful speech. Finally, they are willing to take the awesome risk of allowing legislators and governmental regulators the freedom to delineate the bounds of discourse. By doing so, they unwittingly take a weaker position against harmful speech than civil libertarians, who encourage counterspeech and education as part of a comprehensive approach to fostering free inquiry in an atmosphere where discourse is valued, not punished (Calleros, 1995). By leaving the problem for the government to solve, this outspoken group of scholars has effectively abandoned discourse.

The reliance on speech codes to punish harmful speech in the university presents a troubling rejection of the curative effects of greater discourse. More troubling to academia, however, is that the punishment of harmful speech undermines the primary mission of the university. Here I attempt to illustrate the incompatibility between critical liberal science, with its reliance on discourse as an avenue to the truth, and university speech codes, which reject and even punish such discourse, as a case study of how the Court's outmoded jurisprudence encourages the denial of societal discourse of unpopular thought. I do not debate the constitutionality of the many hate speech codes on the books; most fail even cursory traditional First Amendment analysis. Instead I review the three historical models of education that have emerged from the leading judicial opinions on freedom of speech in the academic environment to illustrate the Court's outdated approach to academic discourse.

The first step in restoring the primacy of discourse in academia is to recognize the reliance on outdated historical values inherent in the Court's treatment of academic speech. Three distinct models emerge from the leading judicial opinions on freedom of speech in the academic environment.

The earliest model, named the *civic education model,* stresses the role of education as an instrument of community life that teaches respect for government and its rules (Post, 1991, p. 319, citing *Pugsley v. Sellmeyer,* 1923). The second model, which dominates the Court's philosophy regarding the purpose of public education, is dubbed the *democratic education model* and holds that the public school is "in most respects the cradle of our democracy" (*Adler v. Bd. of Ed.,* 1952). Support for this model is found in such cases as *Tinker v. Des Moines School District* (1969) and *Healy v. James* (1972). Finally, scholars have identified a third model, best described as the *critical education model*,[6] that views the university as an institution whose primary function is the discovery of knowledge through research and teaching ("Report on Freedom," 1975).

The critical education model requires no less than "unfettered freedom, the right to think the unthinkable, discuss the unmentionable, and challenge the unchallengeable" ("Report on Freedom," 1975, p. 337). Thus, freedom of speech is the central value of critical education, without which the university cannot fulfill its purposes. Under this model, the university is viewed, not as a repository for the values of democratic society, but as a true marketplace of ideas where any idea can be tested, rejected, or accepted regardless of its popularity. Indeed, proponents of the critical education model view the university as a marketplace within the marketplace of ideas, which must be insulated from the authoritarianism of the majority outside its walls if it is to contribute to knowledge. The critical education model protects academic speech, which encompasses scholarship and teaching, including extracurricular and intramural activities, and includes students, teachers, and university staff.

Obviously, the critical education model stands in stark contrast to the view of the university espoused by a typical university speech code providing that students be disciplined for the following:

> Racist or discriminatory comments, epithets or other expressive behavior directed at an individual . . . [that] intentionally: 1. demean the race, sex, religion, color, creed, disability, sexual orientation, national origin, ancestry or age of the individual or individuals; and 2. Create an intimidating, hostile, or demeaning environment for education, university-related work, or other university-authorized activity. (Wisc. Admin. Code @ UWS, 1990)

Indeed, adoption of the critical education model would make it virtually impossible for universities to punish harmful speech by requiring the toleration of all ideas, however uncivil or repulsive to society at large.

More important, adoption of the critical education model would signal a return of discourse as the primary social value to be protected by the law. Distinctions based on content would be eliminated, as would justifications for speech codes based on egalitarian or equality grounds. Instead, unpopular speech must be confronted by increasing the quantity and quality of discourse. The critical education model, I argue, furthers discourse as an instrument of social reform and as such must be the appropriate response if society is to right itself through speech and not through government intermediaries.

THE THREE MODELS OF EDUCATION

The Civic Education Model

In addressing the First Amendment rights of students, teachers, and other players in the educational environment, the courts have struggled to define the ultimate purpose of the classroom. In the early 1900s, the courts viewed public education as little more than an indoctrination of community values—a place where respect for authority and reverence for national symbols were handed down from the elder to the child.[7] The civic education model, as it was named, took root in a period of war and nationalist paranoia when the dominant values of democracy, God, and country were shared by the vast majority of Americans. Facing the perceived threat of insurrection from the many "un-American" groups of the era, Americans asked their schools to inoculate children from such harmful ideas. The courts supported this philosophy, regulating speech that strayed from society's interest in democratic indoctrination.

As the Arkansas Supreme Court said in a 1923 case involving a student's refusal to pledge allegiance to the American flag, "[R]espect for constituted authority and obedience thereto is an essential lesson to qualify one for the duties of citizenship, and the schoolroom is the appropriate place to teach that lesson" (*Pugsley v. Sellmeyer,* 1923). The courts clearly viewed the schoolhouse as a training facility for democratic citizens and could hardly envision a school regulation as a First Amendment violation so long as it advanced some principle of democratic self-governance, such as respect for the flag.

Use of the civic education model has generally been limited to elementary schools and high schools. In *Bethel School District No. 403 v. Fraser* (1986), the U.S. Supreme Court upheld the suspension of a high school student for delivering a speech deemed "offensive" and "indecent" by school officials. In an opinion that best summarizes the civic education model, the Court declared that the mission of a public high school includes "the inculcat[ion of] fundamental values necessary to the maintenance of a democratic political system" (p. 678). The *Fraser* Court allowed that a certain amount of freedom of expression must be available to students but reasoned that such freedom must be balanced at all times against "society's countervailing interest in teaching students the boundaries of socially appropriate behavior" (p. 681, citing *Ambach v. Norwick,* 1979). Schools, as instruments of the state, may sanction any speech that interferes with the essential lessons of the shared values of a civilized social order. Tolerance is scarcely mentioned in an opinion that dealt largely with the potential harm posed by a student's prank-filled speech at a school assembly.

The U.S. Supreme Court's deference to high school administrators was further strengthened in 1988 by *Hazelwood School District v. Kuhlmeier.* In *Hazelwood,* the Court upheld restrictions by a high school of the editorial content of a school-sponsored student newspaper, relying primarily on the "legitimate pedagogical concerns" of school administrators (p. 288). Thus, it was reasonable, in the Court's view, for the Hazelwood school system to censor a story about teen pregnancy out of fears that readers would be exposed to material inappropriate for their level of maturity.

The civic education model was never applied equally to all levels of the American education system, however; the courts recognized essential differences between speech in the grade school and in the university. In a pair of desegregation cases in 1950, *McLaurin v. Oklahoma State Regents*[8] and *Sweatt v. Painter,*[9] the U.S. Supreme Court relied on the importance of the academic marketplace of ideas at the university level to determine that segregated educational systems were unconstitutional. In *McLaurin,* the plaintiff was a black doctoral student forced to sit in a separate row in class, at a separate table at the library, and at a separate booth in the cafeteria (p. 642). In striking down these restrictions, the Court found that the student's freedom of expression, both in class and within the boundaries of campus, were "a valuable aspect of the educational process" protected by the First Amendment (p. 640).

In *Sweatt,* a case involving a black candidate denied admission to the University of Texas Law School, the Court, relying largely on the function of free speech in the academic environment, struck down the racial barriers, stating that "few students and no one who has practiced law would choose to study in an academic vacuum, removed from the interplay of ideas and the exchange of views with which the law is concerned" (p. 631). Under the civic education model, campus speech codes clearly would be permitted. *McLaurin* and *Sweatt,* however, recognize the importance of free speech in the university by holding that an equal education requires access to the academic marketplace of ideas. Courts recognize that the mission of the university is not furthered by the civic education model. Indeed, speech deemed harmful at the elementary level and even the high school level is considered integral to the discourse of a university. This distinction, based on judicial and societal views of the differences among elementary, high school, and college students, underscores the utility of free speech in higher education.

The Democratic Education Model

Another view of the educational system, closely related to the civic education model, has been described as the *democratic education model* (Post, 1991, p. 321). Unlike the civic education model, which views the academic setting as a tool for bestowing all positive social values, the democratic education model limits the public school's primary mission to the creation of democratic decision makers, fully informed and ready to participate in the public debate. Under the democratic education model, schools must refrain from indoctrination of state values and simply teach students to think for themselves. The model embraces expression that furthers the goal of self-governance but limits its protection to the discourse of public issues.

Tinker v. Des Moines School District (1969) offers the clearest example of the democratic education model advanced by the Supreme Court of the late 1960s and early 1970s. In *Tinker,* the Court ruled 7 to 2 that the First Amendment prohibited the Des Moines school system from barring students who wished to wear black arm bands to protest the war in Vietnam. In a majority opinion written by Justice Fortas, the Court said that the arm bands were a form of symbolic expression similar to "pure speech" protected by the First Amendment (p. 505). The Court said that freedom of expression must be protected in the school system because the classroom is peculiarly the marketplace of ideas. "The Nation's future depends upon leaders trained through wide exposure to that robust exchange of ideas which discovers truth out of a multitude of tongues, [rather] than through any kind of authoritative selection" (p. 512, citing *Keyishan v. Board of Regents,* 1967).

Although the *Tinker* Court rejected the civic model of education for high school students, the Court did not rule that high school students enjoy absolute freedom of expression. It concluded instead that speech can be restricted if it materially disrupts classwork or involves "substantial disorder or invasion of the rights of others." Of note is the Court's discussion of the purpose of public education as preparing students for the "sort of hazardous freedom that is the basis of our national strength and of the independence and vigor of Americans who grow up and live in this relatively permissive, often disputatious, society" (pp. 508-509). In other words, the *Tinker* Court held that so long as expression furthers the public discourse of self-governance, school administrators must tolerate it and must not dictate the content of the debate. The democratic education model was short-lived, however; as noted above, the *Hazelwood* Court returned to the civic education model for high school speech in 1988.

The Critical Education Model

The final model of education recognized by legal scholars, the *critical education model,* has been limited in application to institutions of higher learning. First identified in American jurisprudence in the Supreme Court's 1972 decision in *Healy v. James,* the critical education model has actually existed for centuries. Jonathan Rausch (1993) traces the model, which he labels "the game of liberal science," back to René Descartes' reaction to the skepticism movement championed by Michel de Montaigne in the late 16th century. Descartes sought to repudiate skepticism's guiding principle—that for man to attain certain knowledge was hopeless because man is directed by his own thoughts and prejudices—by arriving at one indisputable truth that would prove man's ability to think independently. Rauch argues that Descartes' indisputable truth—that he thought and thus knew that he existed—failed because his awareness of his own thinking proved nothing to critics (p. 44) Nevertheless, Descartes' method of skeptical criticism flourished in the late 18th and early 19th centuries. In rejecting the science of induction, which bases predictions about the future on observations of the past and present, David Hume created a "new" skepticism that grew in 19th-century academe. Instead of arguing that we have no reason to believe anything, Hume stated only that we can have no certain knowledge of the objective world. Because we all believe something, Hume argued, we must draw conclusions while simultaneously remembering that we might always be wrong (Rausch, 1993, p. 45). This shift in philosophy placed new emphasis on public discourse as a means to an end, rather than as a challenge to established thought. As such, it placed new emphasis on speech as a method of discovery and refinement of knowledge.

This "new skepticism" provided the basis for the critical model of education. Hume and other philosophers of his era provided the theoretical background for what Karl Popper (1966) has called "the principle of falsifiability." This new view of science contained two constant rules: (a) Any statement is subject to criticism, debate, and testing; and (b) the test of the statement must provide the same results for whoever tests it. Once embraced by science, the skeptical revolution gradually took root in academia, where critical education formed a community of people looking for each other's mistakes. The university became synonymous with debate, experimentation, and free speech, and academicians were granted "academic freedom" to insulate scholarship and teaching from extramural political interference (Rausch, 1993, p. 49; see also Byrne, 1989).

As described by its supporters, the critical education model would provide protection for students and professors; indeed, the model would incorporate anyone expressing anything in the university. As one academic body noted:

> [I]f a university is a place for knowledge, it is also a special kind of small society. Yet it is not primarily a fellowship, a club, a circle of friends, a replica of the civil society outside it. Without sacrificing its central purpose, it cannot make its primary and dominant value the fostering of friendship, solidarity, harmony, civility, or mutual respect. To be sure, these are important values. But it will never let these values, important as they are, override its central purpose. We value freedom of expression precisely because it provides a forum for the new, the provocative, the disturbing, and the unorthodox. Free speech is a barrier to the tyranny of authoritarian or even majority opinion as to the rightness or wrongness of particular doctrines or thoughts ("Report on Freedom," 1975, pp. 357-358)

The Critical Education Model: Case Law

The promise of the critical education model is frustrated by the courts' piecemeal approach to academic speech cases. American courts have given constitutional protection to only certain aspects of campus speech, applying the critical education model only as a variable in balancing conflicting interests, rather than as the embodiment of a model of legal protection for university work. The leading judicial pronouncements on university speech view the critical education model as providing only protection for the professional autonomy of the individual professor when engaging in academic work within the university. They ignore the larger context of critical education as a model of legal protection that views the university as an institution whose primary function is to discover and disseminate knowledge and that prizes discourse as the conduit among the university, its students, and society at large.

The few cases that embrace the critical education model demonstrate its potential as a system of legal protection for freedom of expression in the university. The first discussion of the critical education model appears in 1957 in *Sweezy v. New Hampshire,* in which the Court reversed the conviction of Marxist economist Paul Sweezy for refusing to answer several questions asked by the state attorney general as part of an investigation of "subversive persons" (p. 235). Although Chief Justice Warren's plurality opinion reversed the conviction under procedural grounds, the Court suggested for the first time that academic freedom was protected by the First Amendment:

> The essentiality of freedom in the community of American universities is almost self-evident. No one should underestimate the vital role in a democracy that is played by those who guide and train our youth. To impose any strait jacket upon the intellectual leaders in our colleges and universities would imperil the future of our Nation. . . . Scholarship cannot flourish in an atmosphere of suspicion and distrust. Teachers and students must always remain free to inquire, to study and to evaluate, to gain new maturity and understanding; otherwise our civilization will stagnate and die. (p. 266, Frankfurter, concurring)

Justice Frankfurter's concurring opinion went even further, arguing that academic "thought and action are presumptively immune from inquisition by political authority" (p. 262). Frankfurter reasoned that because academic freedom—for faculty and students—is a positive constitutional right, the government would have to show a compelling interest to question the content of any expression in the university. The plurality opinion, however, declined to ground its opinion on a positive right of academic freedom, leaving lower courts and university administrators with little guidance as to the protections afforded faculty members.

The ambiguity of the *Sweezy* decision reemerged 2 years later in the Court's decision in *Barenblatt v. United States* (1959), affirming the conviction of an academic for criminal contempt for refusing to respond to questions from a congressional committee investigating Communist activities at the University of Michigan. *Barenblatt* was a defeat for university freedom of expression and is distinguishable from *Sweezy* only because it did not involve teaching or writing. Nevertheless, as one commentator has noted, *Barenblatt*'s impact on subsequent cases has been minimal because the Court ignored it in *Keyishan v. Board of Regents* (1967; see also Byrne, 1989).

In *Keyishan,* the Court recognized the principles of critical education in protecting a group of University of Buffalo faculty who had challenged a state statute requiring them to sign loyalty certificates stating they were not Communists (pp. 591-592). The Supreme Court, in striking down the statute, noted that critical education has strong ties to the marketplace of ideas traditionally discussed in First Amendment theory: "The Nation's future depends upon leaders trained through wide exposure to that robust exchange of ideas which discovers truth 'out of a multitude of tongues, rather than through any kind of authoritative selection'" (p. 603, citing *United States v. Associated Press,* 1943). The *Keyishan* Court rejected the opportunity to define the constitutional parameters of academic freedom and limited its ruling to the loyalty oath statute at bar, holding that regulations affecting academic speech must be sufficiently clear so as not to infringe on constitutional freedoms. Its ringing endorsement of academic freedom and the critical education model, however, is noteworthy. The Court predicated its decision on the effect that a loyalty oath would have on the discussion of unpopular or even radical political theory and concluded that the threat of communism was not a compelling enough reason to restrict political discourse on campus. In fact, the Court noted that its decision was based on a belief that such discourse was an invaluable component of the educational process. In short, the Court gave public discourse primacy over the potential effects of such discourse—a true example of the critical education model at work in the courts.

Following *Keyishan,* the critical education model developed solely through lower court opinions. *Keyishan* and *Sweezy* are credited with effectively ending the intrusion of non-academic governmental officials to prescribe political authoritarianism in university teaching and research (see Byrne, 1989, p. 298), but the lack of a comprehensive model for protection of academic speech has contributed to the rise of academic speech codes and other threats to freedom of expression in the university. Some commentators predicted, in the wake of *Keyishan,* that the Court would soon formally establish a constitutional status for academic speech, but the cases involving speech codes themselves indicate a judiciary unwilling to cast such restrictions in broad constitutional doctrine, choosing instead to attack the regulations on the more narrow grounds of overbreadth and vagueness ("Developments in the Law," 1968). The continued threat of academic speech codes demands an answer to this pressing question, and the critical education model provides an answer unique to the university setting.

THE CRITICAL EDUCATION MODEL REVISITED

A pair of recent federal district court cases underscore the potential for an independent model of free expression for universities. In each instance, the court rejected powerful societal interests in preventing harmful words in favor of discourse deemed essential to the university's educational mission. The cases merit discussion not only because they mark the rebirth of the critical education model but also because they apply the model to the topic at hand: academic speech codes.

Doe v. University of Michigan

In *Doe v. University of Michigan* (1989), the United States District Court for the Eastern District of Michigan became the first court to apply the First Amendment to an academic speech code, striking down the University of Michigan's hate speech code as violative of the First Amendment rights of university students and faculty. Like many campuses across the nation, the University of Michigan had enacted a speech code in response to a series of racist incidents.[10] The policy prohibited in academic buildings any expression that "stigmatizes or victimizes an individual" on the basis of race, ethnicity, religion, gender, sexual preference, and a list of other sensitivities, and that either "threatens or forseeably interferes with a student's education or other campus-related activities."[11] Offenders faced sanctions ranging from mandatory attendance in special classes to expulsion (p. 857). Doe, a graduate student in biopsychology, filed suit seeking to enjoin enforcement of the policy and arguing that his right to discuss openly certain controversial theories positing biologically based differences between sexes and races was impermissibly chilled by the policy.

The court's opinion begins with a comparison of the state's broad powers under the First Amendment to regulate discriminatory conduct with the narrow scope of permissible regulation of "so-called pure speech" (p. 861-862). Beyond the limited categories of unprotected speech—fighting words and libel—the court held that the university may not restrict speech on the basis of its content.

The court stated that some racial epithets clearly fall into the category of "fighting words" and might constitute group libel but found that the policy was not limited to such utterances. Reviewing three complaints against students under the policy, the court held that the university's failure to dismiss immediately each complaint proved that the policy was overbroad because each incident involved classroom discussions of an intellectual nature (p. 866). Two incidents involved allegedly antigay remarks; the third involved an allegedly racist remark. In one case, the university administrator forwarded the complaint to a hearing panel, which cleared the accused student. In the other cases, the students were, respectively, forced to apologize and to attend a "gay rap session." The court concluded that "the manner in which these three complaints were handled demonstrated that the University considered serious comments made in the context of classroom discussion to be sanctionable under the Policy." Thus, the court found the policy overbroad because it ignored both the First Amendment protections afforded the students and the context in which the comments were made. The court also declared the policy unconstitutionally vague, citing the university's reliance on "terms that elude precise definition" such as *stigmatize* and *victimize* (p. 867).

Although the court struck down the speech code on overbreadth and vagueness grounds, its adoption of the critical education model in the university setting drove its rationale. Most important is the court's recognition of the chilling effect of the Michigan policy. Although critical of the vague language used by the university, the court stated that if the plain language of the policy were all it had to review, Doe might have failed to demonstrate a reasonable probability that the policy endangered freedom of expression (p. 858). Instead, the court based its decision on the experiences of those students who had been penalized under the policy, and it concluded that enforcement of the policy clashed with the educational mission of the university by encouraging self-censorship in classroom discussions. By focusing on the practical effects of the policy instead of analyzing the university's intent in drafting the restrictions, the court was able to compare the policy's actual enforcement with the First Amendment principles that "acquire a special significance in the University setting, where the free and unfettered interplay of competing views is essential to the institution's educational mission" (p. 863, citing *Keyishan,* 1967). Citing *Keyishan* (1967), *Sweezy* (1957), and *Papish* (1973), the court embraced the broader doctrine of free speech embodied by the critical education model.

Of critical importance to the court was the impact on discourse in the classroom. By focusing primarily on the secondary effect—self-censorship and overbreadth—the court demonstrated the real danger of such micromanagement of speech. That students engaged in what their professors later described under oath as legitimate classroom discussions could be subject to administrative punishment by the university serves as prima facie evidence of a government-imposed limit on academic discourse.

UWM Post v. Board of Regents
of the University of Wisconsin

Despite their modern appearance, academic speech codes present no new First Amendment questions. In fact, courts addressing the codes have failed to address doctrinal issues because the cases lack the legal complexity of, say, a broadcast regulation case involving new media technologies or a freedom of religion debate involving the public schools. Content-based restrictions on speech make for brief judicial opinions. This limits the expansion of the critical education model, but its judicial endorsement is clear.

In 1991, the United States District Court for the Eastern District of Wisconsin provided the most recent judicial endorsement of the critical education model in striking down the University of Wisconsin's hate speech code in *UWM Post v. Board of Regents of the University of Wisconsin.*

Like the University of Michigan, the University of Wisconsin drafted its speech code in response to a series of racially motivated campus incidents (p. 1164). With the help of noted hate speech expert University of Wisconsin-Madison law professor Richard Delgado, the university drafted and approved the UW Rule, a detailed policy declaration prohibiting any type of expressive behavior meeting the following criteria:

(1) racist or discriminatory comments, epithets or other expressive behavior;

(2) directed at an individual;

(3) demeaning the race, sex, religion, color, creed, disability, sexual orientation, national origin, ancestry or age of the individual addressed;

(4) and creating an intimidating, hostile or demeaning environment for education, university-related work or other university-authorized activity (Wisc. Admin. Code @ UWS 17.06[2])

In addition to the rule, the university circulated a brochure explaining the rule and providing examples of situations where the rule would apply (p. 1166). In March 1990, several plaintiffs, including the UWM Post and several students punished under the UW Rule, filed suit seeking to enjoin enforcement of the rule and to vacate disciplinary actions previously taken against the plaintiffs under the rule (p. 1163). The plaintiffs argued that the UW Rule was unconstitutionally vague and overbroad. The court began its discussion by determining whether the speech regulated by the UW Rule falls within the fighting words doctrine, as argued by the university. Reviewing the U.S. Supreme Court's decisions under the doctrine, the district court found that the doctrine had been narrowed substantially through the years to include only words that tend to incite an immediate breach of the peace. Because the court found that the elements of the UW Rule do not require that the regulated speech, by its very utterance, tends to incite violent reaction, it held that the rule went beyond the scope of the fighting words doctrine (p. 1171).

The court likewise rejected the university's argument that *Chaplinsky* (1942) requires lower courts to balance the social value of offensive speech with the values in favor of restriction, ruling that such balancing is appropriate only in cases involving content-neutral restrictions. Nevertheless, the court engaged in a balancing test, if only to show that even under the balancing test proposed by the university the rule is unconstitutional. The court's adoption of the critical education model emerges largely through the discussion of the benefits of allowing the speech regulated by the UW Rule. The court reasoned that, by restricting speech as lacking social value, the university rejected the marketplace of ideas in favor of dominant social values (p. 1176). Although it agreed that increasing campus diversity and toleration is a noble ideal, the court found that the UW Rule "does as much to hurt diversity on Wisconsin campuses as it does to help it" by limiting the diversity of ideas among students. Because the UW Rule failed under both the fighting words and the university's proposed balancing test, the court found the rule overbroad and therefore in violation of the First Amendment.

As in *Doe* (1989), the court's decision was based on constitutional categorization, and not on the critical education model, but the court's view of the educational mission of the university was strikingly similar to earlier decisions adopting the model. Taken together, *Doe* and *UWM Post* illustrate the potential for an independent model of First Amendment protection for academic speech. Given the current makeup of the U.S. Supreme Court, however, the model is more likely to develop in future lower court decisions. For this reason, *Doe* and *UWM Post* provide the best guidance for colleges and universities looking to protect First Amendment principles from those who would censor harmful speech.

The Future of Speech Codes in the Critical Education Model

The constitutional strength of the critical education model is more than simply doctrinal; it contains a realistic hope in social change and faith in the democratic process of change through discourse. True, adoption of the critical education model would greatly restrict the ability of universities to punish harmful speech, but more important it would mark a return to discourse on campus, an important step toward a community of scholars bound by a commitment to toleration, which I believe is the core concept of academic inquiry.

Critical education would require the toleration of all other ideas; so, it appears, would the Supreme Court. Any future speech code must limit its scope to those unprotected classes of speech outlined by the Court, avoiding vague and overbroad terms such as *stigmatize, intimidate,* and *hostile.* By restricting only expressive behavior that fits within the Supreme Court's narrow class of unprotected speech, universities would not only adhere to judicial pronouncements but also involuntarily adopt the critical education model, for the constitutional limits on speech codes coexist with the philosophical ideals of critical education.

Indeed, critical education might require universities to refrain from promulgating any form of academic speech code. Although limits on harmful speech are allowable under the First Amendment, they may be prohibited by the critical education model. The goal of critical education differs from traditional First Amendment theory in several respects. For example, self-governance and the discussion of public issues are central themes of the First Amendment literature; however, they are but by-products of the critical education model. The key value in critical education is the pursuit of truth, rather than the preparation of autonomous citizens. As Thomas Emerson (1970) noted, such a pursuit must remain free of values to achieve its goals (p. 432). Any academic speech code seemingly would inject artificial civil values into the marketplace. Instead, the critical education model demands that universities create an atmosphere of unbounded, value-free discourse where any idea, no matter how repulsive, can be tested by the rough-and-tumble of Popper's (1966) "falsifiability."

Those who would punish harmful speech have an entirely different view of the university. They long for an "unintimidating" academic workplace where civility and decorum rule the day. The educational system—and indeed, any true system protective of free discourse—does not work that way. Rausch's (1993) description of liberal science perhaps best describes the inherent conflict between the attainment of knowledge and academic speech codes:

> Somehow the idea has grown up that "liberal" means "nice," that the liberal intellectual system fosters sensitivity, toleration, self-esteem, the rejection of prejudice and bias. That impression is misguided. The truth is that liberal science demands discipline as well as license, and to those who reject or flout its rules, it can be cruel. It excludes and restricts as well as tolerates. It thrives on prejudice no less than on cool detachment. It does not give a damn about your feelings and happily tramples them in the name of finding truth. It allows and—here we should be honest—sometimes encourages offense. To advance knowledge, we must all sometimes suffer. Worse than that, we must inflict suffering on others. (p. 19)

As for harmful speech, the critical education model demands its expression so that the proponents of racism, sexism, and other abhorrent philosophies can be challenged and ultimately defeated in the game of science. No venue in American society is better suited for this contest than the university: Would we rather repress such expression until its proponents have graduated and entered the workforce? Should we teach the toleration of only limited types of expression while pretending to engage in the process of liberal science? Until the university, and the courts that protect its expressive activities, embraces the critical education model, true tolerance is an impossible goal. The critical education model is the only system of freedom of expression that protects each tenet of academic speech outlined by Justice Frankfurter in *Sweezy* (1957): "to determine for itself on academic grounds who may teach, what may be taught, how it shall be taught, and who may be admitted to study" (p. 263). Anything less than absolute toleration endangers each of these four cornerstone ideals.

THE FUTURE OF PUBLIC DISCOURSE

We can, of course, reject the notion that public discourse changes public attitudes or that public attitudes manifest themselves in public policy. But we must first admit that rejecting the power of discourse means embracing the power of governmental intervention, with its many vagaries of implementation and enforcement. Speech codes and other governmentally created limits on public discourse may or may not bring about the magical changes in public viewpoints that their creators wish to accomplish. Legal change may encourage political change, but in a democracy the law is insufficient to force political change.

In a democratic society, fashioning permanent social reform is impossible. The thoughts and passions of the minority viewpoint—no matter how unacceptable to the majority—will not change by decree of law. The legal creation of reproductive choice (*Roe v. Wade,* 1972) and of educational equality certainly did not create unanimity of discourse; their social acceptance today is a product, not of law, but of social change brought about by vigorous, often rancorous political discourse.

The future promises even greater challenges to public discourse. The rapid proliferation of new media technologies—which shows no signs of slowing—means that tying the degree of protection to the identity of the medium will necessarily promote further confusion as to speech inside and outside First Amendment protection (Freedman, 1996, pp. 956-967). History shows that each new medium is seen at first as uniquely dangerous and therefore a new and uniquely appropriate target of censors. The speech codes of the 1980s have given way to the current hysteria surrounding the viewing of computer technology messages even remotely related to sexuality (Lewis, 1996).

Just as with speech codes, we see the widespread fear that current First Amendment law is inadequate to deal with emerging problems. This repetitive pattern of legal response to new forms of communication reflects the age-old rejection of discourse in favor of governmental intervention. The issues differ only with regard to content—in one instance, hate speech; in the other, sexuality—but the rejection of discourse is no less obvious.

The danger in both instances is the ability of the courts to declare certain forms of expression "outside" the First Amendment. This provides those who reject discourse as a means of social change the avenue to impose otherwise impermissible regulations on discourse in which the public has the highest degree of interest simply because they disagree with the speaker (Freedman, 1996, p. 964).

This is unjustifiable, but it represents the First Amendment working exactly as the courts have interpreted it to date. As the rapid pace of modern communications works to shorten the interval between speakers, discourse will present new challenges to this unworkable system. The question whether speech falls inside or outside the First Amendment will gradually yield to the inevitable recognition that the First Amendment exists to further the will of the people. The will of the people, in turn, will be reflected through instantaneous communications that the law is not equipped to challenge.

Discourse on university campuses benefits from this realization. The scholarship surrounding the constitutionality of hate speech codes continues with lively debate from both camps, but reality demonstrates that speech codes face severe constitutional limits. The critical education model serves as a useful starting point if we are to agree that discourse, and not governmental intervention, is the ultimate answer.

My position, then, is that neither side of the speech code debate benefits from the rejection of discourse. Counterspeech may or may not be wholly effective in removing the stubborn vestiges of racism and bigotry from college campuses, but neither will the law. By rejecting a legal response to the problem, I turn to the critical education model as a way to restore the notion of unfettered discourse to primacy in the university. It is flawless in its simplicity, and for that it will suffer at the hands of those who reject discourse. Yet, it represents the only constitutionally viable solution to the problem in an era of increasing advances in our ability to disseminate communicative messages, not just on our campuses, but across the globe.

NOTES

1. See, for example, *Chaplinsky v. New Hampshire,* 315 U.S. 568 (1942) ("fighting words" fall outside the First Amendment's protections); *Beauharnais v. Illinois,* 343 U.S. 250 (1952) (group libel is a form of speech outside First Amendment protection).

2. In recent years, more than 250 American universities have reported incidents of bigotry, from racism to anti-Semitism to sexism to homophobia. Nearly one million students are reportedly victimized by bigotry annually (Riccio, 1991).

3. A tremendous amount of scholarship details the hate speech issue and attempts to regulate its use on college campuses. See Smith (1995), Yardley (1991), Delgado (1991), and Riccio (1991).

4. More than 200 universities have enacted speech codes. See Strossen, N. (1990). Regulating hate speech on campus: A modest proposal? *Duke University Law Journal,* pp. 541-543.

5. At least two university speech codes, however, have been struck down by the courts as unconstitutional. See *Doe v. University of Michigan,* (E.D. Mich., 1989) and *UWM Post v. Board of Regents of Wisconsin,* (E.D. Wisc., 1991). Likewise, in 1990, the University of Connecticut's regulations were severely curtailed in a court-approved lawsuit settlement from a suit brought by a student kicked out of her dorm for a hate-speech offense.

6. Post (1991) identifies the critical education model as the only judicial doctrine fully protecting the mission of liberal science in the university. I agree with Post but take issue with the scope of his model.

7. For an excellent discussion of the history of free speech during this era, see Chaffee (1954).

8. 339 U.S. 637 (1950) (holding that the Fourteenth Amendment prohibits the segregation of an enrolled graduate student by a state university based on race).

9. 339 U.S. 629 (1950) (holding that a black student may not be denied admission at the University of Texas Law School because the legal education at the black law school was not substantially equal).

10. The university cited several incidents of racist speech, including one in which a flyer declared "open season" on blacks, whom it called "saucer lips, porch monkeys and jigaboos" (*Doe v. University of Michigan,* p. 854).

11. The policy exempted student publications and behavior in dormitories, limiting its application only to academic buildings.

CASES CITED

Adler v. Bd. of Ed., 342 U.S. 485 (1952).
Ambach v. Norwick, 441 U.S. 68 (1979).
Barenblatt v. United States, 360 U.S. 109 (1959).
Beauharnais v. Illinois, 343 U.S. 250 (1952).
Bethel School District No. 403 v. Fraser, 478 U.S. 675 (1986).
Chaplinsky v. New Hampshire, 315 U.S. 568 (1942).
Doe v. University of Michigan, 721 F.Supp. 852 (E.D. Mich. 1989).
Hazelwood School District v. Kuhlmeier, 484 U.S. 260 (1988).
Healy v. James, 408 U.S. 169 (1972).
Keyishan v. Board of Regents, 385 U.S. 589 (1967).
McLaurin v. Oklahoma State Regents, 339 U.S. 637 (1950).
Papish, 410 U.S. 667 (1973).
People v. Huss, 241 Cal. App. 2d 361 (1966).
Pugsley v. Sellmeyer, 158 Ark. 247, 253 (1923).
Roe v. Wade, 410 U.S. 113 (1972).
Sweatt v. Painter, 339 U.S. 629 (1950).
Sweezy v. New Hampshire, 354 U.S. 234 (1957).
Tinker v. Des Moines School District, 393 U.S. 503 (1969).
United States v. Associated Press, 52 F.Supp. 362 (S.D.N.Y. 1943).
UWM Post v. Board of Regents of Wisconsin, 774 F.Supp. 1163 (E.D. Wisc. 1991).

INFLUENTIAL RELATED CASES

Gooding v. Wilson, 405 U.S. 518 (1972).
Hammond v. Brown, 323 F.Supp. 326 (N.D. Ohio 1971).
Lewis v. City of New Orleans, 415 U.S. 130 (1974).
Texas v. Johnson, 491 U.S. 397 (1989).
White v. Davis, 13 Cal. 3d 757 (1975).

REFERENCES

Byrne, J. P. (1989). Academic freedom: A special concern of the First Amendment. *Yale University Law Journal*, p. 251.

Calleros, C. (1995, Winter). Paternalism, counterspeech, and campus hate-speech codes: A reply to Delgado and Yun. *Arizona State University Law Journal, 27*, 1249.

Chaffee, Z. (1969). Freedom of speech in wartime. In Z. Chaffee (1921), *Freedom of speech in the United States* (pp. 24-31). New York: Harcourt Brace.

Delgado, R. (1991). Campus antiracism rules: Constitutional narratives in collision. *Northwestern University Law Review, 82*, C2.

Delgado, R., & Yun, D. (1994). The neoconservative case against hate-speech regulation: Lively, D'Souza, Gates, Carter, and the Toughlove crowd. *Vanderbilt University Law Review, 47*, 1807.

Developments in the law: Academic freedom. (1968). *Harvard Law Review, 81*, 1045, 1051.

Emerson, T. (1970). *The system of free expression*. New York: Vintage.

Freedman, E. M. (1996). A lot more comes into focus when you remove the lens cap. *Iowa Law Review, 81*, 956-967.

Lawrence, C. (1990). If he hollers let him go: Regulating racist speech on campus. *Duke University Law Journal*, p. 431.

Lewis, P. (1996, January 2). About freedom of the virtual press. *New York Times*, p. 14.

Matsuda, M. (1989). Public response to racist speech: Considering the victim's story. *University of Michigan Law Review, 87*, 2320.

Popper, K. (1966). *The open society and its enemies*. Chicago: University of Chicago Press.

Post, R. (1991). Democracy, racist speech, and the First Amendment. *William & Mary Law Review, 32*, 267.

Rausch, J. (1993). *Kindly inquisitors: The new attacks on free thought*. Chicago: University of Chicago Press.

Report on freedom of expression at Yale. (1975). *Human Rights Journal, 4*, 357.

Riccio, R. (1991, September 30). Free speech v. Freedom from bigotry: A look at university speech codes. *New York Law Journal*, p. 1.

Richards, D. A. J. (1987). Free speech and obscenity law: Toward a moral theory of the First Amendment. *University of Pennsylvania Law Review, 123*, 45.

Schauer, F. (1981). Categories and the First Amendment: A play in three acts. *Vanderbilt University Law Review, 34*, 343.

Smith, S. (1995). There's such a thing as free speech. In R. K. Whillock & D. Slayden (Eds.), *Hate speech* (pp. 226-266). Thousand Oaks, CA: Sage.

Whillock, R., & Slayden, D. (1995). *Hate speech*. Thousand Oaks, CA: Sage.

Wisconsin Administrative Code @ UWS 17.06 (2) 1990.

Yardley, R. (1991, February 18). At Brown, a hard lesson in free speech. *Washington Post*, p. C2.

PART IV

MASTER AND SLAVE: POPULAR MEDIA AND THE SHAPING OF BEHAVIOR

From role models to gatekeepers, theories that explain how popular media shape public images are useful, attempting to map how people are affected by what they see and hear. One argument put forth in this book is that the relationship between the producers of mass-mediated messages and the public that attends to those messages often is one of master to slave. In a tangible way, it is about ownership, domination, and profit. The media are not purely expressive but also directed. Messages are formulated, media personalities selected, and images chosen expressly because they match the desires and needs (but only those the media are capable of delivering) of the targeted population. The media give the people what they think they want from a limited and packaged array of selections and use that desire to further their own economic/political/social ends.

This is not a conspiracy argument. We do not mean to imply one locus of control or that "the media" is a single entity. Media images and the treatment given them are often contradictory, spurious, thoughtless, and produced without regard for specific anticipated effects. But that does not mean their efforts are without effects. Nor does it mean there is never an agenda or a point of view taken and expressed.

Media expressions are made profitable by fitting the messages to the demographics. Popular films are produced for their appeal to the paying

public. Drawing crowds to whom products can be sold supports the television industry. Rockers and rappers pull and hold a following by merchan-
dising their music, images, messages, and styles. The profit motive is strong
and possibly central.

Equally powerful is the innocuous ways we are drawn into sympathy for
various points of view. In Chapter 10, David Whillock helps us understand
what we absorb while sitting in Plato's modern caves—the movie theaters.
Whillock argues that "cinema, like the computer, has repositioned our
discourse in such a way as to change our concept of reality." It is not reality
that we see, nor reality that matters, but rather the images of reality thrown
by the firelike shadows on the wall. And yet those shadows can become
public reality although they are not realities made on any judgment scheme.
They are effective primarily because when we watch movies, we anticipate
being entertained. We relax; we let down our defenses; and we suspend our
disbelief, allowing ourselves to be seduced by images that reach deep into
our psyches to create "real" worlds out of shadows. Using chaos theory,
Whillock explains how this seduction takes place and how, as a result of
these hyperreal images, we are living in a world where images no longer
help us mediate reality: We have stopped participating in the discourse
expressed in the images.

On the opposite end of the spectrum, in Chapter 11, Glenn Geiser-Getz
explores a unique communication phenomenon by examining the shock
rock genre. Using the group GWAR as his example, Geiser-Getz examines
a culture that fully accepts the premise of this text: that real exchange is
nullified in the contemporary communications environment. For these
modern critics, communication is flaccid. The highly commercialized, ever
tender, and ingratiating messages are ruses. He argues that "the many
technologies of communication promoted today do not necessarily improve genuine communication, the kind of interaction that creates,
strengthens, and maintains healthy communities, identities, and relationships." Identities are consumer choices assumed and maintained or exchanged with today's styles and projected through ritualized performances.
Geiser-Getz argues that shock rock helps us understand that traditional
discourse has failed and that these performers are finding a means of
expression that is more real, even if it is more violent and offensive.

The final chapter of the book examines one of the newest and most hyped
mediums—the Internet. In Chapter 12, David Slayden investigates the
actual communication taking place within a medium that still exists largely
as possibility, using words, images, and performances as a means to
establish social identity. This was the medium touted as the salvation of

discourse, the one that would help people reconnect, that would provide a forum for public dialogue now lost in a world too large and too hurried to meet in person in some physical space. This chapter serves as both a summarizing of the issues addressed in this book and a social commentary, scrutinizing the claims and possibilities expressed about this new, virtual world that dispossesses the old, physical one. Discourse on and about the Internet resides primarily in imagined spheres, largely as a "means of self-indulgence and escape, a theme park of the mind." The Internet in its current manifestation presents a pseudo-solution to real problems of discourse.

So much of our performance and image-oriented culture depends on simulated experiences far removed from physical reality. Our images of ourselves are distorted, disembodied, with control elusive and often imagined. All three chapters in this section essentially grapple with the same enduring questions about our attempts at (linguistic) control over an unrestrained world. Although we would like to assert that people are (a) in command of their responses to, and uses of, mass-mediated images; (b) capable of sorting through the morass of information to make wise, responsible, and self-directed choices; and (c) not easily led, we cannot find substantial, encouraging evidence to support such conclusions. Instead, we find a flood of images and pseudo-discourse dominating a society too overworked and too saturated with compensating noise and entertainment to pause, reflect on, and respond mindfully to, much less be aware of, the absence of discourse in existing and new media.

CHAPTER 10

Negotiable Realities

Chaotic Attractors of Our Understanding

David Everett Whillock
Texas Christian University

We have to consciously interact with the creation of the future in order for it to be other than it was.

—Ralph Abraham, cited in Rushkoff (1994)

In her song "Carnival," Natalie Merchant sings of confusion. Should she accept what her eyes have told her, or should she disavow this created and inaccurate complex existence that surrounds her? As she walks the streets of an illusion, her sense of reality is shaken and consistently questioned.

In the film *JFK,* director Oliver Stone creates a scenario to explain the cause of the president's assasination, one in which history and reality have no influence. Stone's *JFK* uses historical moments, re-created to give cause to his tragedy. This (re)creation of the event allows the viewers to choose between what is known and what is conjecture. This choice creates an illusion that we as an audience, like Natalie Merchant, either accept or disavow, creating our own realities in a postmodern malaise.

Within the context of discourse on any subject, we are constantly confronted with what chaos theory has defined as "attractors." These attractors are points of position and, in essence, comfort. Just as a pendulum swings from one point to another, these attractors draw the action of an event toward them. In discourse, these attractors allow us to find points of known reference and comfort; within the attractors, we find our voice.

One concern of this chapter is to determine what these attractors are in a postmodern world and how these attractors are both created and supported in a world where discourse of any subject is constantly created through new methods, with real communication becoming less and less. Indeed, the conflict of double attractors exacerbates this loss of communication.

ATTRACTORS IN CHAOS THEORY

An old adage says that if a butterfly flaps its wings in China, there will be earthquakes in the United States. In chaos theory, the "butterfly effect" is named *sensitive dependence on initial conditions.* For James Gleick (1987), these are "tiny differences of input [that] could quickly become overwhelming differences in output" (p. 8). Stephen Kellert (1993), in his discussion of the effect, expands on this by stating that "a dynamical system that exhibits system dependence on initial conditions will produce markedly different solutions for two specifications of initial states that are initially very close together" (p. 12). Cinematic discourse depends on a dynamic system that exhibits this dependence on a structured system.

The poststudio system in Hollywood is heavily dependent on formula presentation to receive funding. This formula in film is discussed in terms of genre, specifically in adherence to, or deviation from, a generic form. For instance, *Pulp Fiction* developed a new formula that contains a vein of parody on the 1940s film noir. Films after *Pulp Fiction* take as their conventions elements presented in director Quentin Tarrantino's film. Another generic formula that is replicated in every national cinema is the historical/biographical film. Within these narratives, fact plays an essential role in presentation. The "believability" of the film is an important issue in this genre presentation. When the initial condition is the historical fact of which both a screenplay and the historical literature are written, the competing "truths" of this factual event allow the viewer markedly different solutions. For instance, the premise behind Oliver Stone's *JFK* is clear in its assertion that President Kennedy was going to "pull out" of Vietnam, leaving the military-industrial complex to fend for itself. The end result of this impact, as indicated by the film, would severely disrupt control of big business and curtail the power of the military.

For artistic reasons, reality is often a casualty of such plot structures. As a historical fact, Kennedy did indeed withdraw 16,000 advisors located in Vietnam—as Kennedy's U.S. Secretary of Defense Robert McNamara and others have written—to be replaced not only by advisors and observers but also by members of Kennedy's elite force, the Green Berets. Before he could make the exchange, Kennedy was assassinated, giving artistic license to those who wish to revise history. Stone's use of this historical fact as a way of revising history becomes, for the viewers who are unaware or too young to remember the event, *history* itself. Thus, those who are aware of the event in question will come to a markedly different solution than those who have been influenced by Stone's film. Using Kellert's discussion, the initial state of history, and the revised historical account of Stone, the effect of dissimilarity begins to unravel the true discourse of the event.

Because of its style and recent method of discourse—film and its visual presence—new histories are developed and understood as truth. This concept of *attractors* and their impact on a nonlinear dynamic, such as history,[1] is a major component of chaos theory and is essential in the understanding of how film revises and redefines history.

According to chaos theory (Briggs & Peat, 1989), an *attractor* is "a region of phase space which exerts a *magnetic* appeal for a system, seemingly pulling the system toward it" (p. 36).[2] These attractors magnify sources of crisis within a system. Each dynamic system will pull toward an attractor for creating and maintaining stability. Indeed, other authors of the theory contend that, within chaos, a simplified system exists that has, contrary to its name, stability and predictability (see Cohen & Stewart, 1994; Lewin, 1992). Although this debate deserves attention, this chapter does not expand on this discourse within chaos theory; rather, the discussion here is of a "dynamic system" that concerns the argument about how communication plays a crucial role.

As discussed earlier, a *dynamic system* is a nonlinear system and is more focused on feedback loops than causality. According to Briggs and Peat (1989), the modelers for system dynamics "try to identify the written and mental concepts the people in the organization are using when they do their work, the organization's rules and policies, the actual behavior of the people in the organizational setting, the organizational structure, its purpose" (p. 176). The goal of the modeler is to see what kind of feedback loops the elements form within the system. In most communication models, the element of feedback is essential. Indeed, feedback may influence or change the communication process within the encoder or decoder of the communication model.

In chaos theory, the study of these loops helps develop a list of systems' principles. According to Briggs and Peat (1989), these principles include the following: (a) To permanently change a system, you have to change its structure; (b) any given system has very few high-leverage points where significant change can effect the behavior of the system; and (c) the more complex the system, the farther away cause and effect are from each other (p. 177).

When investigating such a complex dynamic system as culture, the principles above become more than theory. Even though the principles themselves seem simplistic, the application of those principles helps us understand how attractors found in chaos theory are influenced and influence those same principles. The complexity of this influence depends on a variety of variables that are not simply a list of actions and reactions to events. What happens within a dynamic system that has two equally compelling attractors that have, from a surface level, indications of similarity yet are two distinctive and competing positions? In a dynamic system, such as culture, how do these attractors change behaviors and eventually the concept of reality?

As an art form, film has played an essential role in shaping our concepts of reality. From its inception, cinema has changed the way we have perceived our existence. It is said that when Louis Lumiere first projected a film of a train coming into a Paris station, the patrons of this cinema ran screaming out of the building, afraid of being run over. Truth or legend, the point of the story is compelling. The impact of media as a feedback loop and as an attractor has, for the most part, been very successful and remains a vital part of how we invent and interpret the world in which we live.

Where is the danger? With a postmodern society, do we know the difference between what is real and what is fabricated? Film theorists for years have dealt with this question and have published widely on what cinema really means.

Few theorists have examined the impact of film as an elemental loop in the change of perception—not what we perceive, but *how* we perceive. In this chapter, I argue that cinema, like the computer, has repositioned our discourse in such a way as to change our concept of reality. This position is emphasized by Kevin Robins (1996), who states that we "live in a world where images proliferate independently from meaning and references in the real world. Our modern existence is increasingly one of interaction and negotiation with images and simulations which no longer serve to mediate reality" (p. 44). The question of how we know what we know becomes a negotiation between images and simulations, not reality. As we peruse the context of a biographical film of General George Patton, for example, we no longer distinguish between the historical fact and the narrative fiction. The film, written by Francis Ford Coppola, is now the text for which we accept all "truths" about the course of events that we remember. The battles, the inner sanctums of command, the psychological makeup of the man, and the events—all have some context of fact. What is alarming is that these negotiations are not played out in an open arena of discourse or history. These "truths" are accepted by many who have only received one source for this information. Through images/simulations as fact, we have developed a newer *closed* discourse that has, in essence, abandoned an open search for historical accuracy.

From the critical school to the postmodern theorists, much has been written on the impact of the image. It is the postmodernists, however, especially Baudrillard (1990) and Jameson (1984), whose writings have focused on the seduction of the image. Within this discourse are several junctures within the debate on media and reality that the postmodernists and chaos theory have in common. This is emphasized by several literary and cultural critics. N. Katherine Hayles (1991), one such critic, writes, "That language is interactive rather than inert implies that Chaos theory is influenced by the culture within which it arose. . . . Rather it is one site within the culture where the premises characteristic of postmodernism are inscribed" (p. 5). She goes on to discuss how the postmodern theorists have provided chaos the "cultural and technological milieu" that creates a complex system that is nonlinear, disordered, and full of noise (p. 5). It is a dynamic system built on component parts mutually reinforcing each other (the events of that system are not isolated). Thus, for Hayles, the postmodernists have provided chaos with the *butterfly effect*—a small flutter from the insect causes earthquakes.

In the second edition of *The Essence of Christianity* (1843), Feuerbach observed that a society becomes modern when one of its dominant activities is producing and consuming images, when images that have extraordinary powers to determine our demands on reality are themselves preferred over that reality, and when they become fundamental to the health of the economy, the stability of the polity, and the pursuit of private happiness. The concept that concerned Feuerbach at the invention of photography has grown exponentially with the coming of the *post*modernist age. No longer is reality stolen by a single-shot photograph, but through a variety of methods that include film, television, the computer, and virtual reality.

The technologies alone, however, do not create a virtual world where realities are created and disposed of at will. The arrangements of images and their created meaning(s) go deep into the psyche of a created culture that has, through a variety of ways, accepted these images as *real*. Manual de Landa (1994) states that this acceptance of a new reality is directly related to the type and seduction of the attractors provided by a culture. In his essay "Emergence of Synthetic Reason," he places the focus on chaos's attractors for such acceptance:

> Thinking in terms of attractors . . . will lead, in turn, to a radical alteration of the philosophical doctrine know as "determinism." Attractors are fully deterministic: if the dynamics of a given population are governed by an attractor, the population in question will be strongly bound to behave in a particular way. (p. 282)

His discussion of altering determinism continues into the full loss of free will. For de Landa, these attractors control populations. Indeed, they limit the choice of possibilities. He continues his argument, stating that "a population whose dynamics are governed by a strange attractor is bound permanently to explore a limited set of possibilities within the space of possible states" (p. 282). Because attractors are points of comfort, audiences, when given a choice, will continue to move within their comfort zones. Such zones, through mediated information, become deterministic through the limited parameters supported by the economic needs of the media. In television, the economic supporters are advertisers who work on homogenization of the message for consumer reasons. In cinema, the economic needs of the studio system continue to create films that are formulaic with wide audience appeal.

This limited set of possibilities directly influences and defines the concept of *selected* realities. This is echoed in the writings of cyberneticist Heinz von Foerster (1984). His theories in cognition reflect how *realities* are constructed. He considers reality construction a process. Cognition is a process of constructing *a* reality, not *the* reality. Because of its visual nature, film constructs a sense of reality despite its narrative form. Through film's dynamic system of production and the intervention of *real* images, the public can easily accept the visual as truth. Even the film *Jurassic Park* held such an element of truth: One could easily believe that off the coast of Central America exists an island where dinosaurs have been cloned. This belief is supported by the plausible narrative of how, through the use of amber, dinosaurs' DNA was preserved. The real cloning of a sheep in Scotland extends and reinforces this plausible scenario. Thus, the jump from conjecture to reality seems very small. If that jump from fiction to reality is plausible with dinosaurs, consider how easily the confusion and struggle between competing attractors of film and event could be in a biographical film or a film based on a real event.

In *Nixon*, director Oliver Stone gives us a linear, chronological time line of the events that lead to Nixon's rise and fall as an American political figure. Within this progression, both fact and fiction intertwine. Many historical events in the film are all too real to the audience that suffered the events firsthand. But other events not known—and indeed fabricated—become part of the fabric of the film and are interwoven throughout the film in such a way as to become seamless. The events in question can be exemplified by Nixon's Texas connection. One scene follows Nixon going to a large Texas ranch (owned by Larry Hagman's character) to meet several politicos who threaten his presidency if he doesn't comply with their wishes. This is not based on political/historical knowledge; it does, however, comply with Oliver Stone's belief in the "beast." Although these events propel the narrative and allow the audience into the mind-set of the film's lead character, these events are so seamlessly intertwined with real events of the character that they allow a conflict of interpretation or, as chaos theory termed it: selected realities.

In his writing on postmodern theory, Baudrillard (1988) discusses this problem in what he termed "simulacrum." The term has a biblical foundation. In Ecclesiastes, it is written: "The simulacrum is never that which conceals the truth—it is the truth which conceals that there is none. The simulacrum is true" (Baudrillard, 1988, p. 188). A simulacrum creates its own reality from the parts of its existence. The truth created is greater than the sum of the parts that create it.

So how does it work in practice? The film *Nixon* allows us to go behind the "scenes" of Nixon's life. Stone creates several crucial transitions in Nixon's political and personal life to advance his story line. Such scenes include discussions with Pat Nixon that may or may not have happened. These transitions are essential in understanding Stone's interpretation of Nixon and his motives for several events in this public life. The created events become a simulacrum. They become the *truth* for several of Nixon's decisions and play heavily on the character's/man's psychological makeup. These simulacra become the attractors for a very different reading of the events portrayed in the film and events that have historical significance. Although the debate continues between artistic license that helps the narrative and the responsibility for historical factual progression, the audience is in place to sift through that which is fact and that which is simulacrum. These competing attractors become a central issue in the (re)creation of knowledge of any event.

These competing attractors go beyond film. Even in the proliferation of current events through the news media, we also find competing attractors. In the age of immediacy, the concept of analysis and synthesis of material for news is virtually impossible. In the Persian Gulf War, we were witness to the events *as they happened.* This Nintendo war blurred the essence of reality and image. The news media created their own reality based on the information *seen;* little attention was given to what remained *unseen.* Indeed, the news created for the war was manufactured by the Pentagon. To ensure that the plot was followed, cameras were limited. A lottery system was used to determine the coverage of the war by the news organizations. The information about SCUD missiles and the accuracy of our "smart" bombs and the Patriot missile was presented as unbiased news events. In competition with the "mainline" news organizations was another story, which was not largely accepted as an attractor. Ironically, this story came from the same source that presented the accepted visuals to the simulacra presented by the government. After the initial bombing report, CNN reporters, specifically Peter Arnett, were not considered reliable and, indeed, biased or forced in the reporting of events in Baghdad. The issue at hand was the accidental bombing of Baghdad's Amiriya air raid shelter. The conflict stemmed from Iraq's accusation that the U.S. military killed several civilians in the bombing versus the U.S. military's position that the bombs used in the war had such perfect guidance systems that no (or minuscule) variance occurred in the target and the aim of the missile. Cameras carried in the guided weapons relayed pictures to command posts that could and did replay "greatest moments" of the war. This visual evidence proved the technological accuracy of the Coalition weapons. Even with visuals of the air shelter's destruction provided by the International News Agency, the earlier footage of missile exact strikes was so compelling that many thought Iraq's accusations were fabricated.

Alternative versions of this event were discouraged. When CBS attempted to get its "own" story, its reporters were met with resistance from the military and were eventually taken prisoner by the Iraqi Army. Issues of debate were silenced by the visual acceptance of those cameras. Kevin Robbins (1996) discusses the impact of those cameras when he says that:

. . . if the war was on our screens, its truth was screened out. Remote images obscured distant realities. Through the evidential force of the image, we knew about the war, but it was a kind of derealised warfare we were knowing. It was at once a way of seeing and a way of not seeing. It was possible to be a voyeur of an image, and yet to be deaf to its reality. (p. 65)

There still exists no competing arguments on this issue in the national psyche. The simulacrum, the constructed reality, suggests that the only targets hit in the Persian Gulf War were military ones and that no missile missed its target. The use of competing attractors and simulacra is common in rhetoric about war. The conflict between reality and mythology is important to such a discussion (see Beinhart, 1993).

Robert Ivie (1977) contends that the rhetoric of war has to establish a "realistic" image of the enemy's savagery in order to eliminate the possible alternative of peace. Again, consider the Persian Gulf War. When a SCUD missile slammed into the U.S. army barracks in Saudi Arabia, the Iraqis were considered a mythological monster. The use of "enemy as savage" scenes during the conflict was bolstered by scenes before actual combat. In the (re)creation of events in Kuwait after the Iraqi intervention, we learned about the (justified) buildup for war. Stories to Congress and the American people about atrocities in the hospitals, the nursing homes, and on the streets of Kuwait during the Iraqi occupation flooded our television screens. What is interesting about the images of that war is not only the savagery of the Iraqi Army but also the relatively few visual images of Allied atrocity. Tanks rolling over trenches literally entombing live Iraqi soldiers, the slaughter on Basra Road, and the aftermath that war creates were, for the most part, all subverted images. The point is not that war is not horrific; it is. The point *is* the media's impact on creating such attractors. A simulacrum of an event like the Persian Gulf War is so prevalent that the distance between image and reality grows exponentially, creating a chaotic representation of fact, or what the postmodernists have termed "hyperreal."

Hyperrealism begins within chaos's feedback loop of attractors. To understand hyperrealism, a workable definition of *reality* needs to be presented. Using Baudrillard's (1988) definition of reality, the discussion of hyperreality is better focused. For Baudrillard, reality is defined as "that for which it is possible to provide an equivalent representation" (p. 145). This definition provides replication and, thus, scientific validity. Within the process of reproduction, reality and (re)production begin to construct a new and accepted *reality.* Inversely stated, "reality itself is hyperrealistic"

(p. 146). In chaos theory, hyperreality is created through the continuous looping of feedback (representation). The process of television news or cinematic representations of factual/fictional narratives become the reality through their consistent looping and, thus, the hyperreal. Rod Hart (1994) discusses this in his book *Seducing America.* He writes that "the electronic media conflate issues and images almost completely and encourage us to do so as well. Over time, we do, for television's lessons are both powerful and repetitive. Because television is a *visual* [italics added] media, its pictures have a self-authenticating quality" (p. 61). This is also true for cinema. William Palmer (1993) discusses this process when he discusses history as film text. He states, "Like the documents out of which the conventional histories are constituted, the supposed 'facts' or events of history are also 'texts' that 'rework' history" (p. 6). What we view in film begins as a factual or real event or, through narrative cinema, "like-reality." This creates the initial state of the system. This initial state (the viewing experience) begins close together (the event and its presentation). Throughout the process of reproduction (looping), however, this initial state gives way to a struggle of competing attractors. These attractors, the factual reality of the event and the produced hyperrealism, compete for the audience's acceptance of a postmodern simulacrum.

This process is exemplified in Oliver Stone's biographical films on John F. Kennedy and Richard Nixon. In *JFK,* Stone begins with an all too recognizable series of historical events. The film opens with the fateful day in Dallas that an American audience has witnessed over and over again. With the factual event, using news footage, one gets a sense of authenticity, and the real is accepted as truth. As the film continues, the real (the death of the president) and the hyperreal (the plot of the assassination) compete for an authenticity or simulacrum of the audience. In *Nixon,* Stone has a more difficult time but is equally successful in developing a hyperrealism that is *Nixon.* Nixon was one of the more *visual* presidents. His rise and fall from power is well documented in televisual events. From the Checkers speech in the 1950s to his resignation speech in 1974, Nixon was made and destroyed while the American people watched. Even with this very public man, Stone developed competing attractors in his film by representing those few "private" moments of Nixon. The relationship with Pat, the fateful night by the fireplace with Kissinger, and the visit to the Texas "mafia" are conjectures that are imperative to the narrative of Stone's film. Those moments "allow" us to view Nixon's motives and inner concerns. By using those undocumented moments to force the narrative to the ultimate conclusion, Stone creates a hyperreal simulacrum that is *Nixon.*

The process of how we come to accept the simulacrum through competing attractors is compelling.

In his book *Into the Image,* Kevin Robins (1996) states, "Increasingly, we have come to see the world by means of mediated vision, and, as we have done so, we have increasingly been able to distance and detach ourselves from contact with its reality" (p. 21). This process is discussed in Baudrillard's (1984) article "The Procession of Simulacra." Baudrillard argues that the mass media have neutralized reality in stages. He says that the media first (a) reflect reality, then they (b) mask and pervert it, next (c) mask reality's absence, and finally (d) produce the simulacrum of the real. This simulacrum is the destruction of meaning and all relation to reality— the death of discourse.

Narratives that reflect a sense of factual event usually have a sense of identification of the real through what is already known. In *JFK,* the opening sequence of events is lifted straight from historical archives. This identification allows the viewer a false sense of security into the film's intent. The opening of this account of the assassination places the viewer into what is the *real.* Any film that attempts to depict its premise around an actual event allows for such an intent. In *Patton,* for instance, the "sense" of the man is augmented in the opening sequence when he gives a speech in full uniform with the American flag as backdrop. His speech, intended to raise the morale and expectation of his soldiers, places him in such a position that both *his* audience and *the* audience welcome such a patriotic (re)presentation of the following events of his life as fact. This reflection of the real, however, is not predisposed only to films about historical persons in our cultural past and present. Films about historical events lead us to accept the films' simulacra as well. Films about the Vietnam War add realism to their narrative lines by placing some of their events in real time and real places. In Stanley Kubrick's *Full Metal Jacket,* the characters and the events in their lives begin in very real locations such as Parris Island. This all too real boot camp for the United States Marine Corps gives the film authenticity. This authenticity gives comfort to the director and his audience as identification of place serves to validate the fictional story. This authenticity also becomes an attractor throughout the process of the film.

Film by its visual nature, however, does not have to rely on real or biographical events to create this authenticity. An image of a created event authenticates itself. Kevin Robins (1996) considers this when he states that "we live in a world where images proliferate independently from meaning and referents in the real world. Our modern existence is increasingly one of interaction and negotiation with images and simulations which no longer serve to mediate reality" (p. 44). As a filmic event, *Thelma and Louise* is *reality.* To its audience, the characters running from patriarchal control are as real as the events represented in *Full Metal Jacket* or *JFK.* Reality is not what actually occurred but what is perceived as having occurred. Adrian Lynn's representation of the American Southwest is as real as Da Nang in 1968 and Dallas in 1963. This reflection of reality allows viewers to let down their guard and to accept the process of simulacra.

The second component of Baudrillard's process of simulacra is the masking and perversion of reality. Through the visual media of film and television, the possibilities of masking and perverting reality are great. Filmmakers can make an attendance of 50 at a political rally look like a packed auditorium. Through the process of editing, they can also project a clear understanding of cause and effect of an event. This manipulation of and by the media is not new. During World War I, Lord Beaverbrook of the British Army hired American filmmaker D. W. Griffith to film the Battle of the Somme. Griffith, in 1915, directed *Birth of a Nation,* which was in U.S. President Woodrow Wilson's words "history told in lightning" (see Cook, 1996). The first attempt to film the Somme was stagnate. The initial film of the battle was pictures of the slain. The cinematographer, not wanting to be shot, photographed the aftermath of each attempt to cross the line. The film delivered to Beaverbrook was of dead soldiers and life in the trenches. This was not acceptable. Griffith, affected by his own fiction film about the Civil War, thought there was a need to see action and drama. He reshot the film, re-creating the event with camera positions above the trenches while soldiers poured out of their protected holes and ran across "no-man's" land, shooting their weapons and running toward the enemy. The film, produced miles from the front, used British soldiers to "re-create" the event known as the Battle of the Somme. The second film shot was the film of record and was considered a documentary of the event.

We can see in that example how the film begins by reflecting reality through its use of actual British soldiers in the trenches. It goes on to mask and pervert reality by re-creating the storming of the German line. Indeed, many soldiers faked getting shot, sliding back down into the trenches or falling to the ground. Once the shooting was over, these "dead" and "wounded" soldiers were sent back to the real trenches to meet the real possibility of death that they had pretended the day before, a death unseen by the camera. It is the "reenactment" that becomes real to viewers; the audience at home viewed Griffith's film as "real." This hyperreal Battle of the Somme became a simulacrum by its very existence, literally replacing the actual event in the public psyche.

The masking and perversion of the image may not always be so overt. In biographical and historical narrative cinema, small changes within the film are like the butterfly in China. As the narrative continues, the impact of the earlier change grows exponentially to the point that the filmic events take on a reality of their own. The events of Kennedy's assassination in Stone's *JFK* begin to unravel almost immediately when the sole cause of the conspiracy is based on the removal of advisors in Vietnam. His masking of reality begins to focus in such a direction that he must "create" a Colonel X to explain it all. By this explanation, Stone, through Colonel X, creates a new version of truth and reality. The clean and clear reason for such a travesty in American history is simplified to an issue of black and white. This issue is more conducive to the audience because they now have a new knowledge of the event so basic in its understanding that other possibilities are too complex to accept. Stone's simulacrum "the assassination of President Kennedy" replaces the actual event and eliminates discourse on the subject through its revisionary narrative.

Stone does this in his Vietnam trilogy as well. *Platoon, Born on the Fourth of July,* and *Heaven and Earth* explain, in simplistic visual terms, the self-destructive path of the United states during the Vietnam War. For Stone's characters, it is an issue of fatherhood. The struggle is between two fathers: one good and one evil. Although this demarcation is given credence by the separation, in that period, between liberal and conservative, dove and hawk, antiwar and pro-war, Democrat and Republican, his explanations create a new "reality," a simulacrum steeped in images but not necessarily history.

This phase of the image creates what chaos theory has termed "turbulence." Turbulence has always confounded scientists. Indeed, in his seminal book on chaos, Gleick (1987) tells a story. On his deathbed, quantum theorist Werner Heisenberg exclaims that when he reaches Heaven he will ask God two questions: why relativity and why turbulence? Heisenberg says, "I think he may have an answer for the first one" (Gleick, 1987, p. 121). Even though turbulence has confounded scientists throughout history, it is an everyday experience of nature and life.

Turbulence is most easily explained by using the analogy of a stream of water. As slowly moving water gently flows around a stone (an attractor) and reforms behind it, the water gently continues to its natural course. If a second stone is tossed into the stream (a larger second stone) next to the original stone, the water now has to flow around two stones, creating a drag and some form of turbulence. When the water increases its speed around the stones (maybe a storm has increased the water flow), more turbulence is witnessed. Kellert (1993) explains the process in more scientific terms, stating that "the onset of turbulence is this: as the flow rate is increased, the quasi-periodic motion on the two-dimensional torus becomes unstable; some small disturbance will lead to three-dimensional quasi periodic motion, then four quasi-periodic motion, and so on to infinity" (p. 9).

Within this turbulence, the interdependency of each element is crucial. This is emphasized by Briggs and Peat (1989) when they write, "Turbulence arises because all the pieces of a movement are connected to each other, any piece of the action depending on the other pieces, and the feedback between the pieces producing still more pieces" (p. 52). The interrelationship between the process of event (film) and the event itself (history) creates turbulence and confusion between the representation and the event itself. Indeed, Briggs and Peat suggest that the interconnectedness of the two leads to the "breakup of order into turbulence" (p. 52). This process depends not only on the interconnectedness of the elements but also on the symbolic relation to each re-creation of event.

Baudrillard's third element in the process of simulacra is the masking of reality's absence. Paul Messaris (1997), in his book *Visual Persuasion,* uses semiotics to discuss the impact that images have on cross-cultural advertising. Using C. S. Pierce's *iconicity,* he explains that, through images of reality, the audience no longer needs or expects explanation of what they are viewing. The image alone is evidence enough to support the event presented. The icons, signs, and symbols used in a narrative to create meaning become more of the reality than the event itself. Messaris states that "iconicity need not entail a complete surface similarity between a picture and reality, so long as the picture reproduces the visual cues that we use in real-world vision" (p. 54). The image of reality that film and visual media so easily re-create masks reality's absence by its very presence. The visual image accepted by the audience becomes the icon for the real.

This new iconic *reality* is presented through visual symbols and signs within the narrative. In *JFK,* Colonel X gave Stone an icon to explain a theory behind the conspiracy of Kennedy's assassination. Colonel X explained the process by which the decision was made by a group of individuals that represented the military-industrial complex so strongly supported by Eisenhower. Colonel X is an important icon within the film, not only for his explanation but for his image of a character as well. The discussion between Garrison and him takes place on a bench in Washington, D.C., a city rife with American iconography. The discussion that takes place is re-created in many films about conspiracy and governmental involvement, including *Three Days of the Condor, The Firm, Clear and Present Danger,* and *Nixon.* In these and many other movies, it is not the people who control their own destiny within a democratic society, but what Stone has termed "the beast." In the 1997 American Historical Association conference, Stone was adamant that a hidden government developed to support the military-industrial complex exists and is in control. He argues that the democratic ideal is an image that protects those in real power while the "beast" actually controls our destiny, as well as our reality. The very presence of Stone at such an "academic" gathering of historians—and the upcoming journal issue on Stone as Historian—implies that film and the media are masking the reality of history through their iconography and re-creation of factual events. The next level of simulacrum is the loss of reality.

According to Baudrillard, the fourth phase of the image is that it bears no relation to any reality whatever; it is its own pure simulacrum. Baudrillard (1988) states, "When the real is no longer what it used to be, nostalgia assumes its full meaning. There is a proliferation of myths of origin and signs of reality; the second-hand truth, objectivity and authenticity" (p. 171). Within this last phase of the image, discourse is lost. The real is no longer debated as the image has gained full control. Within chaos theory, the double attractors no longer exist and the turbulence has subsided to the new attractor that is image only; the loss of the original attractor (the historical artifact) is complete. To use the earlier example of D. W. Griffith's re-creation of the Battle of the Somme, the audience's history of that event was the re-creation by British soldiers. They accepted what Gregg Easterbrook (1996) calls the "synthesized reality."

Easterbrook discusses how the desire to (re)create actuality with audience-grabbing narratives has created a new realism. He says, "Nearly everybody involved in creative pursuits agrees that reality is a virtue. But real realism—correspondence to actuality—is mostly Dullsville. So a new category, one which might be called synthesized realism, is gathering sway" (p. 41). He goes on to point out that the concern with such synthesized reality is that "the goal is to confuse you about the distinction [between synthesized reality and actuality]" (p. 41). This new synthesized reality is the simulacrum of the event and has thus destroyed all relations to the reality of the event.

Easterbrook (1996) uses an excellent example in his discussion of this new reality. It is an example of how a public may be led to an unreal conclusion based on information gained from film and television. Easterbrook contends that films such as *The Hunt for Red October, Clear and*

Present Danger, and *Patriot Games* are full of (un)realistic technical devices. Despite the fact that they do not exist, the audience believes this technology exists. This is augmented by the earlier example of the Persian Gulf War and how, through military filters, the war was covered and presented as "actual time." The audience is given a synthesized or "hyper-real" version of the event. The audience expectation of such of an event, however, is defined, not by a real situation, but by the mediated version of that event. Because of this, audience expectation is augmented and presidents lose elections when a very real event such as the Desert One operation (Jimmy Carter's fiasco during the Iranian Hostage crisis) becomes less than successful. The high-tech devices used in Tom Clancy's novels and films are expected to save the day. The audience's presumption is that technology would have been successful under a more competent leader.

CONCLUSION

We lose discourse when the image is the referent to historical artifact. The "hyperreal" image has given us a solo act, the act carefully constructed to give us an assumption about the world without actual participation. In the words of Kevin Robins (1996), "The screen has allowed us to witness the world's events while, at the same time, protecting us—keeping us separate and insulated—from the reality of events we are seeing" (p. 71). The images are speaking for us. They are our postmodern language. The reality is that, as an audience, we are not participating in the discourse or activity expressed in the images. The loss of this discourse augments the loss of social content and history that makes up a culture or a society.

Because of its economic structure, the media strive to keep the audience on the same level of understanding. This simplifies the overall message and delivers to advertisers an audience that is on the same level of under-standing. For advertisers, this allows a "homogenized" audience for greater reach. The media create a "hyperrealism," a simulacrum, by competing with the attractor of events with the strange attractor of narrative (re)cre-ation. This creates a turbulence within our own knowledge and belief systems. We think we are an "informed" public when, in fact, we remain disconnected with the rest of our world. Again, the writings of Kevin Robins (1996) succinctly pose the problem of such discourse. He discusses what happens when image controls our knowledge of information. He states that "we live in a world where images proliferate independently from meaning and referents in the real world. Our modern existence is increasingly one of interaction and negotiation with images and simulations which no longer serve to mediate reality" (p. 44).

This book is about the loss of discourse in contemporary society. As we continue to be drawn into the strange attractor of media images *as* reality, we feel fulfilled in our homogenized truths. Our trust in the media as fact continues to draw us farther away from the referents of the real world. As we feel confident in our level of understanding and knowledge of the world events, we no longer reach out to confirm or learn about events from other sources. An analogy I like to use is the stoop theory. Before the proliferation of mediated images, individuals used to sit on the stoop to discuss and exchange ideas about their world. Today, with the impact of television, Nintendo, and the computer, the stoop is missing. Sure, we discuss ideas on the "Net," but without real contact. The loss of this contact begins to alleviate discourse and both permits and emphasizes that solo act of the media.

NOTES

1. "Non-linear models differ from linear ones in many ways. Rather than trying to figure out all the chains of causality, the modeler looks for nodes where feedback loops join and tries to capture as many of the important loops as possible in the system's 'picture' " (Briggs & Peat, 1989, p. 174). I do not accept the historical dialectical model of Hegel: the linear progression of history (thesis) being interrupted by an event (antithesis) creating a third linear progression (synthesis) becoming the thesis until met again by an event (antithesis). Indeed, I accept the more nonlinear historical progression that has been accepted by non-Western historians and the definition above.

2. The term *phase space* is defined as a map that plots the location of a system's movement. This is also found in several texts regarding chaos theory, including Hall (1991, pp. 137-138), Gleick (1987, pp. 29-30), and Lewin (1992, pp. 20-21).

REFERENCES

Baudrillard, J. (1984). The procession of simulacra. In B. Wallis (Ed.), *Art after modernism: Rethinking representation.* New York: New Museum of Contemporary Art.

Baudrillard, J. (1988). Simulacra and simulations. In M. Poster (Ed.), *Selected readings.* Stanford, CA: Stanford University Press.

Baudrillard, J. (1990). *Seduction.* New York: St. Martin's.

Beinhart, L. (1993). *American hero.* New York: Pantheon.

Briggs, J., & Peat, F. D. (1989). *Turbulent mirror: An illustrated guide to chaos theory and the science of wholeness*. New York: Harper & Row.

Cohen, J., & Stewart, I. (1994). *The collapse of chaos: Discovering simplicity in a complex world*. New York: Penguin.

Cook, D. (1996). *A narrative history of film* (3rd ed.). New York: Norton.

de Landa, M. (1994). Emergence of synthetic reason. In M. Dery (Ed.), *Flame wars: The discourse of cyberculture*. Durham, NC: Duke University Press.

Easterbrook, G. (1996). It's unreal: How phony realism in film and literature is corrupting and confusing the American mind. *Washington Monthly, 28*(10), 41-43.

Feurbach, L. (1843). *Essence of Christianity*. London: Paul Kegan, Trence, Truber.

Gleick, J. (1987). *Chaos: Making of a new science*. New York: Penguin.

Hall, N. (1991). *Exploring chaos: A guide to the new science of disorder*. New York: Norton.

Hart, R. (1994). *Seducing America: How television charms the modern voter*. New York: Oxford University Press.

Hayles, N. K. (1991). *Chaos and order: Complex dynamics in literature and science*. Chicago: University of Chicago Press.

Ivie, R. L. (1977). Images of savagery in American justification for war. *Communication Monographs, 47,* 279-294.

Jameson, F. (1984). Postmodernism, or the cultural logic of late capitalism. *New Left Review, 146,* 53-93.

Kellert, S. (1993). *In the wake of chaos*. Chicago: University of Chicago Press.

Lewin, R. (1992). *Complexity: Life at the edge of chaos*. New York: Macmillan.

Messaris, P. (1997). *Visual persuasion: The role of images in advertising*. Thousand Oaks, CA: Sage.

Palmer, W. (1993). *The films of the eighties: A social history*. Carbondale: Southern Illinois University Press.

Robins. K. (1996). *Into the image: Culture and politics in the field of vision*. London: Routledge.

Rushkoff, D. (1994). *Cyberia: Life in the trenches of cyberspace*. San Francisco: Harper.

von Foerster, H. (1984). On constructing a reality. In P. Watzlawick (Ed.), *The invented reality*. New York: Norton.

CHAPTER 11

Worlds at GWAR

Celebrations of Juvenile Resistance in Post-Punk Pop

Glenn C. Geiser-Getz
East Stroudsburg University

Musical forms of pop culture have been among the most powerful of languages to communicate feelings of hopelessness, impotence, fear, insecurity, resentment, and frustration. Punk, rap, heavy metal, and other forms of musical expression enable discourses that both reject/negate and project/advocate. The rejection of dominant value systems and ideologies is at times accomplished in these forms through sign systems antithetical to those of the mainstream, and although such sign systems can prove advantageous by providing symbolic power through difference, they can also make genuine communication problematic. A more difficult task for such languages often lies, not in the rejection of the status quo, but in the projection of alternative value systems. The use of artistic forms (music) in entertainment contexts (live and recorded performances) makes the task even more daunting when art aims for multiple meanings to foster creativity and when entertainment aims for broad appeal to fatten wallets. These forces can both foster and frustrate expressive goals by making meanings more open and messages more polysemic.

In the context of this book, then, it is useful to examine such a discourse to better understand and evaluate its power for communication. As the editors of *Soundbite Culture* have explained, the many technologies of communication promoted today do not necessarily improve genuine communication, the kind of interaction that creates, strengthens, and maintains healthy communities, identities, and relationships. The self and the other are increasingly defined by the images of film and television, by the choices of consumers in a world of commodities, and by ritualized performances that often lack complexity, depth, and meaning.

Young people seem particularly at risk in this confusing world of illusion. Whether it be discussions of cigarette advertisements that target teens or debates over portrayals of girls on television, people are rightly concerned about the role of communication and culture in the development of young identities. To their credit, academics and social critics have studied some forms of youth culture—in particular, those most controversial. Dick Hebdidge's (1979/1994) exploration of punk music reveals important relationships between the pessimistic values of Britain's working-class youths and the symbolic forms of expression found in their clothing styles, forms of address, and music.

Although British punk rock has received noteworthy attention, more recent incarnations of "offensive youth culture" (forms of expression by and/or for the young that defy dominant norms and value systems) remain understudied in the United States. To some extent, this is understandable. First, American youth culture of the 1980s and 1990s may seem lacking in substance and foundation (especially to critics who grew up in previous decades), consisting of historically ignorant flower children, punk wannabes, and Bon Jovi fans whose biggest concerns revolve around maintaining their free-flowing rocker locks. Second, the strategic use of offensive forms of communication has yet to be articulated as a rhetoric, as an influential means of symbolic persuasion used to accomplish both expressive and instrumental goals. Creating such a rhetoric will certainly prove useful in the future but is neither appropriate nor possible to accomplish in this chapter. However resistant scholars are to considering more recent developments in American youth culture (and for whatever reasons), such forms of expression remain as distinctive and informative of a cultural moment and audience as any Sex Pistols concert or 1960s protest song.

One trend in teenage music has been labeled "shock rock" by the talk show circuit; it includes the performances, recordings, styles, behaviors, and audiences of musical groups that purposefully insult, offend, and abuse the icons and values of mainstream culture. Although rejecting authority through musical expression is not new to the 1990s, its latest manifestation has some unique features that are explored later in this chapter. Note the description given to this expressive form by the host of *The Jerry Springer Show* in a recent broadcast:

> Welcome to the show. Today we're going to take a look into the world of shock rock—rock music that is violent, scary, and even perverse. Now some of the performers on my stage today hold concerts where they have sex right on stage, they urinate on the crowd, and perform bloody rituals. Today, these bands will tell us why they do it, and they're going to face off with the moms who say they want them to stop spreading their filth. (Springer, 1997, p. 1)

Although Springer's description obviously sets up the symbolic function of his program, which like many talk shows is to generate argumentative conflict and reveal "deviant" forms of human existence in a kind of side-show display that ultimately promotes mainstream American values, it is still informative of the basic focus of shock rock. Performers such as The Mentors, Marilyn Manson, GWAR, and many other punk, metal, and rap bands use graphic lyrics, violent stage antics, grating musical tones, frenetic rhythms, high volume sound, adult themes, and sexually explicit content in their art. They consistently display an apparent disregard for traditional notions of religion, government, sexuality, morality, authority, security, and family, and they communicate this disregard in a flamboyant and controversial way, often using images of rape, incest, sodomy, abortion, murder, bestiality, cannibalism, abuse, masturbation, live sacrifice, urination, and defecation through both verbal (sung lyrics, spoken words) and visual (concerts, film, and video) means.

In this chapter, I examine one notable representative of the shock rock genre of American youth culture, a band known as GWAR. Although GWAR is typical of the genre in themes and techniques, it is also quite distinctive in ways that make it interesting for analysis. GWAR concerts are highly visual and interactive. They have a strong sense of narrative; discrete songs in concerts and albums are often linked by a single story. Although it has achieved some success, unlike many of the popular rap groups, the band is either unwilling or unable to join the mainstream music industry or generate a broad audience. GWAR has an oddly comic sense of the offensive that does not fit with many bands of this type. Through textual criticism and analysis of fan interviews, I examine GWAR to discover what its central messages are, what it says to us about the current cultural environment, and primarily to learn what, if anything, its American audiences are accomplishing personally and socially through their experiences with the band.

GWAR AS PUNK ROCK OPERA

One notable source of musical creativity involves combining genres, purposefully blurring the distinctions once created by the music industry to
construct audiences for specific entertainment products. GWAR's music
combines the sounds and styles of punk, metal, jazz, and rap into a highly
visual and comical type of punk rock opera. GWAR is a bizarre mixture of
Howard Stern, Halloween, and Spinal Tap; it is a hybrid cultural form that
blends the rhythms of heavy metal, the aesthetics of Dungeons and Dragons, the characters of professional wrestling, the slapstick humor of the
Three Stooges, and the plot lines of bad science fiction.

   Although details of the band's history are sketchy at best, according to
fans and Web site authors GWAR began in 1988 when a group of Richmond, Virginia, art students created some costumes for their rock band, the
X-Cops. They opened an X-Cops concert wearing their creations, huge
gruesome alien outfits made of painted latex and Styrofoam. They established characters for each of the costumed band members and gave them
names and identities, including Oderus Urungus (the lead singer), Beefcake
the Mighty, Balsac the Jaws of Death, Flattus Maximus, Jiz Mac the
Gusher, Slymenstra Hymen (the lone female in the group), Techno De-
structo, Sleazy P. Martini, and The Sexicutioner. The band also developed
a history and overarching narrative for these characters. I refer to the
GWAR phenomenon as a type of opera primarily because of this strong
sense of character and narrative; albums and concerts use songs to tell a
coherent and consistent (though highly outrageous) story, and this story
establishes a context for all of GWAR's musical performances. The story
is told through the music, through audience interaction, and through the
equally important visual aspects of the show (costumes, props, special
effects, lighting, movement).

   The GWAR narrative begins with the Master, the creator of all, who
becomes bored with his creation. War, destruction, and death all fail to
satisfy his need for a challenge, so the Master designs and produces a group
of God-like beings called GWAR, also known as the Scumdogs of the
Universe. For a time, the Master uses these creatures to destroy his enemies,
but GWAR eventually turns against the Master. As punishment, the Master
uses his Death Pod to capture the Scumdogs and banish them to Earth,
where they are eventually imprisoned in an Antarctic iceberg for eternity.
In the 1980s, following the popularity of long-haired rock bands with
serious hairspray needs, the increased use of aerosol products creates a hole

in the ozone layer over Antarctica. GWAR's icy prison melts, and the Scumdogs of the Universe are released to wreak violent havoc on all humanity. Sleazy P. Martini, a shifty pimplike character, becomes the band's human manager, brings GWAR to America, and teaches the group to play musical instruments. GWAR dreams of destroying both Earth and the Master through various schemes, weapons, and creatures, and glories in the wanton destruction of all human life. The band's name does not seem to have a clear meaning, although it was most likely taken from a comic book in which an organization called Gay Women Against Rape is featured. During one scene of a 1993 GWAR video, *Phallus in Wonderland,* a group of characters protesting the band's explicit music, hold signs that bear this name. Other audience members, however, claim that the acronym G-W-A-R either represents "God What a Racket" or stands in for the sound the creatures made upon breaking free of their icy Antarctic prison ("GWARRRR").

Human notions of morality and taste are the enemies of GWAR. Note the promotional discourse from their *Live From Antarctica* (1992) concert video:

> For the first time, you can enjoy an actual GWAR cannibalistic blood orgy invading the privacy of your own home. Finally, you can experience a live performance in relative safety. Those too timid to attend a live GWAR show will appreciate that even though most viewers will suffer permanent brain damage, at least they won't get blood all over their latest trendy outfit. Laugh in abject horror as Oderus Urungus, the Sexicutioner, Slymenstra Hymen and company rape, burn, and pillage their way into your heart. Join them in their never ending quest for exploitational sex and gratuitous violence. Including all your favorite death anthems.

GWAR performances involve simulated beheadings, guttings, killings, fondling, intercourse, urination, and defecation. Sometimes referred to as the Monty Python of splatter, GWAR is aural, visual, tactile, and kines-thetic; it captures the senses of its audience through music, images, narra-tive, and audience participation. The elaborate stage shows are presented for relatively small crowds of young people who invariably swarm toward the front of the stage in the hopes of being chosen for annihilation by the band; audience members are occasionally pulled onstage to be sacrificed to the Wall of Flesh, Gor-Gor (a huge *Tyrannosaurus rex*), the human meat grinder, or any number of other grotesque creatures and machines. Fans below the stage are generously sprayed by band members with simulated blood, urine, feces, semen, vaginal discharge, and other fluids during the show. Later, the audience's stained T-shirts may become treasured souvenirs for the most devoted of GWAR's audience.

In the tradition of Kiss, Alice Cooper, the Sex Pistols, and other controversial groups from past and present, GWAR purposely violates as many conventions of middle-class civility as possible. Images of masturbation, bestiality, and human sacrifice (all simulated using costumes, props, sound effects, and sticky, nontoxic colored liquid shot through plastic tubing) are not unusual events in a typical GWAR show. The punk influence is clear in these more outrageous aspects of the GWAR concert. Band members taunt the audience, swearing and criticizing and spewing liquids into the crowd. Unlike the practices of the most intense punk rockers, however, none of these antics are intended to cause any physical damage to patrons or performers. GWAR is also far more playful and comic than most punk rock or heavy metal bands.

The songs themselves deal with a variety of topics, including drug use, rape, abuse of various kinds, pedophilia, alien life, mutants, morality, the difficulties of performing on tour, and anything involving violence or sex. All topics are expressed in the darkest and most explicit manner possible. Songs include such titles as "Pocket Pool," "Slap U Around," "Fight," "Eat Steel," and "Pussy Planet." In the song "Have You Seen Me?" from *America Must Be Destroyed* (1992), the practice of putting photographs of missing children on milk cartons is explored and parodied from the point of view of the kidnappers: "Mommies I've been stealing your babies/Gag the brat and then maybe/I'll suck out his brain/Dead kids/They make me feel almost hard/Go get one from the schoolyard/He bled like a stuck pig/HAVE YOU SEEN ME?" "The Morality Squad," from the same album, criticizes Moral Majority fundamentalists who attempt to censor GWAR's music: "We're the morality squad/Armed with the wrath of God/My name is Granbo/And here's my holy hot rod/Freedom for all the people/Brave and true and strong/Freedom for all the people/Unless I think they're wrong/ Blasphemy!" In "Pepperoni," from *This Toilet Earth* (1994), the juvenile tenor of their music is expressed: "You like it, you love it/You want more of it/You say that you want some/Pepperoni/Give you a fistful of my/Big Bologna/You say that you want some/Ramma-Jamma/I said I'd treatcha/If I meet'cha in the bathroom/IN-OUT-IN-OUT WHITE BOY." "Slap U Around" reveals a misogyny that is both violent and disturbing: "I wake you in the morning/With a kick in the tit/I treat you like shit/You love it!/Smash you right in the face now baby/Just to show you I care/Then I kick your pregnant ass/Down the stairs/SLAP SLAP SLAP U AROUND/

All day!" Perhaps their most offensive song, titled "BDF" ("Baby Dick Fuck"), weaves a cruel tale of forced intercourse with living and dead children and pregnant mothers.

In all ways, GWAR aims for the scandalous. Like Kiss, band members rarely appear out of costume in public, and although they obviously have to tone down their explicit rhetoric while on the talk show circuit, they refuse to step out of their roles as alien conquerors of Earth when appearing on television. GWAR responded to a recent electronic mail message in which I asked about the band's goals and the relationship between GWAR and mainstream culture. The reply was sent by the band's lead singer writing in character as Oderus Urungus:

> GWAR asks only one thing: blind and total obedience. To oppose our will is to be destroyed. Plus we kill the messenger, then send back his head with a bomb inside. This, plus our platform of "pope rape" ensures our position as the only people with any sense. We don't know what you mean by "mainstream." The approval, support, or even existence of any stream other than our own is beneath our notice. We are the only stream and a stream of pee at that. Well then you might ask, why is he writing back? To which I would say, because sir, I am a big fat liar. Anything can be peddled at a mass level and one day it will be GWAR. It's going to take a few more kicks . . . maybe in 4 years, give or take a millennia. ODERUS. (D. Brockie, personal communication, July 9, 1996)

GWAR has attained some notoriety beyond the ghoulish details of its fictional history, concert performance techniques, and song lyrics. In cooperation with Slave Pit Enterprises and Metal Blade Records (Time-Warner), GWAR has produced several albums, including *Hell-O, Rag Na Rok, Scumdogs of the Universe, America Must Be Destroyed, The Road Behind* (EP), and *This Toilet Earth.* They have also produced concert and narrative videos, including *Live From Antarctica, Phallus in Wonderland* (1993), *Tour De Scum,* and the most recent *Skullheadface* (by the creators of The Toxic Avenger). The band has received two Grammy nominations, one in 1993 for its video *Phallus in Wonderland* and one in 1996 for Best Metal Performance for the song "SFW" ("So Fucking What"). The lead singer, Dave Brockie (Oderus Urungus), was arrested in Charlotte, North Carolina, after a concert and charged with obscenity for simulating a human penis. The police confiscated the offending portion of Brockie's costume, a latex appendage the band refers to as the Cuttlefish of Cthulu. During performances, the Cuttlefish, a large phallus with antennae and pursed lips, hangs between Brockie's legs and is regularly touched and held by various band members. In GWAR's video *Phallus in Wonderland* (1993), the arrest is parodied when the Cuttlefish is put on trial for impersonating a penis by Edna P. Granbo and the Morality Squad.

THE GWAR AUDIENCE

Threatening forms of musical expression are sometimes neutralized in a powerful consumer culture through commodification, in which the offending symbols are rendered profitable and relatively harmless to the dominant culture through a variety of techniques and processes. Rap music, for example, has been adopted by the television and radio advertising industry to sell everything from Sprite soda pop to Pillsbury dough products. After almost 10 years of performing, however, GWAR remains a small-time band that attracts a limited and relatively specific audience. GWAR's concert tours are small operations, and performances sometimes depend on word of mouth for advertising. Concerts tend to occur in small facilities because of the size of the audience and the nature of the interactive performance, and tickets usually sell for just $10 to $15. The band and its fans make use of the Internet to maintain the audience and spread information about albums, concerts, and other band activities. GWAR's music may have so far evaded the commodification process because it has been unable to generate a broad audience, because of the level of its verbal and visual offensiveness, and because band members are unwilling to make the kinds of changes required of groups that enter the cultural mainstream.

GWAR employs an alternative form of expression highly critical of, and less than palatable to, the dominant culture. Although it may not be an effective example of cultural assimilation or commodification, however, it does not necessarily follow that GWAR constitutes a positive force in the lives of its audiences. The complex issues of audience popularity, pleasure, use, and interpretation have yet to be explored and are crucial to answering this question. As we know from British and American cultural studies, audiences are creative sensemakers who employ a variety of experiences, understandings, texts, intertexts, and contexts to construct meaning from symbolic environments. It is useful to now turn away from the aural and visual products of the GWAR performers and toward the internal and symbolic products of the GWAR audiences.

Why do people, especially young people, like GWAR? What pleasures does it provide? What needs or desires does it fulfill? What meanings do audience members construct from the complex set of signs that constitutes GWAR performances? Are GWAR's critics correct when they select individual song lyrics as evidence of some immoral, devilish plot to corrupt young minds? Or is something else at work that moves a normally sedate middle-class teen audience to purchase albums and concert tickets and revel in violent language, profane imagery, and fake blood?

The GWAR audience, like the audiences of heavy metal music, is mostly white and mostly male. Fans range in age from 15 to 25 and come from a variety of class backgrounds. Many of them, however, appear to be middle-class teenagers who reside in the eastern third of the United States. GWAR also has a European following that is not examined for this chapter.

I interviewed three audience members for this study, and although I make no scientific claims about the larger audience population based on this data, I believe that these fans illustrate concerns, pleasures, and interpretations that are typical of GWAR's constituency. During the interviews, I explained that I was doing a study of the music group GWAR and obtained permission to tape-record the interviews for later transcription and analysis. I asked interviewees about their experiences with the band, likes and dislikes, interpretations of GWAR's message, views of the band over time, reasons for being fans, and opinions of other audience members. I also asked about the mainstream public's reaction to GWAR. Each audience member interviewed was male and considered himself to be a fan. It is important to point out, however, that they also claimed that most audience members are fans. Apparently, few GWAR listeners are casual about their participation in the phenomenon. Apart from the friends of GWAR fans who may attend a concert or two, most audience members follow GWAR faithfully, attending concerts whenever possible, checking one of several Internet Web sites for information about new albums or television appearances and watching their concert and narrative videos. A popular MTV program, "Beavis and Butthead," features GWAR music videos occasionally on cable television, as the band is the favorite of the two controversial animated characters.

During GWAR's recent appearance on *The Jerry Springer Show,* video footage of interviews with fans was shown by way of introduction. Note the diversity of comments from these four:

Unidentified Man #1:   I like GWAR because—I mean, they just rock, man. They're—they're awesome.

Unidentified Man #2: Because it's something different. You don't just go watch a show; you can get involved.

Unidentified Woman #1: It's—It's really loud. It lets you be who you want to be. It's for freedom. It may not be good for kids, but it's really good, man, because you can have fun. You can scream; you can yell; you can let out all your aggressions.

Unidentified Man #3: GWAR's the best because they're just the sickest, dementedest things you can think of, and it just lets you let out all your inner fears, pleasures. Anything you would want to do, it's just—that is that. GWAR is just that. (Springer, 1997, p. 10)

Sentiments such as these were typical of the interviews I conducted. Fans described the GWAR experience as "different," "intense," "raunchy," "fun," "outrageous," "cathartic," and just plain "bizarre." All agreed that most people did not correctly understand the artistic purposes of the band or the entertainment value of its music. They commented that GWAR was satisfying in many ways, although I focus here on the five features most often mentioned in the interviews: (a) GWAR's highly narrative and inter-active form; (b) GWAR's ability to stimulate multiple senses; (c) GWAR's shocking and vulgar sense of humor; (d) GWAR's existence as an alterna-tive to more commercial forms of pop culture; and (e) GWAR's emotionally charged, emotionally cathartic performances.

GWAR performances are tailored to fit an audience that was raised on television but has ultimately become bored with it. This became clear throughout the interviews, but in particular the first two features of GWAR address this point. First, fans often commented on the narrative, interactive form of GWAR's music. GWAR creates an operalike experience in its concerts through the combination of emotional music, strong characters, and coherent stories. One fan commented that "all their albums seem to follow a story line," and another claimed that "it's more of a play or some sort of production as opposed to just a heavy metal concert." It seemed particularly important to the fans that GWAR songs were not discrete musical expressions but were linked together in coherent ways. Sometimes the stories involved a central negative, a villain creature, concept, or community that GWAR labored to destroy. Examples of villains include corporate America, the Moral Majority, and a *Tyrannosaurus rex* named Gor-Gor. The desire for stimulating narratives seemed more important to some fans than the music:

Fan #2: Each song is a little story in itself, and you can see that story acted out on the stage, and you almost become a part of it just because you know with the blood spraying out into the audience and uh you know seeing things happen firsthand, it adds to the excitement, it adds to the whole experience you know, visual as well as the sound.

Although the stock narratives of melodrama that constitute GWAR stories maintain the audience's interest and make the performances more entertaining, a more captivating quality for these fans seems to be GWAR's interactivity:

Fan #3: The audience becomes part of the show . . . it's their hour and 45 minutes of fame kind of thing, the theatrics that they pull on stage, like spraying the blood out, and whatever sordid materials comes out of the characters at the time, kind of brings kind of a contact with the fans and the fans feel that they're really part of the show.

This fan further noted that GWAR performers address audience members directly, selecting specific people in the crowd through eye contact and shouted words to insult and taunt them. Verbal contact with the audience is not the only way these shows are interactive, however. Audience members are sprayed with liquids regularly during the performance, especially as characters performing in the drama are killed or mutilated, feel a need to relieve themselves, or experience a sexual climax. Audience members are also regularly asked to participate in the production and are even pulled onstage to be dramatically "killed" by various means. Each of these features adds to the excitement of fans who, as a result, feel that they have become part of the performance in some meaningful way.

Second, fans expressed great pleasure that multiple senses were stimulated by the performance. Although none of them made an explicit comparison to television, in a subtext evident throughout the interviews fans compared GWAR to other forms of popular culture with which they were familiar and that they found less compelling. One fan made the following comments about another heavy metal band:

Fan #2: The first concert I went to was a Metallica concert, and sure that was charged full of energy and stuff, but we pretty much just stood on the seats and watched as Metallica put on this little show and sung their thing and they just walked around and you know played their instruments. Whereas, at a GWAR show you know there is actually something to think about what's going on.

Part of the stimulation being referred to here is the fact that GWAR pays equal attention to what audiences hear, see, feel, smell, taste, touch, and think during concerts. The senses are aroused in multiple ways as fans watch and respond to the performers, as they feel the crowd pressing against them, as they hear the booming sounds of the music, and as they taste, smell, and feel the liquids blasted at them from the stage. Consider the following interview excerpt:

Fan #3: They not only bring it to you aurally, but also visually. Whereas other bands just hearing what they have to say, but with GWAR they are putting graphical representations to it.

The same fan describes some of the sensations he felt during a GWAR concert:

Fan #3: I also think it's just the environment of being in the, you know, down on the floor in front of the stage. It's so hot and sweating and you're fighting for your life and people are falling all over you and all this crap's flying and its loud and it's, you know, it's just, it gives you a chance to experience something you don't experience every day.

Unlike the shallow sound, weak images, and harmless, passive experience of watching television, attending a GWAR concert is a dramatic struggle between audience members and the band that verges on sensual overload. Fans are enthralled by the overwhelming nature of the GWAR concert and the fact that their bodies and minds feel fully involved. GWAR concerts give them "something to think about" and bring them a message that is a "whole experience."

For first-time observers of this cultural curiosity, the drenching of audience members with simulated blood is perhaps the most confusing and troubling element of the GWAR concert, and yet for fans it may be the most pleasurable. Fans explain that this part of the show makes them feel more like active performers, rather than passive spectators. The experience is, of course, also highly unusual and fascinating for fans in its novelty alone. The blood adds to the overall experience of the concert by stimulating the sense of touch and by bonding the audience members together more fully as a group. Although audience members rarely suffer injury at GWAR concerts, surviving a concert intact seems to be a "rite of passage" for fans, a bizarre ceremony that is compelling, challenging, and sometimes frightening. It is not unlike when a group of teens enter an archetypal haunted house, sometimes created by service organizations to raise money on Halloween, and survive its simulated terrors, emerging from the experience intact. Such events enable the vicarious experience of danger while simultaneously creating a bond between those involved. Consider another fan's comments on this aspect of the blood ritual:

> **Fan #2:** I definitely got sprayed on. I saw the show at the Trocadero in Philly, and you know that's a pretty small club and everybody is pretty much right there on the floor, and it was just, people were pushing each other out of the way so that they could get sprayed with the blood. After we came out of the concert, we were all red and dripping and drenched with this, you know, sugary fake blood thing, and we went to Denny's afterwards and at another table there was another group of kids who were also at the concert, all looked exactly the same as us. And you know we walked in and they saw us and we saw them and we were just like "yeah!" and we had to make a big commotion and stuff. It was really a good time.

Not only is the experience of the GWAR concert a group bonding ritual, but youths actually bear its mark after leaving the concert hall. Drenched in ghoulish red, they congregate to admire their common appearances. The choice of Denny's as a meeting place, a restaurant highly symbolic of middle America, seems more than ironic. Imagine the reaction of the waitress taking Grand Slam breakfast orders from a group of energized teens apparently coated in fresh blood. This fan further explained that his friend "didn't wash his shirt just so he could keep the red stains on it."

A third important feature of GWAR mentioned in the interviews was the band's use of humor. According to the fans, a newcomer's initial reaction to GWAR is almost always one of shock and horror at the band's boldness and vulgarity. For those who become fans, however, the feelings of disbelief are followed by an appreciation for GWAR's exaggerated sense of parody and humor. At times, GWAR is juvenile and slapstick; at other times, the band targets specific social groups for satirical public critique. Note these interview excerpts:

> **Fan #1:** What got me interested in it was the, uh, the offensive humor. It's not really aimed at being offensive, it's aimed at being funny through being that disgusting. You think, you sit back and think, wow, how did they write these lyrics?

Fan #3: It really blows you away the first time you see it, but the more and more you get used to it, you see how they take themselves as a whole, it's really funny.

All of the fans admitted that the messages of GWAR's songs are disturbing and even obscene but that they must be interpreted in a context of a "joke." GWAR is almost always about making fun of something in a vulgar way. One fan explains:

Fan #1: The humor that comes out of it is so oddball that, I mean you just sit there and just laugh and laugh and laugh. You really wouldn't think of the offensiveness so much, because it was kind of like, "This is so offensive that it's like out of whack with normality!" You know what I mean, and it just, it makes you laugh.

In general, humor involves unusual juxtapositions, the pairing of things not normally perceived together. GWAR's humor, in part, seems to lie in its ability to confront what this fan refers to as "normality" with something completely different. Like the characters of the band, the experience of GWAR is an alien one, so different from everyday life that it calls forth laughter from its in-group fans. One fan refers to GWAR's music as "twisted stuff" so bizarre and disturbing that it fails to make sense and is, therefore, to be interpreted as a "ridiculous" joke. The alien characters; the costumes; the elaborate, involved, and highly inconceivable plots; the stage devices; and the special effects (heavy use of the fog machine) create a context of the ridiculous and the grotesque. Other fans claim that "GWAR is not serious whatsoever" and that outsiders should "lighten up" when they encounter a GWAR song or concert. Another fan explains:

Fan #3: When first seeing it, it's like you get shocked, you're kind of like, "Oh, my god, I can't believe they're doing this!" But after listening to the band for so long . . . they don't take themselves very seriously and they have kind of a comedic undertone to them. So its shocking and they're dealing with this incredibly bad social taboo like mutilation at the same time they're funny about it. They don't take it seriously. It's kind of like they're mocking something that is so socially unacceptable at the same time trying to, like, see how far they could take it.

Pushing the limits of taste has an additional pleasure for many teenage males who make up GWAR's dominant audience because it allows them to rebel against their parents and against mainstream culture. So, while they experience humor through the extreme contrast between what they have been taught is socially appropriate and what they experience at a GWAR concert, they also experience a youthful pleasure at engaging in taboo activities by simply witnessing the spectacle. This seems to be another common characteristic of offensive youth culture.

A fourth important feature of the fans' enjoyment and interpretation of GWAR relates to their perceptions of themselves. According to the group of fans I interviewed, the audiences of GWAR are primarily people who consider themselves different in some way. They are "nonconformist teenage males" who "don't fit in" and are "looking for their own group" or seeking an "alternative" to the forms of culture many of their high school peers enjoy. One fan described many audience members, including himself, as "rebellious metalheads." In general, the GWAR audience seems unsatisfied with everyday life in some way, whether because of family problems, universal frustrations of youth, questions about and struggles with sexuality, feeling that they aren't taken seriously by others, or a general mistrust of society. One fan explains:

> **Fan #2:** Most of the listeners are people who are really, you know, who really don't think on the way like an average person would think, you know. They have their own ideas about how things should be done, and they like anything that goes against the norm, pretty much. 'Cause anybody who is a loyal church-going person or someone who wants to make it in the career world or you know or any of that, I don't know they might listen to GWAR and they might enjoy it, but they really wouldn't get the whole gist of it.

This fan articulates a clear distinction that he perceives between the GWAR audience and others, explaining that fans are different and that GWAR can only be appreciated by a certain type of person. GWAR's parody feeds this perception of difference and alternative culture by criticizing a variety of mainstream cultural products, celebrities, movements, characters, and ideas. Performers dressed as Bill Clinton or Michael Jackson are beheaded in GWAR concerts. Musicians from other, more commercial bands receive similar treatment in performances and television appearances. GWAR culture offers an alternative that is noncommercial, radically

different from the culture of fans' parents, unusual, and often unpredictable:

Fan #1:   You really just don't know what they're gonna do next.
They're extremely chaotic. . . . It's just chaos, pure chaos. That seems
to be their theme in everything.

The idea of chaos, a lack of order or structure, often finds its way into
GWAR fan interviews. Although not unique to GWAR, this feature of
offensive youth culture illustrates the young rejecting the authority figures,
icons, hierarchies, and ordered processes of their parents' culture.

Fifth and finally, GWAR fans find the music and the concerts charged
with emotional energy and useful in relieving stress caused by anger and
the frustrations of everyday life. GWAR provides a cathartic outlet to
release negative feelings in a group of people who feel similarly. This also
is not a pleasure unique to GWAR, as the fans I interviewed pointed out,
but is a common part of the pleasures involved in heavy metal and punk
rock. In fact, one can probably think of many examples of offensive youth
culture that enable the release of anger in this manner. Such musical forms
appeal to a sense of danger to satisfy rebellious young audiences while
offering an opportunity to express anger in a relatively safe environment.
One fan explains how this type of music has helped him:

Fan #1:   The whole thing with heavy metal music seems to be that you
can express rage that you have when you are a teenager through the
music and you're not hurting anyone. You're just banging your head
(laughs). The more music you listen to, the more levelheaded you
would get.

He further explains that his problems dealing with anger made it difficult
for him to communicate with others or deal with relationships construc-
tively. Heavy metal music has a calming, cathartic influence because it lets
him release energy. Another fan, whose was an active GWAR audience
member as a high school student, explains why he is no longer as interested:

Fan #2:   It's definitely for younger people, people who are really
displeased with what they see every day and what they hear and what
people are telling them, what people are telling them to do. I don't

know, I can still identify with it, I just don't feel the same sort of, uh, I don't know, it's hard to explain . . . .

Although he has difficulty expressing himself, it seems clear that, for this fan, the GWAR text is most valuable for people in a relatively specific situation with some specific needs. When asked to explain further, he responded that he believes music fits different moods. GWAR is most satisfying when he is angry:

Fan #2: Angry, say, like somebody was driving in front of me and they were some old biddy doing 30 and she's, you know, weaving in and out of the lane so I can't get by and stuff and just really irritating me. You know, I'd love to put it on and then just like sing along with the lyrics like all them were meant for her. And she turns off the road and I just take off going real fast. Like all music, it helps you get through certain things.

He claims that it feels good to have his anger acted out violently on stage and in GWAR songs. Another fan explains the physically and emotionally cathartic response he has to the musical experience:

Fan #3: You go go go for about an hour and a half or however long they've played and you get out of there and you're like, "Oh, man, that was great" and you rest. You just kinda, not necessarily purge everything from you, but a totally different experience.

Although the fan does not fully articulate a rhetoric of catharsis in this section of the interview, it seems clear that the physically demanding experience of being an audience member at a GWAR concert provides some type of cleansing relief from the dullness and anxiety of everyday life.

CONCLUSIONS AND OBSERVATIONS

Does GWAR symbolize a new low in communication through music? Or does it offer a powerful experience for a frustrated young audience? Both and neither are true. Certainly, there is more going on here in the interaction between audience and text than is initially apparent. An awareness of the audience pleasures of interactive musical drama, aural, visual, tactile, and kinesthetic stimulation, shock and humor, cultural parody, and emotional catharsis should force critics to consider seriously the needs and concerns of fan audiences. It should also motivate scholars to consider various points of view when examining cultural texts. Meaningful discourse may appear absent or in 'decline' when seen from one perspective but highly meaningful and culturally significant when examined from another. GWAR and other forms of offensive youth culture appear to provide energetic, satisfying opportunities for the release of anger, as well as intense feelings of community among fan audience members.

Although I found much to consider and even commend in GWAR's music and audience, there are clearly some potentially damaging elements in offensive youth culture generally and in GWAR specifically. Articulated throughout the music, lyrics, and performances of such groups are images of hate, racism, xenophobia, violence, misogyny, drug abuse, spousal abuse, pedophilia, homicide, and suicide. Even if most GWAR fans understand the joke at work in this form of culture, this pushing-the-envelope hyperbole that ultimately parodies itself, GWAR's art can also be interpreted in a much different and more disturbing way. Confused young audience members who lack a stable sense of self or strong relationships with parents or peers may come to GWAR seeking a primary source of identity. One fan I interviewed cautioned against this volatile combination, warning that heavy metal music, Dungeons and Dragons, and GWAR are inappropriate for "unstable" people. Like many of those who look to popular culture to construct the self, those who come to GWAR hoping for a firm foundation for their identities may be sorely disappointed at the least, and highly disturbed at the worst.

GWAR could be further criticized by considering two types of popular culture: involving and escapist. Although these types may not always be mutually exclusive, they reveal tendencies present in the worlds of American culture. Involving culture appeals to the intellect to move audiences to a thoughtful consideration of their everyday lives, experiences, and relationships. Escapist culture stimulates the imagination to remove audiences mentally from the trials of the everyday for moments of respite. Involving culture brings audiences closer to the marketplace, home, and society for active engagement. Escapist culture distances audiences from the often confusing and difficult worlds of the worker, the family member, and the citizen through the relatively passive experience of spectacle. Communities of escapist culture develop through common experiences with texts and can develop bonds which depend on a very specific context. Communities of involving culture are based on similarities in life situations, rather than only the mutual purchase of cultural commodity.

Although both types of culture fulfill important needs at different times and in different situations, GWAR's escapism, combined with a powerful rhetoric of rejection, may limit its usefulness in the everyday lives of fans. Although GWAR clearly satisfies its audience in significant ways, the feelings of connection and community it develops seem to be highly contextual and, therefore, momentary and fleeting. Fans mention that GWAR can be important to them only at certain times of their lives and in certain places. As primarily an entertainment form lacking a consciousness of class or politics, GWAR's performances do not aim for or enable significant personal or social change. Audiences have common interests as consumers—as album, T-shirt, and concert ticket purchasers, and as survivors of the GWAR concert ritual, a ritual of violence (however simulated) that creates a bond between the concertgoers. These connections, however, are dependent on an entertainment form that parodies but fails to provide an alternative to the mainstream culture, the culture of fan parents. Bonds created in the GWAR experience may not last beyond the concert context; once the simulated blood, sweat, and tears are showered off and the masks are removed, what remains other than a group of exhausted, entertained, and still confused teenagers?

In a general sense, it seems useful to ask how forms of strategic offensiveness such as those in youth culture like GWAR work as a rhetoric. What is its dynamic? What are its defining characteristics, social functions, and influences? When is it effective or ineffective? Strategic offensiveness might be defined as the conscious and calculated use of signs and codes to insult, shock, or annoy, usually by violating or failing to observe dominant codes of appropriateness. What do the many examples of strategic offensiveness tell us about the world today? Do shock rock concerts, obscene graffiti, hate speech, ACT UP demonstrations, news footage of wartime atrocities, dirty limericks told during church, flag burning, and Sinead O'Connor's pope photo shredding have anything to tell us about contemporary culture?

More important here, is strategic offensiveness in the public realm to be considered part and parcel of a decline in discourse, or as a genuine communicator of feelings, states of mind, political views, and ideologies that contribute in some constructive way to cultural conversations about values, issues, ideas, relationships, changes, and technologies? Do such forms of expression function differently in the cultural realm? What role has the sick or grotesque occupied in the past, and how does this role compare with the present? If such expressions have changed over time, as they surely have, what can those changes tell us about contemporary culture? In an era when "political correctness" and "cultural sensitivity" are often discussed, if not always practiced, why does GWAR emerge on the fringe to capture an audience of young white males? Each of these questions deserves thorough study as scholars attempt to understand the dynamics of vulgarity in a confusing and chaotic world.

REFERENCES

GWAR. (1992), *America must be destroyed* [Album 26807-4]. Metal Blade Records.

GWAR. (1992). *Live from Antarctica* [Video]. Metal Blade Videos.

GWAR. (1993). *Phallus in Wonderland* [Video]. Metal Blade Videos.

GWAR. (1994). *This toilet Earth* [Album P2-53889]. Metal Blade Records.

Hebdidge, D. (1994). *Subculture: The meaning of style.* London: Routledge. (Original work published 1979)

Springer, J. (1997, January 31). "Shock rock." *The Jerry Springer Show* [Transcript]. Livingston, NJ: Burrelle's.

CHAPTER 12

Vicarious Realities

Internet Discourses and Narratives of the Future

David Slayden
University of Colorado at Boulder

Possibly there are contradictions in writing about the Internet, and an even further contradiction in writing about it for publication in a book. Whatever is written here will be out of date by the time it is read. Such is the way with the vehicle of this message's transmission (the book) and the subject discussed (the Internet): the first being associated with a physical, analog past and the second linked inextricably with a digital, virtual future. Accepting such a judgment about the outlines of both the past and the future—and whether accurate or not, such a judgment is now commonplace—this chapter can perhaps be regarded most usefully as a document that will later comprise some sort of history of some aspects of where we were now (the time of this writing) and some speculations about what it meant—all of which seems more than a little quaint. I would like to claim more, but accepting the exigencies of the Internet and values attached to it, those of us engaged in scholarly writing published in books for an admittedly limited audience must acknowledge the antiquary nature of how we spend our time. At least this is one narrative shaping a variety of discourses about telecommunications and microelectronics in general and the "Net" in particular. To the array of generalizations and assumptions already introduced in this introduction, I would add another that is routinely embraced in much scholarly and most commercial discourses about the Net: that we are in the process of moving beyond one communicative practice (writing) and to another (images) and that the computer and the capability of worldwide connectivity provide the means. I have neither the desire nor the intention to be characterized as a Luddite. The assumption that the computer has and is transforming communicative practices worldwide is a valid one, as far as it goes. But more interesting than entering into a debate that can be decided possibly only by time is an examination of the narratives and values (and/or meanings) that have been evoked and attached to the Internet and the accompanying worldwide connectivity that it makes possible. Also at issue is the currency of such narratives within commercial discourse; whenever the Internet is evoked, narratives of convergence and transcendence (and the accompanying salvation they imply) arise as well. This chapter asks why and what this means.

THE END OF PRINT AND THE RISE OF THE "BOOK"

A popular narrative is that we are at the end of one thing and the beginning of another. Discussions about the decline of the word and the rise of the image have been with us at least since the introduction of mass media, and like one of its possible precedents, the argument over ancients and moderns, it is likely to be with us for some time. Perhaps it is the imminence of the millennium, but the claim that we are undergoing profound changes in perception and cognition (transformation) because of the computer is now an everyday and commonly accepted utterance. Whatever communication practices preceding are now called into question. Within this context, to write a book is no longer enough; to call what has been written a book is inadequate because writing is itself a failed, because limited, project.

Consider *Imagologies* (1994), for example, by Mark C. Taylor and Esa Saarinen, who in their "Acknowledgments" refer to the "reflections assembled in this 'book.'" The quotation marks around "book," of course, signal the authors' awareness of the irony of their using such antiquated terminology. Any credible or hip book on cyberculture (which exhibits at least this modernist trait of always having to be new and improved) and the cognitive as well as communicative effects that technology is exerting must acknowledge—in form as well as content—the limitations of being a book and push into the realms of being a "book." Such "books" are highly graphic, immediately signaling that they intend to provide or reference a visual as well as a verbal experience, looking more like the cut-and-paste, nonlinear design of David Carson for *RAY GUN*. Blocks of type are set sideways, typefaces are mixed, text type trades places with display type, black out and reversed-out type are together on the same page, type sizes are inconsistent, blocks of type are exorbitantly leaded out—all in an effort to let you (the reader? the viewer?) know that this book is free from typographical convention, that the tyranny of chronology and grammatical control is absent or seriously compromised here. Boundaries are being broken down; limitations surpassed; new ideas must have a new form of presentation as the authors (if we can use such an archaic term) state in the multiple headnotes (functioning like hooks or teasers on sitcoms) to the "book." As follows:

> In simcult, the responsible writer must be an imagologist [What must the irresponsible writer be?]. Since image has displaced print as the primary medium for discourse, the public use of reason can no longer be limited to print culture. To be effective, writing must be imagoscription that is available to everyone. (p. 4)

A prevailing trait of this discourse about the new, possible discourse is its replacement of what has come before. Also, what has come before is characterized as being tyrannical, and the new means of discourse is seen as being more democratic. The new reality of the new medium calls into question all previous communicative practices. To paraphrase and adapt Marshall McLuhan, not only do we use the new medium, but it in turn uses us. Everything—communicative practices and the realities and boundaries within which they exist and operate—is now in question and must be reconceptualized. Or, as Taylor and Saarinen (1994) state, "The electronetwork that mediaizes the real we call the mediatrix" (p. 5)

Clearly, one requirement of being adept at imagoscription is the routine turning of nouns into verbs, but why quibble? In the world of cyberspeak, this is an old practice (one inputs datum). The real is reversed out here in sans serif type against a black, blobbish brush stroke, which is an imagologist's way of saying "the real," which is in effect a wink or an aside to "the reader" because, as we all should now know, the printed word is highly suspect and this act of "reading" is heavily ironic (because even though we are reading, we all now know that we can no longer simply "read").

If nothing else, the renaming and the new names and the jargon communicate the point, perhaps THE POINT (imagine these "words" to be reversed out and in display type with a yellow, pulsating background) that they are exploring a new means of communicating. As one jacket blurb in *Imagologies* claims: "This profound and prescient 'book' enacts and enunciates a new philosophy of communication . . . a form and content of reflection that points to the role of philosophy in a global economy of telecommunications and micro-electronics" (Taylor & Saarinen, 1994, inside front cover). The book is from the past, and we must move toward and into the future. In this sense, *Imagologies* is a modernist manifesto, attempting to distinguish itself in any and as many ways as possible from the past, from any traditions extending from the past into the present.

Before continuing, a few questions: Have we all become too hip? Have we overdosed on irony within a heavily mediated environment where everything is experienced from an ironic because mediated distance? Is communication now more or less an entertainment, a presentation of a public self with any number of knowing asides to an imaginary, clued-in audience? What sort of discourse can occur within such an environment and by such means?

Before considering these questions, consider yet another promotional blurb from *Imagologies*. This one comes from Thomas Krens of the Guggenheim Museum:

> It is almost a banality to say that the information age demands new paradigms for communications, in form as well as in content. Yet the accuracy of the observation is driven home with palpable energy and insight in this "book" by Mark Taylor and Esa Saarinen. Taylor and Saarinen conduct a verbal and visual dialogue, collage ideas, and develop insights within a framework and format that is simultaneously rigorous and spontaneous. This expansive text is not so much read as experienced. It is the work in the print medium that closely captures the process of creative development that generates from inspired associative thinking. (unnumbered, first bound page)

The above is, among other things, marketing speak, and my calling it such immediately places on it a limitation that I do not intend. But regardless of such a blurb's origin' (prepublication review, letter, press release), its excerpted function is to summarize and lend weight to the book—in short, to sell it. And the marketing strategy for *Imagologies* is to position it against what has come before, to characterize it as part of an ongoing development in the rise of the new and the decline of the old. Well. Within marketing, there is nothing like riding a trend, but we need to put into perspective the oppositions and affiliations stated in this litany of the new against the old. The new arrangements made possible by cyberspace are also characteristic of urban space, and it is more instructive to see the one (cyberspace) as following from the other (urban space) and being contained by it. Much of what Taylor and Saarinen (1994) cite results from a long process of global urbanization and the proliferation of media, rather than the Internet. There are precedents. In *High and Low: Modern Art and Popular Culture* (1990), Kirk Varnedoe and Adam Gopnik discuss the kiosks in the highly commercialized environment of early 20th-century Paris:

> [T]he local newsstand was a fountainhead of urban modernity, the focal point of a new kind of massive daily disgorgement of information and persuasion run together, in fast changing styles of type, layout, and political and commercial appeal. The displays of these kiosks had in fact become so crowded and opulent by 1911 that they were considered to be contributing to the downfall of bookstores, and the Prefect of the Seine was considering a law to suppress the foldout "wings" on which these arrays were set forth. In tearing scraps from newspaper pages around 1912-14, Picasso and the other practitioners of *papier colle* were dipping their cups directly into the commercially simulated flow of sensation, of simultaneity and fast-paced change, with all the threats of political unrest and the seductions of consumer allurements that made up contemporary urban consciousness. (pp. 30-32)

Taylor and Saarinen's (1994) futurist manifesto is, in fact, typical and somewhat reactionary in its rejection of the past and embracing of the future. The dividing line between what has come before and what will be is not at all clear, certainly not as obvious as we are asked to believe. They are correct in suggesting that after cybercommunication nothing will ever be the same, but their version of what is to come is, in fact, a narrative of the future that has been with us for some time. It is also a narrative embraced and exploited repeatedly by advertising for the Internet: on vicarious experience and the transcendence of physical limits.

NOSTALGIA FOR THE FUTURE

On the television right now (1997) is an MCI commercial for the Internet. Never mind that it's filmed in black and white, cuing us visually that what we are watching is classic and/or somehow associated with the past or that it tells us that because of the Internet, we are now free to be "only minds"; this commercial is about the future. But this presentation of the future is nostalgic. I suppose it makes perfect sense that advertising, whose stock-in-trade is to appropriate the mythic, should exploit the Adamic myth in its message to an American audience to evoke the desire for an ideal place and the longing for a return to it; but what is notable in this particular commercial for MCI as a connection to the Net is that the lost Eden to which MCI will return us is a conceptual rather than physical space. The desire for movement westward to a mythic renewal has been an essential factor in the development of the United States. So it is with myths, whose power derives from their mobility, from a faith in the goodness and power of change. Although any desire for a return to something could be said to have about it the quality of nostalgia, the nostalgia evident in the MCI commercial and cued by the black-and-white film treatment is not for a simple past; it is for a simple future, a future like the one we used to imagine back when there was a we, before the use of "we" was politically difficult and socially risky. Here, self-transformation is possible and the question of societal transformation is not simply avoided but rendered irrelevant. The social space where problems of difference and discrimination were located—gender, age, race—is now gone, surpassed, transcended. We can all connect because we are only minds; social difference has been eradicated by technological advancement. Why this removal of context in the world of connectivity, the world of only minds where we are signals exchanged? Does it matter?

This is the anomalous part of the ad; it tells us that because of the Net—brought to you by MCI—we will live in a world where there are only minds. Because the quality of this future perfect existence is amorphous and inexact—a positive because its very open-endedness allows us as consumer/viewers to project what we will onto it—the commercial defines this service by what it is not. Because of the Net, which MCI makes possible to you, there will be no races, no genders, no ages, only minds—in other words, freedom and escape, a cyber-utopia that solves the problems of the physical world by transcending them. This is a tremendous leap: from fiber-optic cable and the access it allows to personal transcendence of social identity. What necessarily takes us from connectivity to transcendence of social difference? Such a freedom is comparable to that of the fair, as noted by James Gilbert in *Perfect Cities* (1991), his discussion of Chicago's utopias of 1893.

Michail Bakhtin in his remarkable discussion of *Rabelais and His World,* also focused upon the fair as a place of liberation from restraints, where the marketplace liberated and democratized the experiences of those who entered it. In such democratic places, popular genres penetrate higher culture and speech itself is released from norms, hierarchies and prohibitions. The result, in the Renaissance age he describes, was innovation and temporary freedom from the pressures and duties of social hierarchy. (p. 14)

In MCI's terms, the Internet becomes, not just a new place, but a new way and type of being, a new and nonphysical social identity that can change as quickly as the market economy that allows it. If the physical marketplace of the Renaissance "liberated and democratized the experiences of those who entered it," what can be said of the multiple-screen-name experiences of cyberspace and the variety of border crossings (e.g., geographic, national, ethnic, gender, age) made possible by surfing the Web? What discoveries can actually be made rather than packaged and purchased? And should distinctions even be made any more between making and buying, between being and shopping?

NEW FRONTIERS AND HEAVEN ON EARTH

In considering what we are being told the Internet is and where it might be taking us, another period comparison is useful here. The new space (conceptual) that the MCI commercial charts is conceptual or virtual or both: We are to see the Internet as a new type of frontier, a realm of discovery and possibility, fueled finally by a raw optimism that the future will be better than both the present and the past. Those very qualities deliberately associated with this designation are the same as when John F. Kennedy's 1960 presidential campaign pushed the "New Frontier" theme line, as historian Richard Slotkin points out in *Gunfighter Nation* (1992), to challenge the incumbent Republican administration of Dwight Eisenhower and to end the continuity of power to Richard Nixon. But the utility of the Frontier and its coupling with the New, as Slotkin reminds us,

was not simply a device for trade-marking the candidate. It was an authentic metaphor, descriptive of the way in which they hoped to use political power and the kinds of struggle in which they wished to engage. The "Frontier" was for them a complexly resonant symbol, a vivid and memorable set of hero-tales—each a model of successful and morally justifying action on the stage of historical conflict. (p. 3)

A fundamental American desire for the new and the improved elected Kennedy to office, but this desire for rebirth as a sales appeal in American advertising dates back to the late 19th century for products as diverse as the everyday convenience of household goods and the conquering of domestic space and the early sales pitches for horseless carriages that naturally sold both speed and the ability to give consumers dominion over time and distance. The same mythic symbol resonates in the MCI ad and throughout competitive ads (e.g., AT&T, Magnavox) that depict the Internet as offering consumers new worlds to discover, new people to become. But why should the resonance of this symbol continue? Why is it so long-lived? In *Gunfighter Nation,* Slotkin (1992) writes that myth plays a significant cultural role because of its general utility in ordering social and personal existence. "Myths are stories," he writes, "drawn from a society's history that have acquired through persistent usage the power of symbolizing that society's ideology and of dramatizing its moral consciousness—with all the complexities and contradictions that consciousness may contain." It is the tendency of a society's consciousness, however, to conventionalize and abstract the original mythic story—through tellings and retellings—until it becomes stylized or "reduced," as Slotkin says, to a "deeply encoded and resonant set of symbols, 'icons,' 'keywords,' or historical clichés" (p. 5).

Advertising exploits myth to sell products and services, and the utility of the myth for advertising is both in the meanings it carries for and attaches to the product or service and the means by which it performs this associative transference: "a deeply encoded and resonant set of symbols, 'icons,' 'keywords,' or historical clichés" (Slotkin, 1992, p. 5). Although MCI's version of the future made possible by the Internet would seem to be totally new because of the technology it is pushing, the promises it makes and the problems it will solve are more or less perennial longings in the popular psyche, following in a direct lineage from such utopian fantasies as the White City of the World's Columbian Exposition of 1893. Compare MCI's future world of no minds and no boundaries to this description (borrowed from Slotkin paraphrasing contemporary accounts):

> The centerpiece of the Exposition, and the culmination of the typical itinerary, was the "White City," an architectural extravaganza of ersatz marble representing the pinnacle of Euro-American civilization, the original "alabaster city ... undimmed by human tears," a little ideal world prophetic of "some far away time when the earth should be as pure, as beautiful, and as joyous as the White City itself." (p. 63)

The promise or possibility of Heaven on Earth has long been a recurring narrative within personal and social remembering, and it is natural and perhaps obvious that the transcendence of physical limits would be a key selling point for a technology that generates virtual realities. But the ideology and moral consciousness attached to the Internet, as with the hopes and longings attached to the White City, are not necessarily transcendent and providential. Nothing essentially one way or the other about the Internet and/or computers demands that they be seen as anything more than a means to increased speed of communication and data transfer, yet such attachments are profuse in commercial discourse on or about the Internet.

CONNECTIVITY AND VICARIOUS TRANSCENDENCE

MCI's version of the Internet takes us beyond a temporary liberation found in the marketplace or experience of the fair. MCI's vision of the Internet is transformational and, finally, transcendent. This is heady stuff to speak of: a new age on Earth in which the technologies we interact with—and by and through which we interact with others—transform us. In short, connectivity leads to liberation of self, of society, of world relations and the very conception of how things work and are. But how exactly are we connected, and what is being exchanged? Is the problem of intolerance of social difference being solved in this new medium or circumvented? Again, beyond the material claims that connections are made and that information is exchanged—both of which are supportable propositions—nothing tangible supports the almost millenarian transformational aura of the Internet. (The presence and number of click-throughs in white supremacist Web sites alone calls attention to connectivity's dystopic as well as utopian side.)

The newness and amorphous nature of the medium allows speculation about the Net's possibilities—in both academic and commercial discourse. But consider this newness, coupled with the intended audience—middle-class professionals—along with the fact that the actual primary use of the Internet by consumer audiences is entertainment, and the discourse on and about the Internet is perhaps less about what is possible than what is imagined or desired. It is less a means of self-realization than a means of self-indulgence and escape, an electronic theme park of the mind. What I am most interested in here is how technology resolves social tensions by dissolving them in a virtual world—and why it seems possible. The commercial utility of the Net as a solution to social problems suggests simultaneously a real need to acknowledge such problems (and a consequent desire for their resolution) but an inability and unwillingness to address them in tangible and actionable ways.

American culture has ample historical precedents for the embracing of pseudo solutions to real problems, but one recent notable analysis of this practice will suffice. In Alan Taylor's study of power and persuasion in the early American Republic, *William Cooper's Town* (1995), he writes, "In the eighteenth century, novels offered readers a vicarious opportunity to experience the tests of achieving and preserving gentility" (p. 23). The vicarious nature of these novels as entertainments is comparable with current uses of the Internet. As this book goes to press, less than 20% of current Net usage is by consumers, and they use it primarily for entertainment. A recent commercial for Lotus references this practice of playing on the Net, suggesting that if you are using the Net for anything other than serious gathering and analyzing of information, then you are wasting both the technology and your time. (This jab at those shallow enough only to "surf the Net" evokes Newton Minow's characterization of television as a "vast wasteland.") But other than this one series of commercials, the Net, like much early television advertising, is in the process of being domesticated for middle America, and part of this domestication, as played out explicitly in the MCI commercial, is the vicarious experience of personal resolution of complex social problems simply by being connected. All of which returns this discussion to some of the fundamental considerations of this book: Is the Net a discursive or performative space? And if it is performative, is this performance a soliloquy rather than an exchange? What actual social end is served by the format of the Internet and the exchanges it makes possible?

CONSUMPTION AS VICARIOUS EXPERIENCE

Perhaps the basic contradiction of the narratives about the Net is to be found in the linking of the experience of consumption, the exchange of goods and services, with the exchange of ideas and viewpoints; this is, after all, a conflation because although the two experiences—intellectual and commercial exchange—can both be called exchanges, fundamental differences reside in both the process of exchange and in what is exchanged. Certainly, an argument can be made that, within the variety of media now available to us, the exchange of ideas has become so dominated by ritualistic and stylistic performances (frequently dictated by the channels of discourse themselves) that discourse has effectively disappeared, that it has been replaced by the illusion of discourse, that true exchange has devolved into image-oriented performances, promotions, and presentations.

Discussing the rise of the culture of consumer capitalism, William Leach writes in *Land of Desire* (1993):

> By World War I, Americans were being enticed into consumer pleasure and indulgence rather than into work as the road to happiness. The roots for this enticement lay deep in American and European history. For generations, America had been portrayed as a place of plenty, a garden in which all paradisical longings would be satisfied. Many Protestant settlers even thought that the millennial—the Second Coming of Christ—was destined to be fulfilled here and that the New Jerusalem would bring not only Salvation and spiritual bliss but also temporal blessings and the end of poverty. By the early 1900s this myth was being transformed, urbanized and commercialized, increasingly severed from its religious aims and focusing ever more on personal satisfaction and even on such new pleasure palaces as department stores, theaters, restaurants, hotels, dance halls, and amusement parks. These institutions still carried much of the former mythic message—the message that said Americans can be renewed and remade—but where the old ideas often conceived of America as a millennial land in which many different types of dreams might come true (spiritual, vocational, and political as well as material), this new era heralded the pursuit of goods as the means to all "good" and to personal salvation. (pp. 3-4)

ON BEING AND WATCHING

Consumption may be seen as a form of expression, even as a construction of social identity, but it is not discourse. The consumer at large in the public, commercial spaces—malls, fairs, theme parks, the Internet—nevertheless inhabits a private world of personal desire and individual satisfaction, a self-absorbed being alone and possibly adrift in a world of purchase decisions. It is a world where personal satisfaction is substituted for public exchange: shopping for discourse. The experiences of the Other that are offered within this world are vicarious, looped back to the consumer who is left entertaining a projection, an experiencing of variations of ourselves.

For example, at the end of the film *To Die For,* a teenage girl who has been making the talk show circuit because of her accessory role in the murder of a television weather woman's husband, explains as she talks directly to the camera:

> Mrs. M. [the weather woman] used to say that you're not really anybody in America unless you're on TV. 'Cause what's the point of doing anything worthwhile if there's nobody watching. So when people are watching, it makes you a better person. So if everybody was on TV all the time, everybody would be better people. But if everybody was on TV all the time, there wouldn't be anybody left to watch. That's where I get confused.

One theme of *To Die For,* a movie repeatedly commenting on a society organized by television and consequently driven by image, is the circular logic evident in the advertising blurb "As Seen On TV!"—a claim that draws support from the assumption that television is a means of authentication within a culture where produced and programmed experience is often considered to be more real than actual, lived experience.

DISCOURSES OF IDENTITY IN COMMODITY CULTURE

The film *To Die For* is about television culture, about a world where word is displaced by image, where immersion and absorption triumph over discernment. The Internet—Magnavox's WEBTV, for example—is in many cases being marketed as improved or interactive television; it is the next best thing beyond the passive dream worlds offered by television, but still, the commercial discourse about and on the Net sees it as belonging in a continuum with television.

In his study *Culture and the Ad,* anthropologist William O'Barr (1994) writes that, by discourse, he means

> a flow of ideas that are connected to one another. Discourse can refer to related ideas that an author develops in a written text or that occur in a conversation between two people. In the case of advertising, I mean something broader. When referring to the discourse of advertising I mean the flow of representations about commodities and society over a period of time, even as long as a century or more. (p. 3)

This phrase, "the flow of representations about commodities and society over a period of time," indicates narratives, really, the narratives that shape the representations or fill them in and connect them one to another. And advertising has an additional element or dimension, as O'Barr (1994) correctly points out—advertising's self-referentiality, how it refers to, among other things, itself, to other advertisements, to the idea of advertising in general. It is about many things, but it is also about itself; it is reflexive, self-referential. O'Barr says, "New advertisements do not exist in a vacuum. They acknowledge and refer to what has gone before them. They are part of a larger flow, a discourse of advertising" (p. 3).

Flow is another way of saying continuum, of pointing to the connectedness of this to that, of the past to the present and to the future. The point is obvious but one that needs to be made when discussing advertising, an operation whose cultural stance is always promoting the new and improved against the old and outmoded; it is an operation that seems fundamentally opposed to culture and tradition, to history. That advertising is a discourse (on and in many areas) is indisputable. To what end is also not notable. Buy the product is always the message, whether overt or implied, whether hard-sell or image work. What is interesting is how advertising works. And I don't mean how it cajoles, seduces, or directs its audience. I mean that when advertising is at work, what are the tools of the trade? What are the professional apparatuses from which an advertiser draws to set about performing the act/task of advertising? Watching advertising at work—a profession of presenting messages to audiences—what references are used? What correlatives? What associations are made that say to the audience, "The experience of this product is like that experience with which you are already familiar (only better)." And what are those desired experiences within any given time or history of a society? These are the sorts of questions and topics to which a text-based cultural study of advertising can direct itself. The other study of advertising is its audiences, and the advertising industry itself has perhaps done that more thoroughly (or at least very differently and directly) than any academic studies to date. But here the ends have been very different.

O'Barr (1994) continues with his discussion of discourse and a reference to Foucault:

Following Michel Foucault, theorists usually reserve the term discourse for ideas that involve society in some way. Foucault himself was interested in questions such as how ideas about illness or marriage at any point in time are related to a body of other ideas that have preceded them. Our conventions and social practices have histories, he argued. He marked as discourse those flows of ideas over time that depict society and its order. (p. 3)

O'Barr follows with a useful distinction between *primary discourse* (product messages in the ad) and *secondary discourse* ("ideas about society and culture contained in advertisements"). In doing so, he says:

> In depicting the context of use of a commodity, the advertisements also depict a number of things about society, such as who does the laundry, who prepares breakfast while someone else sits at the table. . . . From a marketing point of view, these are incidental messages that serve only to show how a product works. Nonetheless, in doing their primary work, advertisements also repeat such secondary themes and unwittingly construct a discourse about society along the way. (p. 3)

Here it is necessary to deconstruct the deconstruction. O'Barr has it exactly backward in his distinction between *primary theme* (use value) and *secondary theme* (symbolic value); he assumes that the positioning of the audience or market is secondary and that the information about the product is primary. In this age of parity products, image tends to dominate presentation in an advertisement; there is often little or no real functional distinction from one product to the next. How a product works is less important in a utilitarian sense than in its symbolic resonance and the identity it confers to the user. In this regard, the movement of advertising in the past two decades has been decidedly inward, from being about the product to being about the consumer of that product—and within a carefully defined social setting. Far from "unwittingly" constructing a "discourse about society along the way," advertising deliberately identifies and exploits the salient symbols, myths, and stories within contemporary culture and associates them with a product or service, providing a context into which consumers can place themselves. If we can talk meaningfully about advertising as a whole, the most basic and necessary point is that advertising's task is to dramatize a benefit. Benefits arise from the point of view of the consumer, a what's-in-it-for-me mentality; and what is in it for the consumer in much contemporary advertising is the promise of social identity through an array of products and services. Strategies of constructing identities, of insinuating and naturalizing a product into the lives of individual consumers, are made possible by the paucity of means of information and/or advice in a consumer-oriented society/commodity culture and reside at its center rather than incidentally along the way.

Another questionable assumption in discussions of advertising is also frequently made: that advertisers, Machiavelli-like, plan every detail to maneuver consumers who, like so many puppets, respond as directed. Such a critique has overtones of the Frankfurt school and the early association of mass media with totalitarian regimes. Although some advertising can be said to produce trends or fads, much of it merely follows them and is expensively ineffective. This actuality suggests that it is far more instructive to consider discursive alternatives other than the accidental or the thoroughly manipulative. Advertising is deliberate commentary on contemporary society, a society—as well as an economy—whose meanings and objectives are organized by consumption. Advertisements attempt to rationalize consumers by offering narratives about how things work, and at the center of these dramas is the consumer interacting with the product. One way or another all of these narratives have happy endings tied inextricably, through the presentation, to the product. The problem-solution plot of the various dramas playing in consumer culture follows from the recognition that the positioning of the product is less an external, competitive reference to other products than a positioning primarily within the consumer's mind. Advertisements can serve as rich and revealing texts for the values that permeate and organize a society at a given time; because they are selling something, one way or another, they should be regarded as attempts to identify and present effectively the aspirations of individuals en masse within a given cultural context.

TOMORROWLAND AS THE PROMISED LAND

Writing about the Internet can be said to be something like forecasting the weather or making general predictions about the future: Chances of being wrong are relatively great, but the liability is actually quite low. Yet much of the commentary on or about the Net shares the optimistic tone of world fairs, trade expositions, and other commercially driven sites where worlds of tomorrow are seen as possible technological utopias. The Internet fits beautifully into scenarios about "in the world of tomorrow" because it is intangible and amorphous, and this distinct lack of information allows advertising to concentrate on image over information and to pump its mythic qualities. But amid the hype, two basic questions need to be asked. First, Why all this interest and excitement in an unproven medium? Second,

Why the utopian, pie-in-the-sky approval wherein it is the answer to all sorts of things?

According to the MCI commercial, nonvirtual reality, that world that used to be called "real" (without quotation marks) and that is now being shed like so much skin from an earlier growth stage, is identified with the past *and* a flawed project. A brief survey of any day's news lends support to this judgment: Bosnia, China, the tribal battles in Africa, the bombing of black churches and abortion clinics, the bombing of the federal building in Oklahoma City, the rising number of white supremacist groups, all of which support the idea that actual discourse has broken down. The physical world of nonvirtual reality admittedly has its problems, all of which contribute to making virtual discourse possible and attractive; but it does not solve the problems of borders and boundaries and ethnic and religious and gender and national differences so much as circumvent them. The MCI "Only Minds" commercial suggests that the discourse made possible by and through the Internet is a pure discourse, one that transcends personal, social, and national difference. But as for this pure discourse of only minds suggested by the MCI commercial, there is the equal possibility that within its purity and detachment it is not so much a discourse as it is a sequence of unconnected monologues. It is quite possibly, as with other acts within virtual reality, a fantasy without connections or consequences, such as the chatrooms that are often a random collection of individuals watching themselves amuse themselves within a cool world.

THE WAY TO TOMORROWLAND

These are key questions in examining what takes place on, in, at, or with the Internet. The variety of prepositions possible here are indicative of the uncertainty of the Internet as a locale, and my question here concerns context and discourse. What does this physical decontextualization of discourse do to the discourse? Does it purify it as the MCI commercial suggests, or does it merely alter it in a way we have not come to terms with yet? Is the MCI commercial correct or merely one utopian possibility in the abolition of the physical from discursive exchange? Are there others? And then, too, what is the down side? For example, what about self and community? Howard Rheingold, among others, has suggested the idea of virtual communities, but what sorts of communities are on the Internet and what do they mean? What about concepts of community and self and the identities that result from their interactions? These are essential questions, but even when they are asked, they tend to be responded to within the jargon of tomorrowlands and expositions—that is, with techno-utopic fantasies about a perfect future. The leap from technology to social change is far and fast and unconvincing, embracing three fundamental truisms about why the world of tomorrow will be better than today.

1. *Connectivity.* The first is the unquestionable (and unquestioned faith in the value of *being connected*). Being connected makes your voice directly heard in a world that seems to have gotten too large, that seems at every turn to deny or disallow the individual voice. Being connected is put forth as a solution to a basic problem of communication, as a tool that gives you the power to be heard no matter who you are. But acknowledging that a problem exists (and if it has not always existed in one way or another), why should the Internet be any better than the telephone or letters or simply talking? The answer to this somewhat ingenuous question is the democratic appeal and technical possibility of the Internet as the virtual public square where it is possible to meet and talk with strangers. But viewing this as a good thing rather than as a possible threat leads us to an underlying assumption about human nature and to the second truism within commercial discourse on the Internet.

2. *One World.* We're all the same beneath the skin. We will learn this by just talking with one another. So, talking and the being connected that makes talk possible are the secrets to world peace; as only minds and not bodies with different features, complexions, genders, and ages, we would understand this. A certain fluidity of social identity is allowed by such a proposition, and that alone makes it attractive without a modern, urbanized world of anonymity and roles that can and often do shift too rapidly.

3. *It Is Interactive.* The Internet is much better than television. It is regularly marketed on television commercials—for AT&T, MCI Sprint, Magnavox, Lotus, for example—as being just like television but better because instead of making you a moron, it will actually engage you and help you fulfill your human potential—a promise also of early television before it became a vast wasteland. The Internet will do this because it is interactive, because you are not a mindless, passive geek, but someone who is engaged and learning, doing, and reacting. Possibly this is true, but it inhabits the commercials as part of a position against strategy, defining the Internet by telling you what it is not: It is not television, so you can feel superior because you surf the Net rather than the channels.

The narratives that inform the Internet ads on television chart the desires of much of the contemporary world, but they provide simplistic consumer solutions to a set of complicated political, economic, and social problems, what Leslie Savan in *The Sponsored Life* (1994) calls "surreal solutions" to "real problems." They are essentially image work that taps into fundamental concerns about the ordering of daily existence within a commodity culture—issues of family, the economy, unresponsive, unmanageable government—but provide private, separate, and individual consumer solutions rather than actual community building, socially workable solutions. They serve to do what advertising for technologically oriented services and products have traditionally done: to warm up public perception of the product, lower resistance to adopting a new or unfamiliar practice, and provide guidance on how to use it and what it is for—in short, insert it into the daily life of the consumer. In regard to its social aspects, the Internet is in much the same position that television was in the early days of its installation into the home. A comparison here is apt: Lynn Spigel writes about early television advertising in *Make Room for TV* (1992):

> In the case of television these kind of advertisements almost always showed the product in the center of the family group. . . . The product-as-center motif not only suggested the familial qualities of the set but also implied a mode of use: the ads suggested television be watched by a family audience. (p. 43)

DOMESTICATING CYBERSPACE

WEBTV by Magnavox is being sold in the same way as early television and, interestingly enough, addresses some of the same basic concerns about domestic space. In these commercials running on television, we see the family gathered around the television set, but now it's not just a television, it's access to the wide world—and it's interactive. The sale here is based on the assumption—beyond the ease of use because this Internet connection is no more difficult than turning on the television—that the family will want to get onto the Web/Net (so that they can't be left out) and that they can do it via a means already familiar to them: watching television. The Web is positioned as the television was once positioned, as a window to a wide world of discovery, possibly educational and certainly mind expanding. By showing the family gathered around the television, which is now

WEBTV, family values (as in family television, too) are appropriated, promoting family togetherness and countering the isolation obliquely referenced and suggested in the act of spending time on the Net. Also, parental supervision or participation or both is demonstrated. This is something the whole family can do together. No isolated, underage surfing of porn sites here. Within this commercial are several elements and arguments to domesticate cyberspace, much in the same way television was domesticated, addressing the problematic polarities of family versus individual and community versus self.

We see in the Magnavox ads the offering of consumer solutions to social problems to accommodate the remapping of domestic space by the Internet. Rather than disrupt the home, WEBTV will reorganize the home and family and eliminate problems of parental authority and unsupervised children. This is nothing new. In fact, the humanizing of technology has been a persistent commercial theme throughout this century, especially in relation to consumer goods. Again, Spigel's (1992) writing on early television in the home is useful:

> Television was the great family minstrel that promised to bring Mom, Dad, and the kids together; at the same time it had to be carefully controlled so that it harmonized with the separate gender roles and social functions of individual family members. This meant that the contradiction between unity and division was not a simple binary opposition; it was not a matter of either/or but rather both at once. Television was supposed to bring the family together but still allow for social and sexual divisions in the home. In fact, the attempt to maintain a balance between these two ideals was a central tension at work in popular discourses on television and the family. (p. 37)

Together but separate, out in the world and not just in the home, are issues within the marketing of the Internet as well. In regard to WEBTV, the television is no longer a television; it is a connection to the Web and makes the whole daunting process of connection as easy as simply turning on your television. But it is also reassuring in matters of control because surveillance is now possible in a social rather than an isolated setting, meaning that the WEBTV is social rather than private. Within this configuration, it becomes acceptable and public, rather than dubious and solitary. But we should wonder why being public and social is depicted as inherently better (more virtuous) than private experience. And the message of togetherness in the WEBTV commercial contrasts significantly with the meeting of only minds that is posited in the MCI commercial.

WHERE WE ARE NOW

Writing about television and the transition from "wartime to postwar life," Spigel (1992) notes a set of "ideological and social contradictions concerning the construction of gender and the family unit" (p. 42). I think within our own time, the "now" within which this book is being written, we are looking at similar contradictions concerning individual and community, federal and state control, country and corporation, self and other. And these contradictions have manifested and been resolved in much of the commercial work for the Internet. But the solutions are themselves less actual solutions than fantasies about what might happen drawn from popular narratives about how things work. Although it is difficult to make credible general statements about advertising and what it does and how it does what it does, most ads follow a narrative pattern of problem and solution, with the product, of course, always being the solution, the requisite happy ending some time in the future. Generally, within the Internet ads, the future depicted—in style of presentation as well as thematic content—is a '50s kind of future, a Reagan "Morning in America" or a Disney-like Tomorrowland. The existing commercial narratives about the Internet have more in common with the worlds of tomorrow presented at trade shows, consumer fairs, and mall displays.

Yes, the MCI commercial for the Internet depicts it as the place that goes beyond physical appearance/boundaries and says that "there are only minds." This is significant, this leaping past or over or beyond or around physical limitations (which is also what *Imagologies* does in its putting an end to the book) because it sees this as somehow doing away with cultural problems, as if mind were somehow pure of culture, rather than being conditioned by it. The Internet, according to MCI, will take us around or beyond cultural differences and distinctions that keep people/nations/races/genders/age-groups apart and separate. But this solution of going around or beyond is a matter of concern because of its working of the personal as political. Politics becomes no more than a matter of people talking, one with another, rather than through and by governments. I suppose one should take heart in such a scenario. But rather than a solution, such commercial discourse dramatizes the end of constructive exchange within public political discourse—instead, seeing citizen discourse as private consumer entertainment—and does so by exploiting contemporary lack of confidence in government and a general distrust or loss of faith in politicians and the possibility of constructive outcomes of political discourse.

The commercial version of the Internet is utopic, offering connectivity, transcendence, and possible salvation. If the Internet is to be a transforming medium, connectivity beyond the bit stream must occur. As with television, tremendous possibilities are inherent in the Internet's structures: public forums, private exchanges, access to information, and access to political and industry leaders.

A few years ago, I visited the headquarters of Saturn when the company was still in the start-up phase. Although I was meeting with top-level management, we ate in the lunchroom where anyone who worked at the company could eat. The idea, my host explained, was that even the lowest-level employees could be sitting next to, and possibly with, the heads of the company. The hope was that exchanges would occur between low and high, although this description inaccurately conveys the sentiment because the company's goal was to reduce or eliminate hierarchical thinking and allow concentration on the merits of an idea, rather than on who said it. I don't know whether this plan worked or has continued, but the lunchroom model is appropriate for the Internet as well; a dissolving of hierarchies and conceptual frames is perhaps one way to create a free flow of opinions and ideas, what the MCI commercial describes as only minds. But if minds are to participate in a free flow of uninterrupted and nonjudgmental exchange, an unprejudiced discourse, then equal access to the medium will have to be made possible. And this is only one element in a whole field of elements that influences and shapes those minds. The Internet is less a panacea than a mirror, reflecting the ugliness of our world and all of its discriminatory and divisive, border-mongering elements, as well as the hope and promise resident within the technological developments. Bypassing the physical limitations will not solve the problems. An exchange of only minds will not bring us to the One-World realization. The notion must be entertained that the minds that MCI dramatizes in its techno-utopian fantasy are equally the problem and not separable—or to be liberated—from the social and physical realities; and until both of these contexts or sites are addressed, the Internet notwithstanding, no matter what narratives of convergence, transcendence, and salvation are brought to bear, the real issues of everyday, nonvirtual reality will continue both to exist and to be neglected.

REFERENCES

Gilbert, J. (1991). *Perfect cities: Chicago's utopias of 1893.* Chicago: University of Chicago Press.

Leach, W. (1993). *Land of desire: Merchants, power, and the rise of a new American culture.* New York: Pantheon.

O'Barr, W. (1994). *Culture and the ad: Exploring otherness in the world of advertising.* Boulder, CO: Westview.

Savan, L. (1994). *The sponsored life: Ads, TV, and American culture.* Philadelphia: Temple University Press.

Slotkin, R. (1992). *Gunfighter nation: The myth of the frontier in twentieth-century America.* New York: Atheneum.

Spigel, L. (1992). *Make room for TV: Television and the family ideal in postwar America.* Chicago; University of Chicago Press.

Taylor, A. (1995). *William Cooper's town: Power and persuasion on the frontier of the early American republic.* New York: Vintage.

Taylor, M. C., & Saarinen, E. (1994). *Imagologies: Media philosophy.* London: Routledge.

Varnedoe, K., & Gopnik, A. (1990). *High and low: Modern art and popular culture.* New York: Museum of Modern Art.

Index

ABC network, 9-10, 49
Abel, E. L., 71, 99
Adler v. Bd. of Ed., 206
Advertising:
  as controversial issue, 10
  culture and, 278-281
  for Internet on television, 271-275, 284
  myth exploitation and, 274
  political figure, 19
  society and, 281
Advocacy, inquiry vs., 176
Affirmative action, 117-120
Alcoff, L. M., 145, 148
Ambach v. Norwick, 209
Anderson, M., 188n13, 188
Anti-Semitism, 128, 222n2
Anzaldua, G., 19, 28
Aphasics, 5-6
Aronowitz, S., 196, 200n1
Art:
  American society and, 108
  film, 232. *See also* Film
  graffiti as people's, 69
  music. *See* Music
  negative and positive, 66
  urban guerrilla, 75
Artists, images of, 109-111
Attractors, 230-244
Audiences, 7
Autoethnography, 164-170, 181, 187n9

Back, L., 66, 69, 83, 99n1n9, 100n10, 100, 101
Baer, S., 53, 62
Bailey, D., 192, 201
Barber, B., 99n6, 100, 101
Barenblatt v. United States, 213
Basquiat, J. M., 75-77
Baudrillard, J., 233, 235, 237, 239, 242-243, 245
Becker, C., 66, 103, 196
Behar, 188n9, 188
Behr, M., 107
Beinhart, L., 237, 245
Beniger, J., 26-27
Benjamin, W., 155, 188
Bennett, C., 89, 101
Bennett, T., 196
Bennett, W. J., 116-118, 120, 148
Berman, M., 77, 99
Bernier, F., 132
Bernstein, S., 126, 148
Bethanis, S. J., 188n15, 188
Bethel School District No. 403 v. Fraser, 208
Bethnal Green Trades Council, 99
Bezansom, J., 8, 27
Bhabha, H., 143, 148
Birdsell, D. S., 44, 58, 62
Bitzer, L., 45, 62

Black Theology of Liberation, A (Cone), 141
Blankenship, J., 62
Blasting, 162-164
Bochner, 188n9, 189
Bolce, L., 32, 41n2, 41
Bonchek, M. S., 21, 27
Bonnett, A., 133, 139-140, 148
Booth, W. C., 18, 27
Border:
    academy on discourse, 151-224
    Mexican-American, 122-127
    "New World," 143
Borja, J., 78, 99
Bradlee, B., Jr., 124, 148
Briggs, J., 231-232, 242, 245n1, 246
Brockriede, W., 187n4, 189
Brodkey, L., 200n1
Buckley, B. E., 71, 100
Burke, K., 158, 189
Bushnell, J., 71, 93, 100
Butler, J., 193
Butterfly effect, 230, 233
Byrne, J. P., 212, 214, 224

Cain, W., 195, 200n3, 201
California Voter Foundation (CVF), 20, 27
Calleroos, C., 224
Callinicos, A., 130-131
Campbell, K. B., 19, 28
Capitalism:
    culture of consumer, 277
    racism and, 130-131, 133
    transnational, 195
Carlin, D. B., 52, 63
Cashmore, E., 129, 148
Castells, M., 78, 100
Castillo, A., 19, 27
Castleman, C., 74, 100
CBS network, 32, 40, 55
Censorship, 65-150
Cerullo, K., 41n2, 41
Cesaretti, G., 74, 100
Chaffee, Z., 223n7, 224
Chalfant, H., 74, 99n8, 100
Chaos theory, 230-244
Chaplinsky v. New Hampshire, 218
Chatroom:
    discourse in scholarly, 155-189

strategies, 163
Chayko, M., 41n2, 41
Cinematic discourse, 230-244
City, graffiti in racialized, 69-102
Civic education model, 206, 208-210
Civilization and Its Discontents (Freud), 104
Class:
    graffiti as marker of, 86
    sports talk radio and, 32-35
    warfare, 117
Closed discourse, 233
Cobb, J., 101
Cockcroft, E., 71, 100
Cognition, reality and, 234
Cohen, J., 231, 246
Cohen, R. E., 14, 27
Coleman, T., 32, 41
Collectivity, 108
Collins, R. K. L., 62
Color blindness, 118-120
Combative imagery, 168
Commodity racism, 39
Common person, 6
Communication:
    exploring new means of, 270
    graffiti as, 66, 69, 97-98
    lack of collaborative, 171
    more vs. meaningful, 7
    music as, 247-266
    personal, 26
    quality of graffiti, 95
Community:
    discourse norms of, 182-184
    graffiti and, 72, 76, 78-88
    organic vs. pseudo, 26
    scholarly. *See* Scholarly community
    sports talk radio, 40-41
Cone, J. H., 141, 148
Conflict:
    escalating, 170
    graffiti and, 78-88
Connectivity, 275-276, 283
Conscience of the Eye, The (Sennett), 72-74
Consumption, 276-277
Conway, M., 19, 27
Cook, D., 240, 246
Cooper, M., 74, 76, 99n8, 100
Corey, F. C., 156-157, 189

Corrigan, P., 82, 100
Cranberg, G., 8, 27
Cresswell, T., 71, 100
Crimmegrantes, 122
Critical education model, 206-207, 211-
    220, 222n6
Critical pedagogy, 191-202, 198
Cross-disciplinary discussion, 180
Cultural pedagogy, 194
Cultural politics, 198
Cultural studies, 191-202
Culture:
    advertising and, 278-281
    chaos theory and, 232
    commodity, 278-281
    white, 133. *See also* Whiteness
Culture and the Ad (O'Barr), 278
Cyberculture:
    books on, 268
    See also Cyberspace; Internet
Cyberspace:
    domesticating, 284-286
    See also Cyberculture; Internet
Cybriwsky, R., 79, 85, 101

Davis, C., 153, 203-224
Davis, O., 6, 27
De Landa, M., 234, 246
De Montaigne, M., 211
Debates, presidential, 44-53
Degler, C. N., 48, 62
Delgado, R., 205, 217, 222n3, 224
DeMaio, G., 32, 41n2, 41
Democracy:
    death of, 29-42
    "hyperactive," 60
    neoliberal, 121
    sports talk radio and, 31, 33
Democratic education model, 206, 210-211
Denzin, N. K., 188n12, 189
Depoe, S. P., 48, 52, 62
Derrida, J., 197, 201
Descartes, R., 211
Destructive gemeinschaft, 73
Détournement, 71, 96, 99n2
Dhanwant, K. R., 89, 101
Dictating, 176
Discourse:
    academy at edge of, 151-224

chatroom, 155-189
cinematic, 230-244
closed, 233
color blindness and, 118-120
dynamics of, 176-181
elite, 159-160
future of public, 220-222
identity and, 278-281
illusions of, 13-18
Internet, 267-288. *See also* Internet
male styles of, 173-176
norms of community, 182-184
otherness as positive, 145-147
presidential campaign, 43
public, 204, 220-222
rebel, 181
schoolhouse, 203-224
unpopular public, 204
Disney, 10
Dissent, alienation of, 7-12
Diversity:
    difference vs., 114-115
    discourse of, 121
Doe v. University of Michigan, 215-218,
    222n5
Dowd, M., 56, 62
D'Souza, D., 224
Dundes, A., 71, 100
Dynamic system, 231-232

Eagleton, T., 105, 111-112, 197, 201
Easterbrook, G., 243, 246
Education:
    civic model of, 206, 208-210
    critical model of, 206-207, 211-220
    cultural pedagogical practice and, 194
    democratic model of, 206, 210-211
    political, 198-199
    politicizing, 199
    role of speech in, 203-224
Electronic media, 16, 59. *See also* Media
Electronic town meeting, 59-61
Elite discourse, 159-160
Ellen, 9
Ellis, 188nn9-10, 189
Ely, J., 57, 62
Emerson, T., 219, 224
Emotional tranquility, 8
Employment Non-Discrimination Act, 10

Entertainment, media and, 108
Entman, R. M., 26, 28
ESPN network, 31
Essence of Christianity, The (Feuerbach), 233
Ethnic identity, 141
Evocation, value of, 178-180
Exchanges, on Internet, 276-277
External allusion, 98

Fall of the Public Man, The (Sennett), 72
Fallows, J., 13, 27
Fashion:
    autoethnography in, 164-166
    sports and, 38
Ferrell, J., 70-71, 100
Feuer, J., 26-27
Feuerbach, L., 233, 246
Film:
    as cinematic discourse, 230-244
    impact of, 232-233
First Amendment protection, 204-222
Fish, S., 195, 200n3, 201
Fiske, J., 187n9, 189
Flesh and Stone, The (Sennett), 72
Flores, L. A., 19, 27
Foucault, M., 279
Frankenberg, R., 132-133, 135, 148
Free speech, 204-222
Freedman, E. M., 204, 221, 224
Freud, S., 103-104, 112
Frith, S., 193, 201
Fulkerson, R. P., 19, 27
Fusco, C., 135, 142, 148

Gangs, graffiti and, 86
Garvey, J., 140, 148
Gays/lesbians:
    gay male pornography, 162-176
    lobbying group, 9-10
Geiser-Getz, G. C., 226, 247
Genocide, graffiti and, 69
Germond, J. W., 11-12, 16, 27
Gilbert, J., 272, 288
Gilliam, T., xii
Gilroy, P., 93, 100, 146, 152, 192, 199, 201
Giroux, H. A., 152, 191, 200n1, 201n3, 201
Gitlin, T., 10, 27, 122, 148
Glazer, N., 72-74, 98, 100

Gleick, J., 230, 241, 245n2, 246
Goankar, D. P., 195, 201
Goldberg, D. T., 2, 29
Goldstein, R., 75, 100
Gómez-Peña, G., 116, 122-123, 143, 148, 197, 201
Goodall, H. L., Jr., 152, 155, 159, 189
Gopnik, A., 271, 288
Gordon, L., 193
Government, "grand narratives" of, 23
Graff, G., 199, 201
Graffiti, 69-102
    controlling, 72
    enhancement vs. defacement, 70
    examples of, 78-87
    gang, 86
    history of, 71
    identity and, 93-96
    internal allusion and, 98
    memorial, 76-77
    outlaw communication, 66, 69
    public space and, 71-77
    racist, 78-82, 89-96
    relations of conflict and, 82
    semantic and linguistic system, 93
Gray, H., 193, 201
Greenstein, F., 19, 27
Grossberg, L., 145-146, 148, 152, 192-193, 196, 200n1, 201
Guernica (Picasso), 110
Gumpert, G., 25-27
Gunfighter Nation (Slotkin), 273-274
Gutiérrez, R., 127, 148
GWAR (rock band), 247-266

Haag, P., 33, 41
Habermas, J., 17, 27
Hagopian, P., 70, 100
Hall, N., 245n2, 246
Hall, S., 185-186, 189, 192, 195-197, 201
Hanh, T-n., x, xiv
Harris, C. I., 118-119, 148
Hart, R. P., 13, 16, 19, 21, 27, 238, 246
Hate groups, Internet, 22
Hate speech, 204-205
Hate Speech (Whillock & Slayden), xi
Hayles, N. K., 233, 246
Hazelwood School District v. Kuhlmeier, 209, 211

Healy v. James, 206, 211
Hebdidge, D., 75-76, 100, 248, 266
Heisenberg, W., 241
Henderson, S., 71, 100
Herbeck, D., 3, 43
Hesse, B., 89, 101
Hicks, E., 121, 142, 148
Hidden Injuries of Class, The (Sennett), 72
*High and Low: Modern Art and Popular
    Culture* (Varnedoe & Gopnik), 271
Hinich, M., 6, 27
Hodges, A., 56, 62
Hogan, J. M., 46, 62
hooks, b., 200n1, 201
How Holocausts Happen (Porpora), 12
Human Rights Campaign, 9
Hume, D., 211
Hutchby, I., 32, 41
Hybridity, postcolonial, 142-145
Hyperrealism, 237

Iconicity, 242
Identity, 66
    authentic forms of, 142
    ethnic, 141
    graffiti and, 78-88
    Internet and social, 283
    neoliberal democratic models of, 121
    politics, 10-11, 161
    reflections, on, 180-181
Ignatiev, N., 140, 148
Illusion(s):
    of democratic self-government, 60
    of discourse, 13-18
    of hope, 18-23
    images and, 66
Image, 66
    of artists, 109-111
    of who is American, 105
Image making, art of subversive, 103-112
Imagery, combative, 168
Imagologies (Taylor & Saarinen), 268, 270
Imagoscription, 269
Inclusion, discourse of, 121
Inquiry, dysfunctional relationship between
    advocacy and, 176
Internal allusion, 98
Internet:
    chatrooms. *See* Chatrooms

connectivity and, 275-276, 283
cyborg personalities via, 6
discourses and narratives of future, 267-
    288
dissolving of hierarchies and, 287
false identification of public on, 19
hate groups, 22
"hyperactivie democracy" and, 60
interactivity of, 283
letter mocking by, 19
"lurkers," 20
MCI ad for, 271-275, 282, 284
netiquette, 182
personae created for, 18
political decision making and, 19-20
political dialog and, 21-22
virtual communities, 25
WEBTV, 278, 284-286
writing about, 281
    See also Cyberculture; Cyberspace;
        Web; Web page
Interrogating, 163, 176
Into the Image (Robins), 239
Ivie, R. L., 237, 246
Iyengar, S., 11, 27

James, J., 193, 201
Jameson, F., 233, 246
Jamieson, K. H., 44, 58, 62-63
Jay, M., 87, 101
Jehl, D., 56, 62
Journalists:
    political debates and, 45-46
    See also Media
Jubera, D., 57, 62
Judeo-Christian racist logic, 132
Judgment, suspension of, 6

Keith, M., 66, 69, 83, 99n, 100
Kellert, S., 230-231, 242, 246
Kellett, P. M., 152, 155-156, 189
Kelling, G., 72, 102
Kellner, D., 62
Keyishan v. Board of Regents, 210-211,
    214, 216
Kinder, D., 11, 27
Kleiner, A., 157, 163, 187nn5-6, 189
Kloer, P., 62
K-mart, 36

Kofman, F., 187nn7-8, 188n17, 189
Krauthammer, C., 53, 62
Krens, T., 270
Ku Klux Klan, 115, 128

Lacy, S., 197, 200-201
Land of Desire (Leach), 277
Langellier, K. M., 188n12, 189
Language:
    as "generative action," 188n16
    music as, 247
    polarizing, 167-169
    politically correct, 7-12
    postmodernist, 105
    skin color and, 137
Lapham, L., 160-161, 189
Lawrence, C., 205, 224
Lazarsfeld, P., 16, 27
Leach, W., 277, 288
Learning to Labor (Willis), 191
Lefebvre, H., 87, 101
Lentricchia, F., 195, 200n3, 201
Leopold, G., 59, 63
Levine, L. W., 201n3, 201
Lewin, R., 231, 245n2, 246
Lewis, P., 221, 224
Ley, D., 79, 85, 101
Li, T., 20, 28
Lichfield, J., 63
Lindsay, J., 71, 101
Linnaeus, C., 132
Lippmann, W., 13, 28
Lipsitz, G., 140, 148
Living Buddha, Living Christ (Hanh), x-xi
Loewen, J. W., 128, 148
Lomas, H. D., 85-86, 101
Lone, M., 89, 101
López, I. F. H., 126, 138-141, 148
Lott, E., 134, 149
Lurking, 163

McClintock, A., 39, 42
McGee, M., 156
McLaren, P. L., 67, 113, 142, 149, 200n1
McLaurin v. Oklahoma State Regents, 209
McLuhan, M., 25, 28, 160-161, 189, 269,
    288
McMillan, S., 19, 28
MacNeil, R., 14, 24, 28

Magnavox, 278, 284-285
Mainstream, 66
Make Room for TV (Spigel), 284
Man Who Mistook His Wife for a Hat and
    Other Clinical Tales (Sacks), 5
Margin, 66
Matsuda, M., 205
May, B., 13-14
MCI, 271-275, 282, 286-287
Media:
    American society and, 105, 108
    behavior shaping by popular, 225-288
    broadcast, 54-55
    explosion, 6
    "feeding frenzies," 13
    "narcotizing dysfunction" of, 16
    "navel-gazing" by, 22
    political correctness and, 8-9
    political debates and, 45-46
    print. See Print media
    public opinion and, 17
    television, 238. See also Television
    See also Electronic media
Media Studies Center, 20
Mediatrix, 269
Meiklejohn, A., 48, 63
Mercer, K., 196
Merton, R., 16, 27
Messaris, P., 242, 246
Messner, M., 36, 42
Metropolitan hybridity, 142
Mexican migrant workers, 122-123, 127
Meyer, J., 52, 63
Millennium Whole Earth Catalog, The, 21
Miller, G. R., 156
Minow, N., 276
Moe, T. M., 20, 28
Moore, J. W., 85, 89, 101
Moral high ground, 172
Morris, M., 196
Morton, D., 200n2, 202
Mosse, G., 96, 101
Movies. See Cinematic discourse
MTV network, 30
Muir, J. K., 48, 59, 63
Muller, H., 112
Multicultural, 66
Multiculturalism, revolutionary,
    113-149

Music:
    creativity in, 250
    teenage, 247-266
Muzzio, D., 32, 41n2, 41

Nakayama, T. K., 156-157, 189
Naming, 167
National Communication Association, 163-
    164
National Endowment for the Arts,
    106, 111
Natural System (Linnaeus), 132
Nayak, A., 99n9, 100
Nazis, 12
    graffiti of, 93-95, 99n1
    swastika, 100n10
Nelson, C., 194-195, 201
Netiquette, 182
Neuman, W. R., 26, 28
New space, 273
News coverage, 13-18
News stories:
    Persian Gulf War, 236-237
    scandals, 13
Nolan, M. F., 57, 63
Non-linear models, 245n1
Noonan, P., 11, 23

O'Barr, W., 278-280, 288
O'Brien, C. C., 125, 149
Offensiveness, strategic, 265
Okley, J., 188n10, 189
Oliver, A. M., 98, 101
Opinion polls, 43
Ordeshook, P., 6, 27
Osborne, P., 193, 201
Otherness, 145-148
Out-groups, 11
Outlaw communication, 66, 69

Page, B., 32, 42
Page, S., 55, 57, 63
Palczewski, C. H., 19, 28
Paletz, D. L., 26, 28
Palmer, W., 238, 246
Papish (1973), 216
Pathology, politics and, 104-105
PBS network, 14
Peat, F. D., 231-232, 242, 245n1, 246

Pedagogy:
    critical, 191-202
    cultural, 194
People v. Huss, 204
Perea, J. F., 124-125, 149
Perfect Cities (Gilbert), 272
Performativity, 193-198
Perley, J. E., 188n15, 189
Perry, R., 71, 101
Persian Gulf War, 15
Peterson, E. E., 188n12, 189
Phase space, 231, 245n2
Phelan, P., 197, 201
Pierce, C. S., 242
Plant, S., 101
Pledge of allegiance, 208
Political correctness (P.C.), 7-12
Political education, 198-199
Politicians:
    campaign vs. governing modes of, 25
    conservative, 128-129
    identity borrowing by, 18-19
    image advertising and, 19
Political Freedom (Meiklejohn), 48
Politicking, 163, 176-177
Politics:
    cultural, 198
    death of public argument in, 43
    identity and, 10-11, 161
    illusion and, 5-28
    pathology and, 104-105
    presidential campaign debates, 44-53
    rhetoric and, 193
    sports talk radio and, 35-38
Popper, K., 211, 219, 224
Populism, acts of resistance and, 65-150
Pornography, gay male, 162-176. See also
    "Sextext"
Porpora, D., 12, 28
Posner, J., 99n5, 101
Post, R., 210, 222n6, 224
Postcolonial hybridity, 142-145
Postman, N., 25, 28, 55, 63
Postmodernism:
    autoethnography and, 165
    chatroom discourse and, 171
    language of, 105
    technology and, 234
Powers, B., 25, 28

Presidential campaigns, 11, 45-53
Primary theme, 280
Principle of falsifiability, 211-212
Print media:
    end of, 268-271
    town hall debate and, 55-58
Progress, changing view of, 23
Protocols of the Learned Elders of Zion,
    The, 128
Psychoanalytic-Marxism (Wolfenstein),
    137
Psychosexual racist logic, 132
Public argument, major themes of, 158-159
Public discourse:
    future of, 220-222
    unpopular, 204
    See also Discourse
Public figures, media consultants of, 16, 18
Public opinion, 13-18
Public relations consultants, 16
Public space, graffiti and, 71-77
Publics, 7
Pugsley v. Sellmeyer, 206, 208

Quinn, M., 100n10, 101

Race Traitor (Ignatiev & Garvey), 140
Racism:
    at American universities, 222n2
    capitalism and, 130-131
    commodity, 39
    defeating, 123, 131
    graffiti and, 69, 76, 78-82, 89-96
    groups, 115
    logic of, 126
    music and, 264
    slavery and, 131
    sports talk radio and, 36-40
    whiteness and, 113-149. *See also* White-
        ness
Radhakrishnan, R., 142, 149
Radio, sports talk, 29-42
Rational choice theorists, 6
Rattansi, A., 126-127, 149
Rausch, J., 211, 212, 219, 224
Reality:
    construction of, 234
    negotiable, 229-246
    synthesized, 243

vicarious, 267-288
Rebel discourses, 181
Reed, M., 63
Rees, N., 71, 101
Rein, I. J., 187n3, 189
Reisner, R., 71, 101
Representation, 66
Resistance, 66
    acts of populism and, 65-150
Resonation, 179
Reston, J., 18, 28
Reuter, T., 45, 62
Revolutionary multiculturalism, 113-149
Rex, J., 89, 101
Reynolds, R., 71, 101
Rheingold, H., 21, 28, 282
Rhetoric:
    consequences of, 12
    politics as, 193
Rhetorical polarization, 10
Ricard, R., 75, 99n4, 101
Riccio, R., 222n2, 224
Richards, D. A. J., 203, 224
Riley, M., 21, 28
Roberts, C., 157, 163, 187nn5-6, 189
Robins, K., 232, 236, 239, 244, 246
Rodriguez, L., 57, 63
Roe v. Wade, 221
Roediger, D., 36, 42, 124, 140-141, 149
Ross, R. B., 157, 163, 187nn5-6, 189
Rothenberg, 20, 28
Roush, M., 63
Ruane, J., 41n2, 41
Rudy's Red Wagon: Communication Strats
    in Contemporary Society (Rein),
    187n3
Rusher, W., 32, 42
Rushing, J., 159, 189
Rushkoff, D., 229, 246
Ryan, S., 187n5, 189

Saarinen, E., 268-271, 288
Sabato, L., 13, 28, 63
Sacks, O., 5, 28
San Juan, E., Jr., 121, 149
Sartre, J. P., 192, 201
Saturn, 287
Savan, L., 284, 288
Schauer, F., 203, 224

Schneider, K., 22, 28
Scholarly community:
    blasting toward, 162-164
    quality of, 176-177
    skillful discussion and, 177-178
Scholarship, autoethnography as, 166-167
Scholl, I., 12, 28
Schudson, M., 14-15, 28
Schuller, D., 19, 22, 28
Scientific racist logic, 132
Sciorra, J., 76, 100
Search for a Method (Sartre), 192
Seattle Communicate Network, 22
Secondary theme, 280
Seducing America (Hart), 238
Segal, L., 193, 201
Senge, P. M., 157, 162-163, 186, 187nn5-8,
    188n17, 189
Sennett, R., 15, 25, 28, 72-74, 95, 98, 99n3,
    101
"Sextext," 155-189
Sexuality, gay/lesbian, 9-10
Shales, T., 56, 58, 63
Shaw, G., 55, 57, 63
Shock rock, 248-249
Shohat, E., 143, 149
Short-Thompson, C., 48, 52, 62
Shulman, S., 57, 63
Siegel, E., 57, 63
Silence, 66
Simcult, 269
Simon, R., 200n1
Simpson, xii, xiv
Simulacrum, 235, 239-240
60 Minutes, 46
Skillful discussion:
    accountability and, 183
    concept of, 187n5
    evocation and, 178-180
    generates skillful discussion, 181-182
    scholarly community and, 177-178
Skover, D. M.,
Slavery, 125, 129-130
Slayden, D., xi, xiv, 224, 226, 267
Slotkin, R., 273-274, 288
Smell of Apples (Behr), 107
Smith, B. J., 157, 163, 187nn5-6, 189
Smith, R., 19, 27
Smith, S., 8

Smolla, R., 8, 28
Society:
    advertising and, 281
    media in American, 105, 108
    privatization of, 15
    pseudo-communities, 26
    television and, 278
Solomos, J., 66, 69, 83, 98n, 100n10, 100,
    101
Soloski, J., 8, 27
Southern Poverty Law Center, 149
Spacks, P. M., 201n3, 202
Speech, role in education, 203-224
Speech codes, 205-206, 219-220
Spigel, L., 284-286, 288
Spin control, 13-18
Sponsored Life, The (Savan), 284
Sports talk radio, 29-42
    race and, 36-39
    uniformity and, 34
    "whitemaleness" expression and, 37
Springer, J., 249, 255, 266
Steinberg, P., 98, 101
Stereotypes, 8, 13, 122
Stevens, A. J., 19, 27
Stewart, I., 231, 246
Stowe, D. W., 131, 149
Strategic offensiveness, 265
Subjectivity, 145
Suburbia, graffiti in, 78
Subversive image making, 103-112
Sussman, E., 75, 102
Sweatt v. Painter, 209
Sweezy v. New Hampshire, 213, 216, 220
Symbolic value, 280
Synthesized reality, 243

Talk, talk about, 65
Talk radio, sports, 29-42
Talk show, The Jerry Springer Show, 249,
    255
Tannenbaum, J., 32, 42
Taylor, A., 276, 288
Taylor, M. C., 268-271, 288
Television:
    interactive, 278
    Internet ads on, 271-275, 282, 284
    society organized by, 278
    symbolist poetry and, 160

"vast wasteland" of, 276
visual medium, 16, 238
Thomas, C., 56, 63
Tinker v. Des Moines School District, 206,
    210-211
Tomlinson, S., 89, 101
Tomorrow, T., x
de Toqueville, A., 48, 63
Town hall:
    presidential campaign debates in, 44-53
    See also Town meeting
Town meeting:
    in electronic age, 43-64
    myth of, 53-58
    self-government and, 48-49
    See also Town hall
Transdisciplinary knowledge, 200n2
Trend, D., 200n1
Turbulence, 241-242

U.S. Supreme Court, on education and
    speech, 204-222
United States v. Associated Press, 214
Universities, crime upsurge in, 204
Urban culture, graffiti and, 71-77
Uses of Disorder, The (Sennett), 72
Use value, 280
*UWM Post v. Board of Regents of the Uni-
    versity of Wisconsin,* 217-218, 222n5

Value, use vs. symbolic, 280
Van Dijk, T. A., 155, 159, 189
Varnedoe, K., 271, 288
Vattimo, G., 23, 28
Vicarious experience, consumption as, 276-
    277
Vicarious transcendence, connectivity and,
    275-276
Violence, graffiti and, 69
Virtual communities, 25
Visual Persuasion (Messaris), 242
Von Foerster, H., 234, 246

Waldman, M. S., 57, 63
Wall writing. *See* Graffiti
Walzer, M., 77

Web:
    personae created for, 18
    See also Internet; Web page
Web page:
    URL as graffiti, 83
    See also Internet
WEBTV, 278, 284-286
Weiler, M., 46, 63
Weltman, G., 85, 101
West, C., 131, 149
What I Saw at the Revolution (Noonan), 11
Whillock, D. E., 226, 229
Whillock, R. K., xi, xiv, 2, 5, 63, 224
White by Law (López), 138
White solidarity, 92
Whitemaleness, sports talk and, 37-38
Whiteness, 67
    America as euphemism for, 115-118
    choosing against, 120-121
    cultural logic of, 131-136
    dismantling, 136-142
    resisting, 113-149
    See also "Whitemaleness"
William Cooper's Town (Taylor), 276
Williams, J., 201n3
Williams, R., 194, 202
Willis, P., 191
Wilson, J. Q., 72-74, 98, 102
Wimsatt, W., 88-89, 102
Winant, H., 117, 149
Witcover, J., 11-12, 16, 27
Withdrawing, 163, 176
Wolfenstein, E. V., 137-138, 149
Wood, E. M., 144, 149
Words, rethinking harmful, 203-224
World Wide Web. *See* Internet

Yardley, R., 222n3, 224
Youth culture, post-punk pop, 247-266
Yudice, G., 145, 149
Yun, D., 205, 224

Zarefsky, D., 44, 63
Zavarzadeh, M., 200n2, 202
Zinn, H., 124, 149